# Why The Pharaohs Built The Pyramids With Fake Stones

Joseph DAVIDOVITS

INSTITUT GÉOPOLYMÈRE

www.geopolymer.org

©2009–2017 Joseph Davidovits
Web: www.davidovits.info

**ISBN:** 9782951482043

1st edition in 2009 (hard cover), revised in 2017 (soft cover).

**Published by:**
Institut Géopolymère
16 rue Galilée
F-02100 Saint-Quentin
France
Web: www.geopolymer.org

Translated in English by Claude JAMES from the French book *La nouvelle histoire des pyramides*.

# Books from the Author

## Archaeology

In French:
2017 *Bâtir les Pyramides sans pierres ni esclaves ?*, éditions Jean-Cyrile Godefroy, Paris. ISBN 978-2-86553-288-9
2009 *De cette fresque naquit la Bible*, éditions Jean-Cyrile Godefroy, Paris. ISBN 978-2-86553-216-2
2006 *La Bible avait raison, Tome 2: sur les traces de Moïse et de l'Exode*, éditions Jean-Cyrile Godefroy, Paris. ISBN 2-86553-190-2
2005 *La Bible avait raison, Tome 1: L'archéologie révèle l'existence des Hébreux en Égypte*, éditions Jean-Cyrile Godefroy, Paris. ISBN 2-86553-182-1
2004 *La nouvelle histoire des pyramides*, ISBN 2-86553-175-9 2e édition en 2006, éditions Jean-Cyrile Godefroy, Paris. ISBN 2-86553-192-1
2002 *Ils ont bâti les pyramides*, éditions Jean-Cyrile Godefroy, Paris. ISBN 2-86553-157-0
1978 *Le livre de la pierre: que le dieu Khnoum protège Khéops, constructeur de pyramide*, ed. J. Davidovits, Saint-Quentin. ISBN 2-902933-02-9

In English:
2008 *They built the Pyramids*, ed. Institut Géopolymère, Saint-Quentin, ISBN 978-2-9514820-2-9
1988 *The Pyramids, an enigma solved*, ed. Hippocrene Books, New York, ISBN 0-87052-559-X (in collaboration with M. Morris)
1984 *The book of stone, Vol. 2: Joseph and Solomon*, ed. Institute for Applied Archaeological Science, Miami, Fl., ISBN 2-902933-10-X
1983 *The book of stone, Vol. 1: alchemy and pyramids*, ed. Geopolymer Institute, Saint-Quentin, ISBN 2-902933-09-6

In Portuguese:
1990 *As Pirâmides, a soluçao de um enigma*, ed. Editora Record, Rio de Janeiro, BR.

In Italian:
2004 *Il calcestruzzo dei Faraoni: cosi hanno costruito le grandi pyramidi*, ed. Mondo Ignoto, Roma, ISBN 88-89084-54-5

In Czech:
2006 *Nové Dejiny Pyramid*, ed. Fontana, Olomouc (CZ), ISBN 80-7336-341-0
2007 *Egypt, tajemstvi pohrebniho chramu, Bible Mela Pravdu*, ed. Fontana, Olomouc (CZ), ISBN 80-7336-354-2

## Science

2008–2015 *Geopolymer Chemistry & Applications*, 4th ed., Institut Géopolymère (Geopolymer Institute), Saint-Quentin, France, ISBN: 978-2-9514820-9-8
2005 *Geopolymers, Green Chemistry and Sustainable Development Solutions*, Proceedings of the GEOPOLYMER 2005 World Congress, edited by Joseph Davidovits, Geopolymer Institute, Saint-Quentin, France, ISBN: 978-2-9514820-0-5
1999 *GÉOPOLYMÈRE '99* , Proceedings of the Second Conference on Geopolymer, 1999, edited by J. Davidovits, R. Davidovits and C. James, Geopolymer Institute and INSSET, Saint-Quentin, France, ISBN: 978-2-9029331-4-3
1989 *GÉOPOLYMÈRE '88* , Proceedings 1st European Conference on Soft Mineralurgy, 1988, edited by J. Davidovits and J. Orlinski, Université de Technologie, Compiègne, France, ISBN: 978-2-9029331-3-6

# Contents

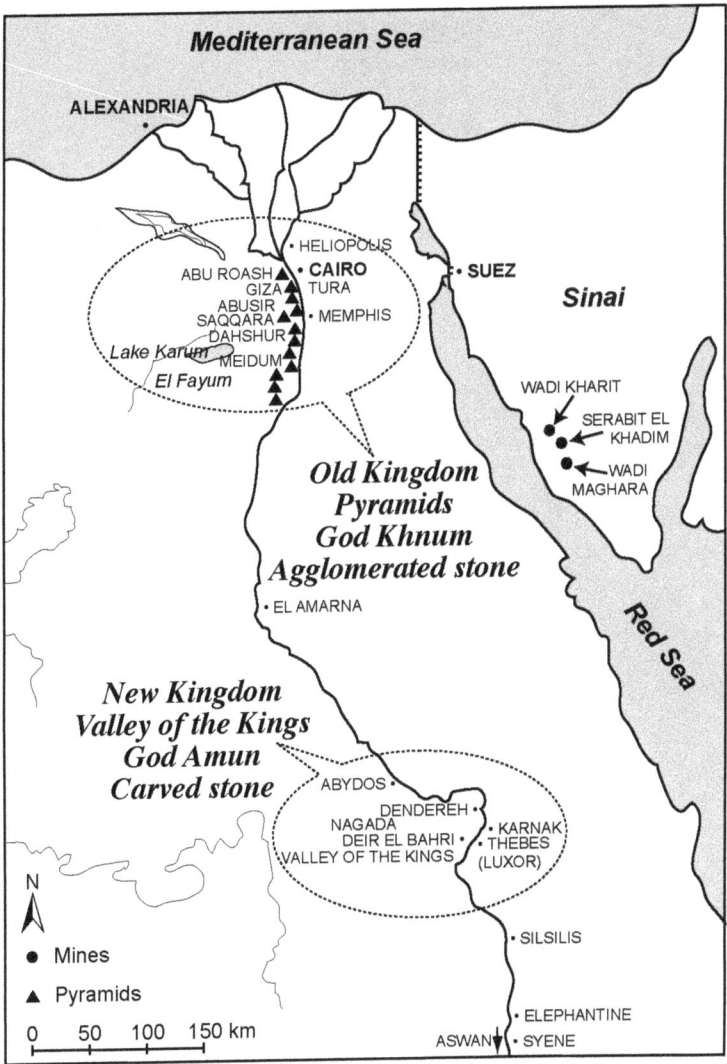

Mediterranean Sea

ALEXANDRIA

Sinai

HELIOPOLIS
ABU ROASH
GIZA
CAIRO
TURA
ABUSIR
SAQQARA
DAHSHUR
MEMPHIS
Lake Karum
MEIDUM
El Fayum

SUEZ

WADI KHARIT
SERABIT EL
KHADIM
WADI
MAGHARA

**Old Kingdom
Pyramids
God Khnum
Agglomerated stone**

EL AMARNA

Red Sea

**New Kingdom
Valley of the Kings
God Amun
Carved stone**

ABYDOS
DENDEREH
NAGADA
DEIR EL BAHRI
VALLEY OF THE KINGS

KARNAK
THEBES
(LUXOR)

SILSILIS

N

● Mines

▲ Pyramids

0  50  100  150 km

ELEPHANTINE
ASWAN · SYENE

# CHRONOLOGY

*selection of pharaohs
and religions*

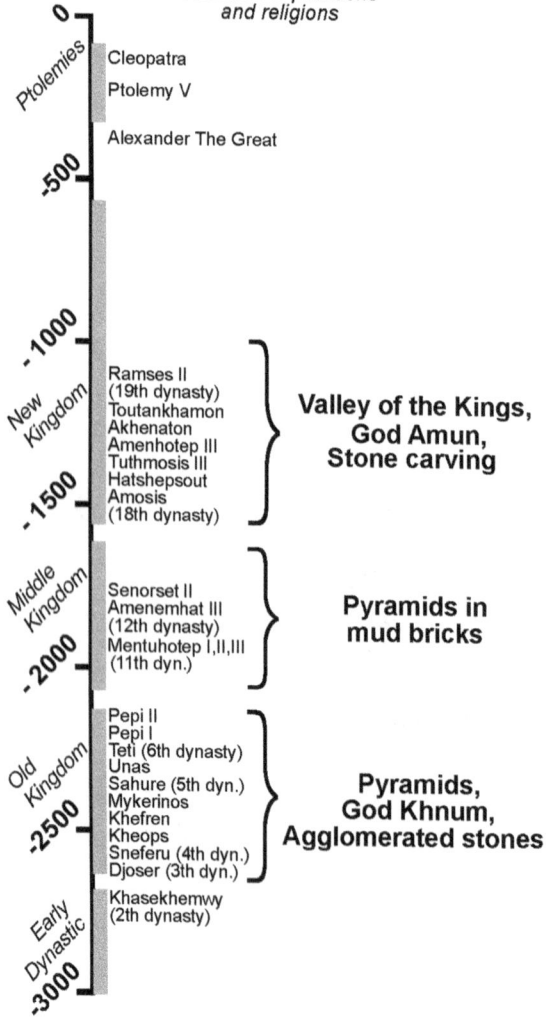

**0**

Ptolemies
- Cleopatra
- Ptolemy V

Alexander The Great

**-500**

**-1000**

New Kingdom

Ramses II
(19th dynasty)
Toutankhamon
Akhenaton
Amenhotep III
Tuthmosis III
Hatshepsout
Amosis
(18th dynasty)

} **Valley of the Kings,
God Amun,
Stone carving**

**-1500**

Middle Kingdom

Senorset II
Amenemhat III
(12th dynasty)
Mentuhotep I,II,III
(11th dyn.)

} **Pyramids in
mud bricks**

**-2000**

Old Kingdom

Pepi II
Pepi I
Teti (6th dynasty)
Unas
Sahure (5th dyn.)
Mykerinos
Khefren
Kheops
Sneferu (4th dyn.)
Djoser (3th dyn.)

} **Pyramids,
God Khnum,
Agglomerated stones**

**-2500**

Early Dynastic

Khasekhemwy
(2th dynasty)

**-3000**

# Chapter 1

# Why a new theory on how the pyramids were built?

*Professor Davidovits, you are a research scientist and you are described as the father of a new branch of chemistry. Throughout the world people are doing research in various fields to extend your work on what you have called "geopolymers"; what exactly are these?*

Geopolymers are mineral substances obtained synthetically, i.e. by chemical processes that are actually also found in nature, but which there take millions of years.

*So you are able to make all kinds of rock and stone identical to that found in the natural state?*

Yes and no. These synthetic stones are in fact re-agglomerated materials. The process is explained in more detail later in the book. Basically, the principle is as follows: starting with a mineral substance such as eroded, disintegrated or naturally disaggregated rock — such as the limestone found everywhere in northern France — we give it a compact structure using a binder, a geological glue that will agglomerate (or re-agglomerate) the mineral particles. The result is a rock that looks perfectly natural: in our case, for example, an extremely solid limestone similar to certain types occurring naturally. A geologist would notice nothing unusual. Only a very close observation of the binder can reveal the synthetic nature of the rock, because the particles themselves are without question limestone — or granite or whatever you like.

*So the fine statues in your laboratory, all depicting the same human head in various stones — these are made of geopolymers?*

1

Yes, they are. They were all cast in the same mould from different mixtures as an example of what we can do.

**Figure 1.1:** Samples of moulded geopolymer stones (limestone, granite, sandstone, arkose, . . . ) (2003).

*Very interesting. But what took you from geopolymers to the Pyramids of Egypt?*

It was partly chance. My work as a research chemist really started in 1972. For two years, in my first laboratory in Saint-Quentin in Picardie, I worked first of all on the chemical reactions of clay minerals. Nobody took any notice of us and with my team we developed the first applications, for the building industry. But in June 1974, I realised that what we were producing were materials that are very close to natural cements, such as rocks based on feldspars, the feldspathoids. One day, as a joke, I asked my scientific partners at the Muséum d'Histoire Naturelle de Paris what would happen if, we buried in the ground a piece of the product that we were synthesising in the laboratory at the time, and an archaeologist were to discover it in 3000 years' time. Their answer was surprising: the archaeologist would analyse this object disinterred from the garden of a ruin in Saint-Quentin, and the analysis would reveal that the nearest natural outcrop of the stone was in Egypt in the Aswan region! It was on that day that I realised that if I did not reveal the synthetic nature of was convinced that if the pyramids had been built as I thought, there must necessarily be, among all the writings left to us by the Egyptians, some trace somewhere. I therefore had to comb through and compare many translations in many languages. And I found what I was looking for: the texts exist and are even well known among specialists. But because they failed to understand what they were transcribing, the translators were forced to use imprecise terms in translation, and sometimes the translation of a passage was completely erroneous. So I went right back to the original writings and began a linguistic investigation on a series of technical words. And you will see in the book that a similar approach was necessary to the history, the religion and even the economy; in short, everything is connected.

*If I am to understand, it appears that the implications of your discovery open up a vast field of investigation for archaeology and perhaps place a question mark over many things that we thought we knew. Did this worry your detractors?*

As far as future work is concerned, you're probably right. As for my "detractors", I don't know. As a chemist, I was considered above all as an "amateur" in the eyes of many Egyptologists and hence not to be taken seriously. And it is this "handicap" which has led me to give more and more depth to my arguments, and which has resulted today in my theory being held in regard by the scientific community, with many ready to defend it.

*Apart from the Pyramids, can you give us an example which shows the utilisation of this chemical science?*

Yes, and quite a spectacular one. In 1999 at the Grand Palais in Paris, there was an exhibition on the ancient Egyptian Kingdom *"L'art égyptien au temps des pyramides"*. Exhibited there were objects from the Old Kingdom (3000 to 2400 BC), such as hard stone statues (granite and gneiss). And among other remarkable objects, I noticed a vase, or as it was called in catalogue number 99 *"coupe"* resembling an ashtray (figure 1.2). The shape of the vase was curiously evocative of ceramic, whereas in fact, it was made in one of the hardest rocks that exist, anorthositic gneiss. It was described thus in the catalogue:

*"... the walls are astonishingly thin, and the folding of the edges is so natural that anybody not knowing that it is made of stone would believe it to be of some flexible material ..."*

With its beautifully shaped curves and its wafer thin walls, how could such a vase have been fashioned? How could such a hard and crystalline material have been worked without being broken by the sculptor's chisel? To this, the experts have no answer, and are content to suggest that the craftsmen would have worked extremely slowly and minutely, chipping away at this very hard material millimetre by millimetre for a whole lifetime. No, clearly, the craftsmen used a technique similar to that of a potter, using instead of clay a stone paste developed through chemical knowledge and worked in a similar way.

**Figure 1.2:** Vase number 99 in anorthositic gneiss. Catalogue of the exhibition *"L'art égyptien au temps des pyramides"*, Réunion des Musées Nationaux, 1999.

*Maybe, but you must admit that to suggest that a people of nearly 5000 years ago had knowledge of the very latest science and technology of today appears unlikely.*

Perhaps, but we can approach things differently. Is it finally so surprising that a civilisation, that so venerated stone, the symbol of eternity (and we shall see that the act of agglomeration is indissociable from religious practice), should turn some of its energy to the observation, study and experimentation of minerals? Their knowledge did not appear from nowhere. It is the product of history, i.e. a long transmission from initiate to initiate, with discoveries, failures and technicians, one of whom, Imhotep, probably the wisest of all, is known to us. This is real science. And this science, like others, has been lost. The history of progress is not a linear history, whether scientific or not. And is it not paradoxical that our modern Western society, which has invested so much in the study of the animal and vegetable kingdoms (from which have come oil chemistry), has done so little with minerals? In other words, your perplexity stems perhaps more from our own ignorance than to the incontestable genius of the ancient Egyptians.

# 2 choices on how Pyramids went up

By John Munch and
Kelly McParland
Toronto Star

The mystery of how the Pyramids were built has entered a new and furious phase.

Touted as the first of the Seven Wonders of the Ancient World, the Pyramids have defied researchers trying to explain how Egyptian workers were able to lug 65-ton limestone blocks to build the mammoth structures that have dotted the Nile Valley for 4,000 years.

Now two Frenchmen believe they each have the answer, they are poles apart.

Joseph Davidovits has the more bizarre theory: The Egyptians built the stone blocks on the spot from a crude variety of fossil shells. He calls the blocks a primitive type of concrete with a casing made of relatively fine shells.

Davidovits, 47, is the founder of the Geopolymer Institute, at St. Quentin, 129 kilometres (80 miles) from Paris, and freely acknowledges that he is the "enfant terrible" among researchers in the field.

Opposing his theory is Jean-Philippe Lauer, 80-year-old Dean of European Eyptologists. Ridiculous, says Lauer, of the artificial stones theory. "There are many ridiculous surveys, not stupid, but impossible. Not many are serious."

## 300 experts

Lauer, who has spent 56 years laboring over a single pyramid, now believes that Egyptians building the pyramid of King Zoser at Saqqara, near Cairo, built short, sharply angled ramps to lift blocks as high as 70 metres (210 feet).

Davidovits and Lauer are among 300 experts attending the International Congress of Egyptology at the Skyline Hotel

until Saturday. The two researchers are to present their opposing theories during lectures this week.

"I am the first person who has ever said the stones are man-made. All the analysis, all the arguments so far were based on the supposition that the stones are natural," Davidovits said in an interview yesterday.

He says that researchers have disagreed on where the stones came from. Traditional archeologists said they came from the far side of the Nile; geologists have pinpointed their source close to the site of the pyramids; while one team of researchers believed they came from all over Egypt.

"The principle of artificial stone obtained by agglomeration of fossil shells allows me to use all these results and to interpret them correctly," Davidovits says in his newly-published book.

### Mysteries remain

Davidovits believes that ancient Egyptians could have produced synthetic stone at temperatures as low as 80 degrees C. He has constructed his own version of a stone chipping given him by Lauer. "We are totally opposed in our theories, but we converse and are friendly towards one another," Davidovits says.

Lauer, officially retired from France's national research centre, scoffs at Davidovits' approach. He believes that a moveable lever was placed on a ramp of about 250 metres (820 feet) in length, ahead of the limestone blocks. Ropes ran from the block to the lever, then reversed and ran past the block to workers further down the ramp. Workers could raise the block by pulling downhill, rather than upwards.

**Figure 1.3:** Third international conference of Egyptologists, Toronto, Canada, September 1982. The article in the newspaper, Toronto Star, on Tuesday 7 September 1982.

# Chapter 2

# Anomalies observed at Giza

*Most tourists visiting Giza are disappointed, because they see only heaps of stones.*

Yes, and at first sight, the pyramids are heaps of stones. Their height and their mass are certainly imposing, but some people think that too much of a mystery is made of them. This is the feeling you get the first time you arrive on the site if you're following a group of tourists hurrying to keep up with the guides. You ought to be able to stop, if only for ten minutes, and begin to gaze up instead of staring at the ground, and start thinking. It is then that you begin to distinguish the blocks one by one, to realise their dimensions, the number of tiers, the number of stones, and the technology used at the time. Maybe then it comes to you: "They were mad, the Egyptians!"

*Where should you look?*

If only they would take their time, the tourists would discover some strange features which defy all traditional theories. But they never have time; they are whisked around these grandiose monuments at high speed. Moreover, they concentrate on the pyramid of Cheops, whereas they ought to be looking elsewhere. Cheops is certainly remarkable in all respects, but it is an exception compared with all the other pyramids that we shall be studying in this book.

## 2.1   Enormous blocks of 30 to 500 tonnes

It is interesting to note that the first tiers of the pyramid of Chephren are built of enormous individual blocks (figure 2.1). In general, in all the great pyramids (Cheops, Chephren and Mykerinos), the

9

first and second tiers have been largely repaired or restored. The stones all have tool marks and lines which are sometimes taken for natural stratification marks. Perfectly fitting curved joints, like the one on the left of figure 2.1 are difficult or impossible to make with traditional carving instruments. This type of joint is found in all the large blocks of the eastern part of the pyramids and in the temples of the Giza Plateau.

Figure 2.1: Blocks with vertical curved joints (A) (1984).

The walls of the mortuary temples, the Temple of the Valley, the temple of the Sphinx in the complex of Chephren, and those of the funeral temple on the Mykerinos site all attracted my attention. These walls were originally covered with granite, or with some sort of cladding imitating granite, but this has disappeared. The parts protected from erosion are smooth and light grey in colour. Where there has been erosion there are variations in density. These blocks are so huge that it is difficult to imagine how they could have been hewn, extracted and transported by primitive means. They are 2 to 3 metres high and can weigh up to 500 tonnes. Sometimes, the eroded part of these enormous blocks has 2 or 3 irregular undulating layers (figure 2.2).

These layers are thinner than the natural layers; geologists maintain that these strata in the blocks are the proof that the stones are natural. They are forgetting that most man-made concrete con-

**Figure 2.2:** Undulating strata in the largest temple blocks (1988).

tains strata. Moreover, the strata seen in the Egyptian monuments are wavy, and not horizontal, whereas geological layers are generally straight.

## 2.2   The surprising dimensions of the blocks of the great pyramids

The list of anomalies found in the Great Pyramids lengthens when we consider the dimensions of the blocks. There exists a false idea perpetuated by archaeologists about the blocks of the pyramid of Cheops, according to which the height of the blocks measured at the base of the monument is always greater than that of the blocks at the summit. Obviously, such a theory would enormously simplify the logistic problems, but it does not apply to the hundreds of blocks weighing from 15 to 20 tonnes around the chamber of the King. The latter, at tier 35, clearly visible in figure 2.3, are so large that they take up the space of two tiers. As it is very difficult to lift such blocks to these heights, these figures, based on exact measurements, are a real challenge to the official theory.

**Figure 2.3:** The large blocks at tier 35 (A). One isolated large block has the dimension of tiers 20 and 21 (B) combined (1984).

## 2.3   The blocks with inclusions

The stones of the temples appear to be better in quality than those of the pyramids. Some of the features of the blocks are quite unusual, such as a large lump trapped within the mass (figure 2.4), the wavy strata, the differences in density between the stones of the pyramids and the natural stones, the absence of any horizontal orientation of the shells in the pyramid blocks, when normal sedimentation would be expected to result in shells lying flat.

The stones of the pyramids are visibly different from those of the Plateau on which the pyramids are built. In figure 2.5, at (A), the fossil shells are oriented horizontally as would be expected in the geological layers that form the base of this pyramid.

At (B), the pyramid blocks that have been adjusted above the geological layer are extremely well jointed. In the blocks, fossil shells can be seen oriented in all directions and fragmented. We can see at (C) the separation between the geological plateau and the pyramid blocks. The natural inclination of the limestone is so well corrected by the sloping base of the blocks that the top is perfectly horizontal. These blocks are each made up of a succession of layers of differing density, the topmost being the lightest.

Figure 2.4: Inclusion in a block of the pyramid of Chephren (1984).

Figure 2.5: The author examining the transition between the inclined geological plateau and the Chephren pyramid blocks that compensate the incline and establish a stable horizontal base (1984).

## 2.4 The location of the quarries is against all logic

Looking at a simplified cross-section of the plateau of Giza, it is noteworthy that the builders did not use the hard limestone occurring near and beneath the pyramids, but a much softer material further away and, surprisingly, lower down (figure 2.6).

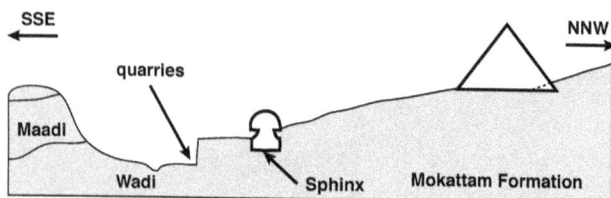

**Figure 2.6:** Simplified section of the plateau of Giza.

Why did the architects prefer to use a limestone found in the Wadi, at the bottom of the hill, requiring a lot of extra work to drag the blocks up an additional height of 40 to 50 metres, on ramps? This is contrary to what we know about the traditional methods for extracting stones used in antiquity. Generally during this period, quarries were chosen in a location above the place where the monument was to be constructed, so as to make transport easy with a minimum of effort, letting gravity do its work. All the quarries worked by the Egyptians — the granite quarry at Aswan, the sandstone quarry at Silsilis to the south of Thebes, the soft limestone quarry at Tura, opposite the pyramids on the other side of the Nile — were chosen according to this criterion. Why should the plateau of Giza be an exception?

Egyptologists do not seem to be unduly bothered by this question. They find it perfectly normal that architects should have deliberately neglected the limestone on top of the hill, close at hand to the west. Yet had this limestone been used, it would have been so much easier, using the natural inclination of the plateau, to transport the blocks to the pyramids.

The Giza site is full of blocks with astonishing shapes that can only be explained by the use of re-agglomerated stone. Here, I have selected the most representative evidence, but the reports of visitors supporting my theory are so numerous that a whole book could be devoted to them.

# Chapter 3

# Criticism of theories

*From all that you have just shown, explanations can still be given for the official theory.*

Yes, but this leads to needless complexity; a way of perfectly carving the blocks has to be found, and remember that the strange blocks were not visible, because they were covered with casing stones which have now disappeared. If the Egyptians really did use the traditional methods ascribed to them, we must admit that they had a perverse pleasure in creating superfluous problems for themselves.

*But isn't this official theory based on the presumed knowledge of the ancient Egyptians?*

Numerous Egyptologists agree that we are well acquainted with the science and the techniques mastered by the Egyptians at the time of the pyramids. But beneath this certainty lies a paradox: why is it that over several centuries, so many generations of architects, chemists, physicists, geologists, historians and Egyptologists have failed to agree among themselves on a single theory of how the pyramids were built? There are several dozen theories covering systems of ramps, hoisting devices, carving and transporting of the stones. If we know all the facts, if our methods of scientific investigation and analyses carried out by advanced techniques give incontestable results, then why is there such confusion? We can see that there is no official theory. All without exception are speculative and have never gone beyond the stage of hypothesis, i.e. from a simple idea to a feasible model founded on scientific and archaeological proof.

## 3.1 Ramps

Of course, to build the pyramids you have to climb up what has already been built, using steps or ramps. As the pulley and the wheel were unknown in Egypt at the time of the pyramids, the ramp would have been the most suitable way of transporting the stones. In 1936, the German Egyptologist Borchardt discovered traces of an access ramp to the pyramid of Meidum. These traces are very modest in size, from three to four metres wide (figure 3.1). Now, in the traditional explanations for the great pyramid, these ramps would have been 2 km long and 10 to 70 metres wide, according to Jean-Philippe Lauer (figure 3.2). They would have required more material with than the pyramid itself!

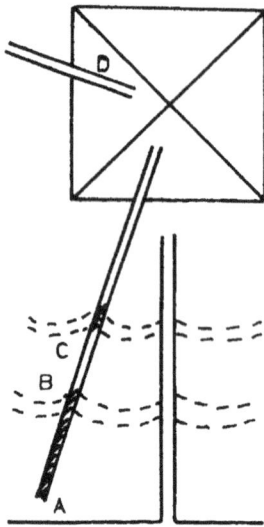

Figure 3.1: The ramps found by Borchardt at Meidum.

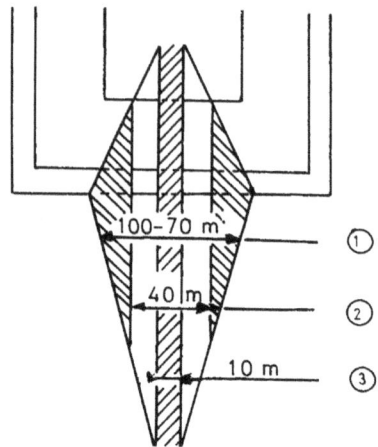

Figure 3.2: Lauer's ramp with a width varying from 100 metres at the base to 10 metres at the summit.

In order to reduce the volume of material, several Egyptologists have suggested the use of an enveloping or spiral ramp (figures 3.3, 3.4; 3.5, 3.6). Even with an enveloping ramp, the length depends essentially on the slope. For example, with a slope of 5 %, it is 2.5 to 3 km long. Workers would have taken more than one day to raise their load of 2.5 tonnes. The lower the slope, the greater the distance, possibly extending up to 10 to 12 km. The transport would take around one week, which seems very long. This is why several experts suggest the use of the alternating ramp, which does increase the slope, but reduces the distance.

**Figure 3.3:** The enveloping ramp of G. Goyon.

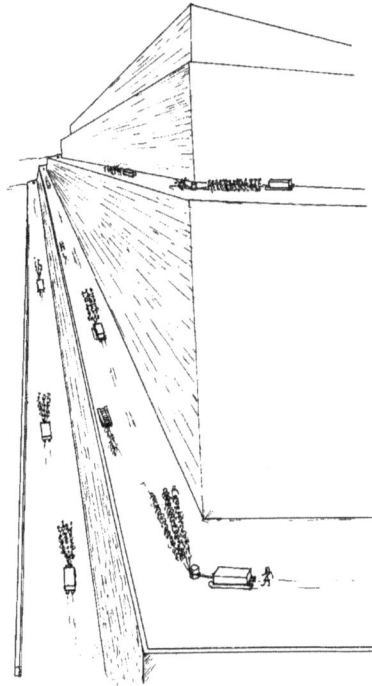

**Figure 3.4:** The problem of the corners.

Others argue against this, arguing that it would have been impossible to manoeuvre safely around the corners. And no archaeological remains of this type of ramp have been found up to now. The only remains found are always of straight ramps. They were obviously used for the transport of small blocks, mortar or stone that was to be agglomerated, because of course, to build a pyramid with re-agglomerated stone, like concrete, you still have to get to the higher tiers. This involves the use of the type of steep, straight, narrow ramps found on sites such as Meidum.

Small ramps in mud bricks have been found, for example at Saqqarah inside the pyramid attributed to the Pharaoh Semkhemkhet of the third dynasty. This pyramid, which was never completed, is made of small stone blocks. A ramp was needed to lay them. But this type of ramp cannot serve as proof of the traditional hypothesis, with blocks weighing several tonnes. Any enormous ramps that

Figure 3.6: The alternating ramp of J.P. Adam.

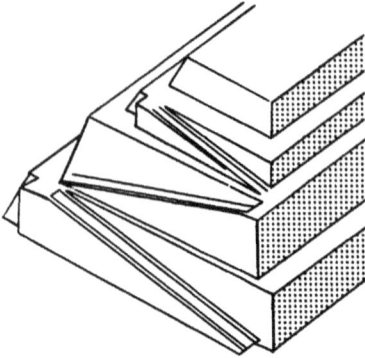

Figure 3.5: The alternating ramp of Hoeschler.

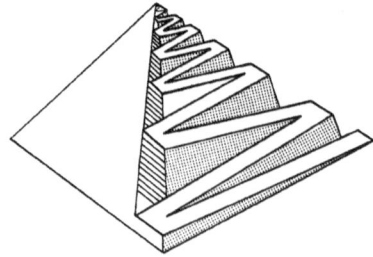

would have been necessary at Giza have left no trace. The only remains of ramps known to us today are suggestive of small ramps used by workers to climb up the pyramids during their construction.

And then, to be of any use, a ramp would have needed a wet clay or silt surface to reduce friction as much as possible, thereby cutting down on the number of haulers. Teams would have been employed continuously sprinkling water. But the ramps are actually made of mud bricks, baked in the sun. The action of water on silt and clay would have transformed the ramp into a slippery mud slope; 50 000 workers slithering in the mud ... they would simply have become bogged down in no time!

Some archaeologists favour the idea of a sledge hauled along on wooden rollers (figure 3.7). There is no evidence to support this. Rollers automatically imply the discovery of the wheel, but the latter was only introduced into Egypt at the end of the Middle Kingdom around 1700BC by the Hyksos during their conquest of Egypt. The only document showing the use of rollers is a bas-relief from the palace of Sennacherib of Nineveh, at present in the British Museum. It dates from 750 BC, i.e. around 2000 years after the building of the pyramids. The Great Pyramids, the most impressive buildings of antiquity, were built before wheels were introduced as a means of transport.

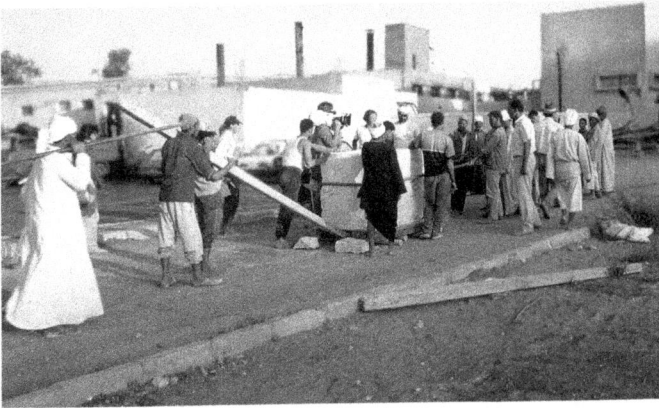

**Figure 3.7:** The experiment carried out by the NOVA team; pulling a large stone on rollers is only possible on a hard, flat surface such as a modern tarmac road. It does not work on sand (1991).

## 3.2   The other machine theories

Instead of a lever, in the nineteenth century the French architect Auguste Choisy suggested a device that he called an oscillating hoist, wooden models of which have been found in several New Kingdom tombs (figure 3.8).

However, according to J.P. Lauer, the fact that these models were found in New Kingdom tombs and not those of the Middle or Old Kingdom contradicts this theory. A German engineer, Louis Croon, following the text of Herodotus, pondered the problem of transporting and raising the pyramid blocks. After using long calculations to show that ramps would have been impossible, as they would require almost as much labour as the pyramids themselves and would not in any case allow the last few metres to the summit to be finished, he concluded that some sort of lifting device would have been necessary. Croon proposed a machine design along the lines of the Egyptian chadouf with which a fellah would draw water from his well; this already existed in antiquity (figures 3.9 and 3.10).

The machine consisted essentially of a beam pivoting in a vertical plane about a pivoting shaft. In 1952, Strub-Roessler ruled out the use of ramps and proposed large wooden gins to lift the casing blocks (figure 3.11).

In 1975, the French archaeologist Jean-Pierre Adam proposed lifting devices inspired by the Greco-Roman civilisation including

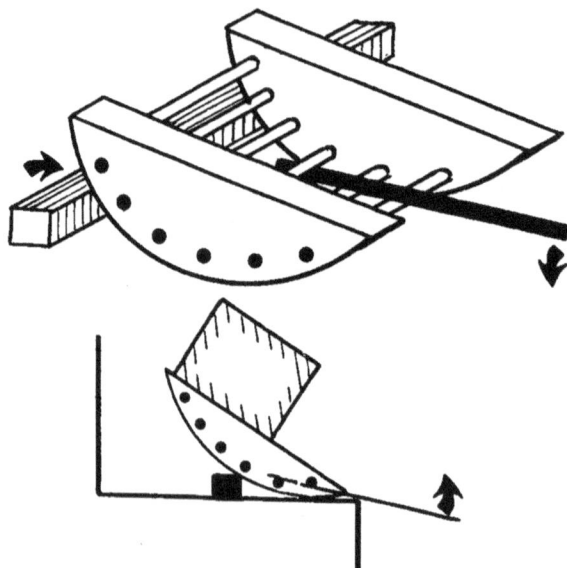

Figure 3.8: The oscillating hoist.

Figure 3.9: The Egyptian chadouf.

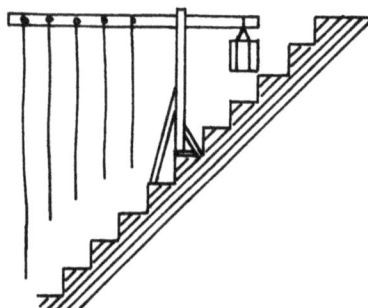

Figure 3.10: Croon's device.

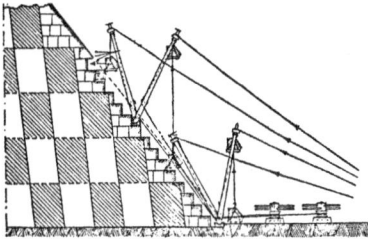

Figure 3.11: Strub-Roessler's gins.

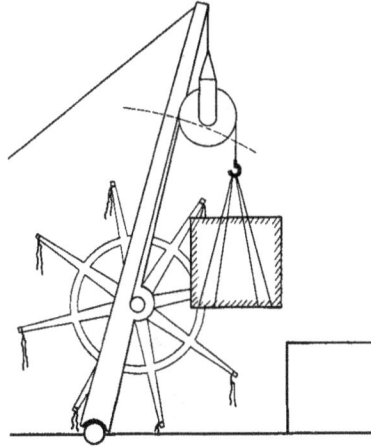

Figure 3.12: J.P. Adam's capstan.

the capstan. But this does not in any way agree with what we know of the means at the disposal of the Old Kingdom Egyptian pyramid builders (figure 3.12).

Among other methods, the most original is the use of hydraulic force. Manuel Martinez came up with the idea of a huge system of locks (figure 3.13). On the assumption that all the stone blocks came from quarries on the other side of the Nile, he had them crossing the river in individual boats, then rising up on a system of ascending locks to where they were needed on the pyramid.

This idea is in major contradiction with what is actually found on the site at Giza:

a) 95 % of the blocks — those making up the mass of the pyramids — come from nearby quarries on the same side of the Nile. These blocks have not therefore crossed the Nile. The gigantic locks are therefore of no use.

b) How did they build these colossal locks made of enormous stone blocks that had to be hoisted along the slope of the pyramid? With capstans? Levers? Clay ramps? More material would have been needed than for the pyramid itself.

## 3.3 Other systems

Hardly a year goes by without somebody dreaming up a new theory, always based on the use of ropes, rails, sledges, oscillating devices or

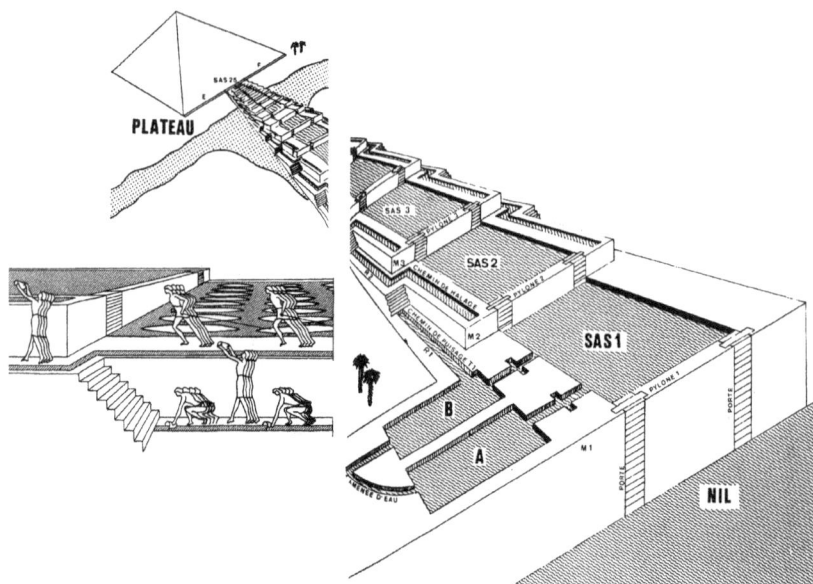

**Figure 3.13:** The huge locks of M. Martinez.

levers. Among others we can quote:

### 3.3.1 Papyrus cylinders

Imitating a technique used by the Greeks to transport marble columns, the stone block is rolled up the inclined plane of the pyramid inside a papyrus cylinder by workers pulling on ropes.

### 3.3.2 The elevator

A tower consisting of two parallel walls is built. At the top is placed a large and perfectly cylindrical tree trunk (the pulley). Men in a basket act as a counterweight, thus raising the block.

### 3.3.3 The funicular

To prevent the workers slipping on the clay ramp, they move along behind the block on wooden duckboards, pulling on ropes attached to the block and slung around vertical or horizontal stakes driven in ahead of the block. The block itself moves on a sledge sliding on wetted clay or on rails. In 1988, I attended the talk given by J.-P. Lauer at the fifth Congress of Egyptologists at Cairo. Recognising that his system of ramps was too voluminous, he presented a device equivalent to a funicular.

The only limit to the number of theories for the lifting and transport of these stone blocks appears to be that of the ingenuity of human imagination. In general, they all come from retired public works engineers or architects, who are, after all, serious people with a considerable intellectual background. But the profusion of their systems hides a fundamental error in their approach to the problem: they are concerned only with how the stones were moved, never with how they were shaped using stone or soft copper tools; neither are they concerned by the dimensions of the blocks, let alone their perfect fit. Thus, they are only interested in the pyramid of Cheops — certainly the most remarkable — and ignore the eight earlier and some 40 later pyramids, each one different. They are interested only in one very precise technical problem, and take no account of the environment and knowledge of Egyptology. It is moreover very easy to show that their ideas do not stand up to archaeological proofs.

## 3.4   The mini pyramid of NOVA

In October 1991, in the USA, I took part in the making of a television documentary on the various experts' theories currently in circulation. The main aim was to actually build a mini-pyramid. Although the experiment was carried out from start to finish with modern tools — a forklift truck, lorries to transport the stones — the programme makers claimed that they wanted to field test certain methods of carving quarrying and transporting. The accent was on building a ramp, a sledge and rollers and on handling with levers. My contribution remained theoretical, since I did not have access to the various sites for raw materials.

The documentary was broadcast in 1992 by the American public channel PBS and entitled "This old pyramid"; it was produced by NOVA (WGBH, Boston), with the American Egyptologist, Dr Mark Lehner as the anchorman. However, the producer deliberately avoided showing the modern lifting machinery or the steel tools being used, leaving the viewer with the impression of having seen a mini pyramid being built by the methods really used by the ancient Egyptians. But during the building of this mini pyramid, which took three weeks, I was able to witness the flagrant weaknesses of the traditional theories. Figures 3.14, 3.15, 3.16, 3.17 shares some of my photos; they illustrate the main problems that the builders had to cope with.

The Egyptian workers employed to build this mini pyramid for NOVA, used modern steel tools that were in no way imitations of the stone tools of the Old Kingdom. But even with these powerful steel carving tools, they were incapable of imitating the perfect jointing obtained by their ancestors. Their casing blocks did not join properly and had gaps 0.5 to 1 cm wide, plus broken corners. By comparison, you cannot insert a razor blade between the stones of the Great Pyramid.

Building this mini pyramid provided no satisfactory answers to the following questions: How, using stone and copper tools, could absolutely flat surfaces on the pyramids have been made? How did the Egyptians ensure that the four surfaces joined perfectly in a single point at the summit? How did they get the tiers to be perfectly horizontal? How could they have quarried stones with uniform and repetitive dimensions? How could they have placed the heaviest blocks in the pyramid at a great height? How could they have made the casing blocks fit so perfectly that a hair cannot be inserted between the joints? And finally, how could they have built this monument in 20 years?

**Figure 3.14:** The NOVA mini pyramid, 1991.

Figure 3.15: Steel tools and a stone tool.

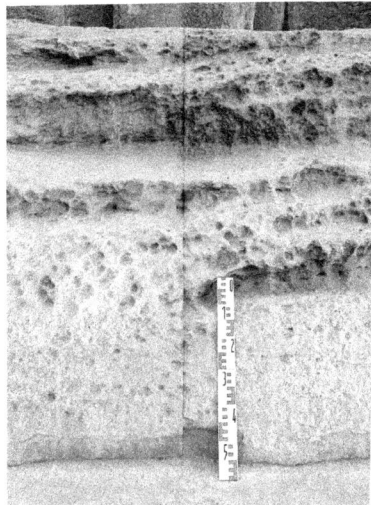

Figure 3.16: The gaps in the NOVA casing.

Figure 3.17: The joints in Cheops (1991).

# Chapter 4

# Alternative and fantastic theories

*We have just seen that the traditional theory on the carving and hoisting of blocks on sledges is neither official nor convincing.*

Yet Egyptologists, architects and engineers continue to devise processes that, though practical and intelligent, have no connection with archaeological reality.

*Then given these weaknesses and impossibilities, the question is still open?*

Yes, which allows various people outside Egyptology circles to publish other scenarios and hypotheses. It is these alternative theories that arouse public interest. In this chapter, I shall give several accounts involving so-called "advanced" technologies and knowledge, with or without the aid of "extraterrestrials".

In the years 1960 to 1970, after the esoteric movement set in motion by the book by Louis Powels and Jacques Bergier, *Le Matin des Magiciens*, numerous authors carried the torch. Thus, Robert Charroux claims that these mysterious monuments, the pyramids, were built by technologically super-advanced ancient civilisations, generally using engineering based on physical science. Erich von Daniken attributes everything to the physical and engineering prowess of extraterrestrials.

Charroux endows Ancient Egypt with a knowledge of ultrasonic and antigravitational forces. These theories, implying a super civilisation that has disappeared today, resurfaced in the Nineties under the pens of Graham Hancock and Robert Beauval.

A short extract from these publications is quite edifying:

"... It is easier to judge the pyramids from a strictly architectural point of view. This investigation provides the proof that no 20th century state would dare to undertake such a colossal project using modern techniques, requiring 200 000 to 300 000 workers, several million cubic metres of hewn stone, and millions of francs. The greatest experts estimate that the Egypt at the time of the pyramids had to feed more than 100 million inhabitants, and to have been able to achieve such gigantic works they possessed machines of a power and perfection unknown in our own century. All explanations, whether they involve scaffolding, infilling, inclined planes or slippery ramps, collapse on examination. A single hypothesis can be the only explanation: the Egyptians must have had as yet unimaginable knowledge of the power of ultrasound and antigravitational forces".

On the use of ultrasound and levitation, we read:

"... Levitation by antigravitation or ultrasound was responsible for the same feats: and if we associate ultrasound with antigravitation, it is because the Egyptian tradition seems to allow us to do so. Sound, which may be an unknown dimension, possesses a power that modern science has only recently studied. An ultrasonic bomb capable of annihilating all animal life within a large town without damaging monuments or objects has been described. In medicine, bones can be broken by ultrasound, and death can be caused by the effect of sound on the brain. Indeed it is certain that the bang of supersonic aircraft shakes up the nerves and may be lethal for those with heart disease ... Whatever the case, from ultrasounds that cause death or levitation, to the ultrasounds that may have caused the fall of the walls of Jericho, there exists a scientific unknown that was exploited in Antiquity ... "

All these fabulous forces proposed by archaeomaniacs only serve to reduce monuments to a heap of rubble: the ultrasonic bomb, the walls of Jericho, death by shaking the brain, the supersonic bang from a wall of sound. We know of no application to building, only destruction. They destroy natural equilibrium, and in their way they rival the hard technology that came in with iron — only they are more deadly. The main application of iron has been weapons. Those who mastered iron were warriors above all else: not builders, but invaders. Those periods in Egypt's history that are the richest in monuments are precisely those during which peace prevailed over the whole kingdom.

One small but significant detail is sufficient to eliminate these "hypertechniques": to capture these energies and make use of them, "resonance chambers" are supposed to be necessary — the chambers, in fact, of the Great Pyramid of Cheops (the Great gallery associated with the Chamber of the Queen and the Chamber of the King). Thus, the Pyramid of Cheops with its immense chambers (of enormous blocks) is built first, with whatever means they have. Then, using the pyramid, weight can be eliminated, thus enabling the later pyramids to be built using this "supertechnique". But how on earth did they build Cheops, with its resonance chambers, in the first place?

As for myself, I prefer the solution proposed in the well-known strip cartoon by Rene Goscinny and Albert Uderzo, *Asterix and Cleopatra*, in which the magic potion of the druid Getafix gives super-human force to the person who drinks it. Every worker who drinks the potion is able single-handedly to lift a block weighing several tonnes, and the blocks are then thrown from worker to worker to speed up the transport; a method that is still used today, but with bricks of much more modest dimensions! The comic book humor-ously describes a rather personal point of view on Egyptian building methods — but one that is perhaps not so far removed from the ideas of more serious authors.

# Chapter 5

# The theory of agglomerated stone

*In the face of all this confusion, a radically different new theory must surely be devised, one that stands up to scientific and historic scrutiny. Does the theory of agglomerated stone get us out of the impasse the egyptologists and amateur archaeologists have shut themselves into?*

I believe so, because the theory of agglomerated stone is the only one that is really holistic — it can be justified from all points of view: theoretical and experimental science, religion and hieroglyphic texts. None of the other theories take into account the whole environment at the time of the pyramids. And for a good reason: they are all technical theories, focused on engineering and ignoring the historical context. To begin with, let us examine a few simple data. The great pyramids were built from real agglomerated stone, i.e. a limestone that has been naturally broken up and reconstituted like concrete (figure 5.1).

But this is not a concrete made with plaster, nor is it a modern cement of the Portland type used to agglomerate ground up stone. My discovery is based on the new science involving surprising knowledge that nobody has dared attribute to these distant ancestors living more than 4500 years ago. This science, which used to be called Alchemy, involves a range of disciplines: geosynthesis, geochemistry, mineralogy and geology; in other words, it is what is known today as geopolymer science[1] . The agglomerated stone hypothesis, relying

---

[1]See the Geopolymer Institute website at www.geopolymer.org.

**Figure 5.1:** The Rekhmire fresco describing the making of mud bricks, depicts a process in very similar to that of real agglomerated stone. Photo: Manuel Delgado.

on scientific, archaeological and religious proofs, is the only one to have made use of the hieroglyphic texts describing the building of these gigantic monuments.

But it is not enough just to present scientific and technical arguments. They must agree with the knowledge existing at the time, with archaeological evidence, and with the culture of the Egyptian people. All this evidence has been discovered and is developed in this book.

Take for example the hieroglyphs. Which symbols refer to the action of building? Do they refer to the method of building by carving and transporting stone?

## 5.1   The hieroglyphic writing of the notion "construct, build"

There are two distinct verbs, *khusi*, and *kedj*, to designate the notion of construct, build. The verb *kedj* represents a mason building a wall or enclosure in unbaked silt bricks (sign A35 in Gardiner's list). The sign is very often found associated with other concepts such as fashion, mould, model, form, construct (a body or statue). (See figure 5.2).

The other verb, *khusi*, which is also pronounced *khuas*, *khesi* is

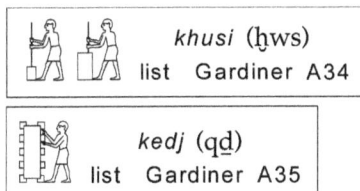

| | khusi (ḥws) |
| list | Gardiner A34 |

| | kedj (qd) |
| list | Gardiner A35 |

**Figure 5.2:** The two verbs for construct, build.

always accompanied by a determinative sign showing a worker crushing material in a mortar or packing it in a mould (see sign A34 in Gardiner's list).

In column 12 of the Famine Stele, which we shall later be studying, we read... "With these products... they built [...] the royal tomb (pyramid)" (figure 5.3).

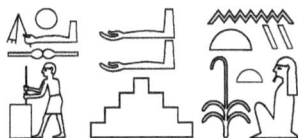

**Figure 5.3:** Khusi — "With these products... they built [...] the royal tomb (pyramid)"

**Figure 5.4:** The adobe technique used today in Africa for building with compacted earth.

This sign is said to come from a word which originally meant the technique of building with compacted earth (adobe). But far from being limited merely to the packing of a wet clay material, this sign can perfectly well refer to the production of blocks using a wet mortar of nummulitic limestone to make agglomerated stone.

The adobe technique is still used today in Mediterranean countries and in Africa (figure 5.4). We see a worker standing barefoot inside a mould of small planks, held together by ropes and wooden laths across the bottom of the mould. The worker is packing the wet material with a pestle. The adjacent blocks form part of the mould, thereby giving imperceptible joints.

## 5.2   The theory explained in a strip cartoon

The cartoon below shows how reagglomerated stones were made for the construction of the pyramids.

(1) Wadi : a desert watercourse that dries up periodically

**Figure 5.5:** Illustration of the theory of the reagglomeration of stone, cartoon drawings by Serge Dutfoy, 2002.

# Chapter 6

# Scientific evidence

*In your introduction you told us how you came to study the pyramids, quite by chance, from your background of science. What exactly is this science?*

Everybody knows that nature is composed of the animal kingdom, the vegetable kingdom and the mineral kingdom. For the last 150 years, chemical science has helped us understand and reproduce the various features of the animal and vegetable kingdoms. This biochemical research has given us plastics, synthetic fibres, biochemistry and modern medicine. But it is only since 1960 that the chemical mineralogical and geological sciences have tackled the synthesis of materials duplicating those of the mineral kingdom.

## 6.1 Chemical formula, geological glue

Materials representing practically all the mineralogical classes can now be made in the laboratory, but the most spectacular results have been obtained in the microprocessor industry (with silicon and germanium), and with geopolymers of the aluminosilicate type. With the latter, many mineral structures equivalent to natural ones such as feldspars, feldspathoids, zeolites and amphiboles can be produced (figure 6.2). It is actually quite easy to produce these minerals; this is done at low temperature, i.e., under normal climatic conditions, or else at relatively moderate temperatures between 45 and 100°C.

We know that the earth is composed of clay-like materials, and that these materials are the result of the climatic erosion of rocks such as granite. In other words, the natural erosion and degradation due to the climate transform feldspar rocks into sedimentary minerals such as the clays. New research in mineralogy and geology has revealed various different reaction kinetics. With this knowledge, we are able in a sense to go back in mineralogical time, i.e. to convert the clay sediment back into a rock, in a word, *to do the opposite of what nature does*. The techniques of geopolymerisation make use of these chemical principles. Thus, any clay materials can be metamorphosed into a set of mineral products having all the characteristics of rocks, that is: water resistance, temperature stability, hardness, resistance to acids, etc.

In general, natural stones are made of crystallised components agglomerated or bound together by a cement or a binder. There are for example, sandstones, granites, puddings, fossil limestones, etc. Similarly, artificial stones are the result of the agglomeration of crystallised materials (from natural stones), with a geopolymer binder (cement) of the same chemical nature as natural cements and binders. When stones from archaeological sites are examined, and the analysis shows the presence of these minerals, we therefore have to ask ourselves whether they are natural or artificial. The answer is not as simple as it may appear, because in fact, we do not know very well how to distinguish between the "natural" and the "synthetic". This is why, as we shall later see, geologists have not detected anything of an artificial nature. When there is any doubt, what we have to look for is anything in the archaeological or historical environment that could be evidence for the use of these techniques. Are there the remains of any industry? Were the necessary chemicals available? Does the technology fit in with the history, the religion and the civilisation of the place?

Every society uses its own natural resources, and above all takes maximum advantage of its ecosystem. Every civilisation is founded around the presence of a unique natural potential specific to the area and not found elsewhere. Mineral and agricultural exploitation ensure the development of this civilisation. When resources run out, the civilisation disappears. The approach I used in studying the pyramids of Egypt was to take an integrated look at the facts of Egyptian culture and civilisation as they were affected by the available resources.

We quickly realised that among the chemicals that are used in the laboratory, a large number were available in Egypt. Take for example, sodium carbonate, commonly called *natron* salt and used in the mummifying process. From analyses of the mummification process, we know that the Egyptians had perfect mastery of chemical processes. Moreover, the limestone from the quarries of Giza readily disaggregates in water, because it contains kaolinitic clay, a very reactive clay. This clay, present in the Giza limestone, swells in the presence of water, making the limestone aggregates break up. It is this naturally disaggregated, cleaved stone which serves as raw material.

## 6.2 Egyptian Pyramid stone, re-agglomerated limestone concrete, 2700 BC

When did the history of concrete begin? Emery Farkas, then president of ACI, American Concrete Institute, contemplated this question in his August 1985 President's memo of the Magazine, Concrete International, entitled, *"How old is concrete? Engineering versus Chemistry."*

*"It is an accepted fact that the origin of Portland cement goes back to the early 19th century when an English bricklayer, Joseph Aspdin, created a cementitious product which when hardened looked similar to building stone found in the island of Portland in England.*

*The history of concrete, however, goes back to ancient times. The Greeks and Romans used calcined limestone and later developed the pozzolanic cement by grinding together lime and volcanic ash called "pozzolan" which was first found near Port Pozzuoli, Italy. The late Henry L. Kennedy, a past president of ACI in the middle 50's, had on his desk a sample of pozzolanic concrete, which had been under water in the harbor of Pozzuoli for over 2000 years.*

*Sometime ago, an article in Omni magazine dealt with a fascinating idea, which would put the origin of concrete much earlier... According to this theory, to built a pyramid, Egyptian workers could have carried crushed limestone to the work site in buckets, mixed it with Nile River for the needed aluminum and silicon binder, and added salts available locally as catalysts to make the solution alkaline. They could have dumped the ingredients into wooden molds and a few hours in the desert heat would have dried the mixture to hard rock. This could have been done with neither massive ramps nor difficult tooling... This is a fascinating theory but it is totally rejected by archaeologists who support the "engineering" aspect against the "chemistry" theory.*

*Whoever is right, it is interesting to note that concrete may be much older than we think and that in ancient structures it might have been "engineering" or "chemistry" while in today's construction it is "engineering" and "chemistry" together which create the marvelous modern structures."*

How the Great Pyramids of Giza were built has remained an enduring mystery. In the mid-1980s, I presented my first analytical results carried out on genuine pyramid stones[1]. I claimed that the ancient Egyptians knew how to generate a geopolymeric reaction in the making of a re-agglomerated limestone (a concrete involving 95 % by weight of natural limestone elements). I was followed by Professor Guy Demortier[2] who analyzed Cheops casing stones with PIXE, PIGE and NMR. The NMR spectroscopy depicts similarities between a Cheops stone and a geopolymeric reconstituted stone. According to Demortier, the Cheops casing stone may hold 15 % of artificial geopolymeric cement.

More recently, Barsoum, Ganguly and Hug[3] used primarily scanning and transmission electron microscopy to compare a number of pyramid limestone samples with six different quarry limestone samples from their vicinity. They provided fundamental information that allowed me[4] to present a final geopolymerization mechanism for the

---

[1]Davidovits J., (1982), No More Than 1500 Workers to Build the Pyramid of Cheops with Agglomerated Man-Made Stone, *International Congress of Egyptology; Toronto*, 1982, 5–11 sept.; CAN; 1982; p. 40.

Davidovits J., Thorez J. and Gaber M.H., (1984), Pyramids of Egypt made of man-made stone, myth of fact?, *Symposium on Archaeometry 1984*, Smithsonian Institution, Washington DC; Abstracts; pp. 26–27.

Davidovits J., (1986), X-Rays Analysis and X-Rays Diffraction of Casing Stones from the Pyramids of Egypt, and the Limestone of the Associated Quarries; pp. 511–20 in *Science in Egyptology Symposia*, Edited by R. A. David. Manchester University Press, Manchester, U.K.

Davidovits J. and Morris M., (1988), *The Pyramids: An Enigma Solved.* Hippocrene Books, New York, 1988.

[2]Demortier G. (2004), PIXE, PIGE and NMR study of the masonry of the pyramid of Cheops at Giza, *Nuclear Instruments and Methods in Physics Research B*, B 226, 98–109.

[3]Barsoum M.W., Ganguly A. and Hug G., (2006), Microstructural Evidence of Reconstituted Limestone Blocks in the Great Pyramids of Egypt, *J. Am. Ceram. Soc.* 89[12], 3788–3796.

[4]Davidovits J., (2006), Le "béton" des pyramides égyptiennes, *Revue du Palais de la Découverte*, Paris, 343, dec. 2006, 47–60.

making of the limestone matrices (see in figure 6.2). Up to that date, geosynthesis involved kaolinite clay (naturally included in the Giza limestone) that reacted with caustic soda. To manufacture this caustic soda, the Egyptians used natron (sodium carbonate) and lime (coming from plant ashes, for example acacia). The so obtained caustic soda, NaOH, reacts with kaolinite clay. The chemical reaction creates natural mineral analogues: pure limestone (calcium carbonate, calcite) as well as Na–poly(sialate), a feldspathoid (hydrated hydrosodalite). This method has a major drawback, it is still caustic and difficult to manipulate with bare hands.

Barsoum, Ganguly and Hug found that the pyramid samples contained micro-constituents ($\mu c$'s) with appreciable amounts of Si in combination with elements, such as Ca and Mg, in ratios that do not exist in any of the potential limestone sources. The intimate proximity of the $\mu c$'s suggests that at some time these elements had been together in a solution. In other words Mg and Ca should be involved in the geopolymerization mechanism. Calcium based geopolymer is well known, but the involvement of Mg was unknown, even in zeolite chemistry.

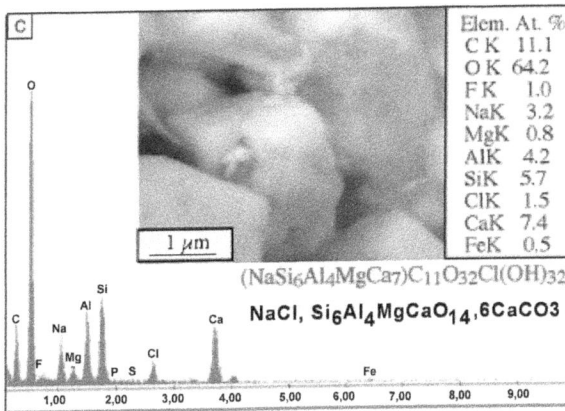

**Figure 6.1:** SEM analysis of pyramid core block MENK, after Barsoum *et al.*.

So far, at least two chemical systems have been identified, one used for the manufacture of the core blocks (the greatest quantity of stones), the second for the casings. In the study by Barsoum *et al.* the core blocks are illustrated by the samples MENK, whereas the casings relate to the Lauer and OC samples. I chose those pyramid stones and selected the MENK samples from a big ashlar at the bottom of one of the Mykerinos (Menkaure) satellite pyramid (See in Appendix A at Stage 12, figure A.27). The casing stones, coined Lauer and OC originated from the Cheops Great Pyramid itself.

SEM analysis of the matrix associated with limestone core block MENK gives the general formula $(NaSi_6Al_4MgCa_7)C_{11}O_{32}Cl(OH)_{32}$ (figure 6.1) corresponding to the solid solution of:

- halite NaCl
- geopolymer of the feldspathoid/mica-chlorite type $Si_6Al_4MgCaO_{14}$
- calcite calcium carbonate $6CaCO_3$

## 6.2.1 Chemistry of the core blocks

The following laboratory experimentation has reproduced the chemistry involved in the making of the pyramid stone MENK of figure 6.1. This example, among others, introduces natural salts found in the Egyptian environment

We have seen above that the mixture is still quite caustic and cannot be used with bare hands. In order to neutralize it, I added to it a special salt[5], for example carnallite (magnesium chloride) easily found in evaporites, in saline deposits like natron, but not at the same place (see chemical equations 3 and 4 in figure 6.2). The excess of caustic alkali is transformed into the neutral salts magnesite and halite, which explains the high content of NaCl found in pyramid stones. Most importantly, the sodium Na in the feldspathoid geopolymer is exchanged with Mg, yielding a new Mg-based geopolymer of type mica-chlorite (equation 3).

In their investigation, Barsoum *et al.* found that between the natural limestone aggregates, the $\mu c$'s with chemistries reminiscent of calcite and dolomite — not known to hydrate in nature — were hydrated. Figure 6.2 illustrates this finding: magnesite $MgCO_3$ produced in equation 4 reacts with calcite $CaCO_3$ generated in equation 1, yielding hydrated dolomite that will crystallize with time into rhombohedral dolomite crystals, another characteristic of this reaction. Several pyramid mortars exhibit this property, highlighted by Regourd *et al.*[6] .

---

[5]Davidovits J., (2006), Le "béton" des pyramides égyptiennes, *Revue du Palais de la Découverte*, Paris, 343, dec. 2006, 47–60.

[6]Regourd M., Kerisel J., Deletie P., and Haguenauer B., (1988), Microstructure of Mortars from Three Egyptian Pyramids, *Cement Concrete Res.*, 18, 81–90.

**1** $Na_2CO_3$ + $Ca(OH)_2$ → $2NaOH$ + $CaCO_3$
sodium + lime => caustic soda + calcite
carbonate (natron)

**2** $Si_2O_5,Al_2(OH)_4$ + $2NaOH$ → $Na_2O.2SiO_2.Al_2O_3.nH_2O$
kaolinite clay + caustic soda => hydrated feldspathoid

**3** $Na_2O.2SiO_2.Al_2O_3.nH_2O$ + $MgCl_2$ → $MgO.2SiO_2.Al_2O_3.nH_2O$ + $2 NaCl$
feldspathoid + carnallite => mica-chlorite + halite

**4** $Na_2CO_3$ + $MgCl_2$ → $MgCO_3$ + $2 NaCl$
sodium + carnallite => magnesite + halite
carbonate (natron)

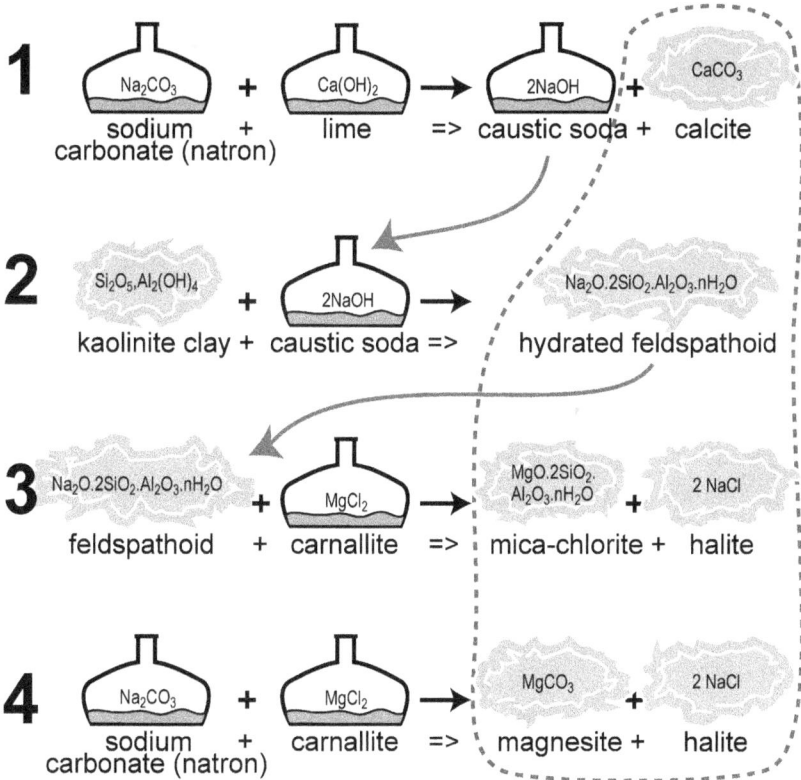

**Abstract of the geosynthesis of an artificial limestone:**

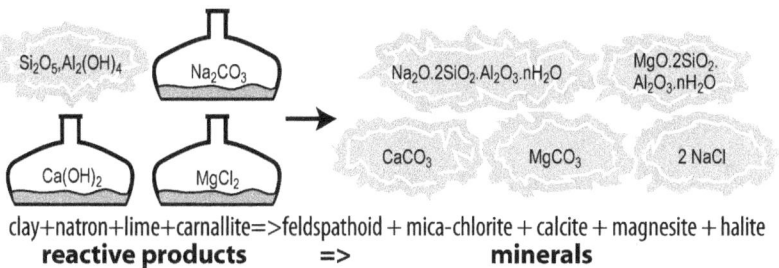

$Si_2O_5,Al_2(OH)_4$ $Na_2CO_3$ → $Na_2O.2SiO_2.Al_2O_3.nH_2O$ $MgO.2SiO_2.Al_2O_3.nH_2O$

$Ca(OH)_2$ $MgCl_2$ $CaCO_3$ $MgCO_3$ $2 NaCl$

clay+natron+lime+carnallite=>feldspathoid + mica-chlorite + calcite + magnesite + halite
**reactive products** => **minerals**

Caption:
reactive product · synthesized mineral · **Geosynthesis:** manufacture of minerals with chemistry, thus natural materials!

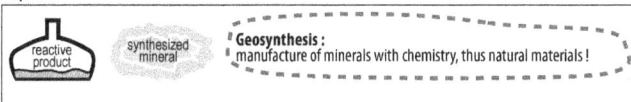

**Figure 6.2:** Geochemical reaction scheme for kaolinitic clay and limestone from Giza, Egypt.

## 6.2.2 Chemistry of the casing stones

The casing stones are harder than the core blocks. They are made of a silica-based limestone[7] containing up to 10 % $SiO_2$. Barsoum *et al.* stressed the ubiquity of Si and the presence of submicron silica-based spheres in some of the micrographs. Transmission electron microscope confirmed that some of these Si-containing $\mu c$'s were either amorphous or nanocrystalline, which is consistent with a relatively rapid precipitation reaction.

In the chemical reaction 2 of figure 6.2, the clay may be replaced partially (or entirely) by hydrous siliceous mineral varieties, such as diatomaceous earth (hydrated amorphous), yielding sodium silicate (water glass), which will react with carnallite according to chemical formula 3, with formation of magnesium silicate. Casing blocks contain much more magnesium silicate than core blocks.

The sophistication and endurance of this ancient concrete technology is simply astounding. In natural stones, we expect to find elements that had the time to crystallize. However, silicates in pyramid stones are completely amorphous (not crystallized). Barsoum *et al.* stated that they were in the presence of a cementitious process. The silicates were formed in a very short period of time.

The re-agglomerated pyramid stone binders are the result of geopolymerization mechanisms that create several natural minerals: limestone (calcite), hydrated feldspars (feldspathoid, mica-chlorite), magnesium silicates, magnesite, dolomite and halite. In addition, Egyptian natron often contains Na-sulfate which causes the formation of hydrated Ca-sulfate, always confused with natural gypsum. We understand why geologists can easily be misled.

## 6.3 Scientific knowledge can be hard to teach

In the concrete industry, geopolymers are revolutionary. Absolutely any kind of aggregate can be used, so concrete fabricated with a geopolymeric binder is very hard to distinguish from natural stone. Some geologists who were unaware of the technical possibilities of geopolymerisation have confused certain geopolymeric concretes with hewn

---

[7]Davidovits J., (1986), X-Rays Analysis and X-Rays Diffraction of Casing Stones from the Pyramids of Egypt, and the Limestone of the Associated Quarries; pp. 511–20 in *Science in Egyptology Symposia*, Edited by R. A. David. Manchester University Press, Manchester, U.K.

stone. The reason why geologists fail to recognise a rock as being geopolymeric is that their analytical methods are based essentially on the detection of crystallised materials.

This technology is unprecedented; synthetic stone produced without the use of extraordinary heat or pressure. Geopolymer concrete hardens rapidly at ambient temperature, forming an artificial stone with interesting properties. A few years ago, I presented this technology, but archaeologists and Egyptologists failed to understand the implication: synthetic stone. Thus a non-objective criticism of my theory as seen by Egyptologists can be summarised in the following remark:

*"... According to J. Davidovits, geopolymer (i.e. synthetic stone) explains how the Egyptians transported and shaped their stone. But I do not think that he has ever said or proved that the rocks at Giza are geopolymeric. In fact, the limestone blocks at Giza contained fossil shells which are intact, proving that they are not made of synthetic geopolymer stone, but that they are natural stone..."*

This statement shows how difficult and frustrating it is to share new ideas with the archaeological community. The argument they are ascribing to me contains the assumption that the Egyptians were capable of making fossil shells by some unknown means! What a mistake! I have never said anything of the sort. I claim that the stones of the pyramids are a limestone reconstituted by man. As I have already explained, the fossil shells are the aggregates in this agglomeration and come from limestone quarries. If this argument is applied to modern concrete, it is as though the aggregates (gravel, pebbles etc.) used in modern concrete are synthetic whereas in fact as we all know they come from ordinary quarries. I have given numerous talks at international archaeology and Egyptology conferences, and published articles in scientific, technical and archaeological journals, all in vain! The interested reader will find several bibliographic references and all the scientific background in the book *Geopolymer Chemistry and Applications*[8].

This incomprehension reveals an important failure in the way contemporary science works: specialists operating in various disciplines do not use the same terminology to describe the same phenomenon.

---

[8] Davidovits J., (2008), *Geopolymer Chemistry and Applications*, 2008, Second edition, Geopolymer Institute, ISBN: 9782951482012

In short, two different specialists do not speak the same language, even though they are trying to represent a phenomenon, a process or an object that is perfectly well-known in their respective disciplines. This is a dialogue of the deaf: the definitions and terms of one fail to match those of the other or, to use the language of linguistics, the "signifiers" (the words) are different, while the "signifieds" (the concepts, the ideas) are identical to the two specialists.

In 1988, the American Egyptologist Mark Lehner used similar arguments to convince the American NOVA television producer that the theory of reagglomerated of stone was worthless. As I have previously mentioned, I was nevertheless allowed to take part in the filming of the documentary "This old pyramid" in 1991, broadcast on American television channels. The following anecdote illustrates the lack of information, fortuitous or deliberate, of the Egyptologists who failed to understand the foundation of the theory.

On the way to the Giza quarries to examine the limestone samples, the fossil shells, that were to be shown in the film, I was accompanied by one of Mark Lehner's assistants. While driving me to the quarry, he turned to me and said: *"We know you are wrong"*. I answered something like this: *"Oh, really, are you sure? I've been studying this question for 20 years now and you claim that I'm wrong. How can this be possible?"* the assistant replied: *"Because there are fossil shells in the pyramid blocks, just as there are fossil shells in the quarries"*. I replied: *"Very strange; where do you think I collected the aggregates (fossil shells), to make my blocks, on the Moon. No, of course not, the fossil shells obviously came from the quarries"*. Wide-eyed, he said no more.

Developing a new branch of chemistry is one thing, but applying this chemistry to ancient history is quite another. How did I come to believe that the stone of the pyramids is geopolymeric? First of all, the theory must be easy to apply; then, there must be evidence on site, and finally, there must be scientific evidence. This being the case, all the problems associated with the building of these monuments should be solved.

46

# Chapter 7

# The geology of Giza

*To make geological glue by geosynthesis requires a special limestone rock containing clay. Is this possible?*

Yes, but the limestone must contain one particular type of clay, in order to react chemically with our system. All clays are not all identical. The one we need is called kaolinitic clay. And we shall see that this special limestone clay is not one that can be easily carved. It breaks up too easily.

*Have geologists found this raw material?*

Yes, they have. The ideal material to produce reagglomerated stone is found in abundance in Egypt. We shall see that a knowledge of geology is essential to understanding why the pyramids were built in one place rather than in another. The pyramid sites were perhaps all chosen from esoteric considerations, but I show that they were also chosen for the abundance of good raw material and water from the Nile nearby. It was not chance.

## 7.1   The geology of the Giza Plateau

Geologically, the Giza Plateau belongs to the Mokkatam formation. This is the name given to an outcrop of limestone containing fossil shells and dating to the middle Eocene period (60 million years ago). Alongside the formation at Mokkatam, bordering the Plateau of the pyramids in the south southeast, is a different limestone bank with fewer fossil shells, the Maadi formation. These two limestone layers are separated by a wide sand wadi created by the south-east inclination of the Mokkatam formation (see figures 7.1, 7.2). It is

47

in this Egyptian wadi, where the Mokkatam formation meets the Maadi formation, that the quarries are situated. It is from here that the raw materials for the pyramid stones were extracted for Cheops, for Chephren, and also for Mykerinos, 50 metres or more lower down from the plateau of the three pyramids.

(a)                                (b)

Figure 7.1: The quarries where the soft limestone was extracted for Cheops.

According to geologist Thomas Aignier[1] and Egyptologist Mark Lehner[2], the surface layer of the Mokkatam formation, which forms the base on which the pyramids were built, is a very hard type of nummulite (the hard limestone and sandstone banks in figure 7.2).

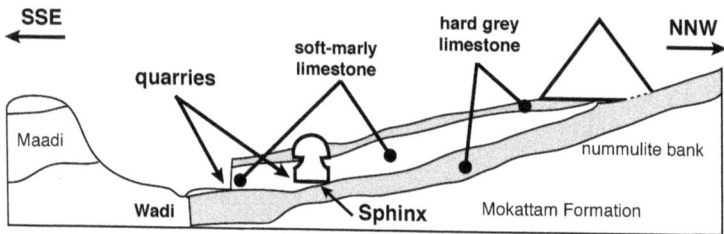

Figure 7.2: Section showing the geological layers of the Giza Plateau.

On the other hand, the layer that plunges down into the wadi, where the quarries, the surrounding area of the Sphinx and the body of the Sphinx itself are found, consists of a much softer nummulitic limestone. There we find alternating layers of marl containing quite

---

[1]T. Aigner, Facies and origin of nummulitic buildups: an example from the Giza Pyramids Plateau (Middle Eocene, Egypt). N. Jb. Geol. Paläont. Abh. 166, 347-68 (1983).

[2]M. Lehner, The Development of the Giza Necropolis: The Khufu Project, Mitteilungen des Deutschen Institutes, Abteilung Kairo (MDAIK), 41, pp. 109-143, 1985.

a large amount of clay (the very soft limestone marl bank sandwiched between the two harder layers in figure 7.2).

It is here that the theory of reagglomeration is particularly well suited to the situation, since:

— the hard limestone at the foot of the pyramids is not suitable raw material for the production of reagglomerated blocks, because this limestone does not easily disaggregate in water;

— on the other hand, the soft marly limestone is a very acceptable raw material for the reagglomeration of limestone blocks, because it disaggregates in water after a certain time. The result is a disaggregated limestone mud (containing fossil shells), to which are added other aggregates of limestone, lime and reactive silicates such as kaolinitic clay, silt and Egyptian natron salt (sodium carbonate).

In October 1991, while taking part in the filming of the American documentary, I was able to demonstrate this unique property of Giza limestone. A lump of limestone taken from the quarry crumbles rapidly in less than 24 hours, the shells separating from the clay part, whereas a lump of hard limestone from the Mokkatam formation does not. The disaggregated material is muddy and ready for the geopolymeric reagglomeration (see in Appendix A, *the Giza Plateau Circuit*).

Using simple stone tools, the Egyptian workers could very easily disaggregate an impressive quantity of limestone to make the pyramid blocks.

## 7.2 The origin of the pyramid stones

The geological formation of the Giza Plateau explains why the great mass of stone materials were extracted from quarries on the edges of the wadi, in the layer containing soft yellow limestone marl. In 1993, the German geochemist Professor D.D. Klemm, from the University of Munich, published his latest analyses on the origin of the stones of the three pyramids, Cheops, Chephren and Mykerinos[3] . His aim was to find where the source of the limestone raw material was. To do this, he chemically analysed various fossil shells and compared the

---

[3]R. Klemm and D.D. Klemm, Steine und Steinbrüche im Alten Ägypten, Springer Verlag Berlin Heidelberg 1993... Klemm's analysis are shown in diagrams plotting the rare elements magnesium (Mg) against strontium (Sr).

results obtained on pyramid blocks and on samples from the quarries. In the reagglomerated stone, the majority of the material is also made up of the same fossil shells, from the disaggregation of the original stone. Klemm's results demonstrate the source of the fossil shells, i.e. the place where the limestone raw material was extracted before being used to reagglomerate the stones. The graph in figure 7.3 shows Klemm's results; these were on 62 blocks of Cheops, 77 of Chephren and 22 of Mykerinos.

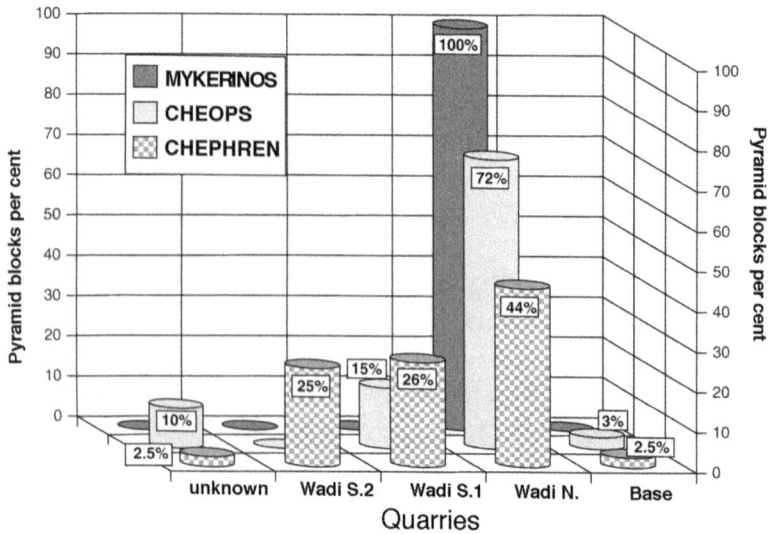

**Figure 7.3**: The origin of the limestone material for the pyramids of Cheops, Chephren and Mykerinos. Adapted from D.D. Klemm (1993).

Thus, the results of Klemm's analyses unequivocally confirm the fundamental geological data referred to above: the pyramid builders did not extract the limestone rocks from the hard grey layer of the Mokkatam formation, making up the platform of the pyramids. They got 97 % to 100 % of the rocky raw material from the soft limestone marl strata situated in the wadi below the plateau. Experimentation therefore had to be carried out using similar limestone. The geologist also observed that up to 10 % of the stones came from an unknown quarry in an unknown location, labelled "unknown" on the graph. Only 3 % of the stones came from the Mokkatam formation directly next to the pyramids, labelled "Base" on the graph. These stones seem to have been added at a later time, and were hewn, probably during the repair and restoration work undertaken by the Pharaoh

Ramses II, or his successors.

The head of the Sphinx was sculpted from an isolated outcrop, belonging to the upper hard grey limestone layer of the Mokkatam formation. For the last 4500 years, it has marvellously withstood the severe climatic conditions. As for the body of the Sphinx, it is what remains from the extraction of stone in the softer, marly parts (figure 7.4) to build a temple of the valley of Chephren, in the same way as that of the temple of the Sphinx.

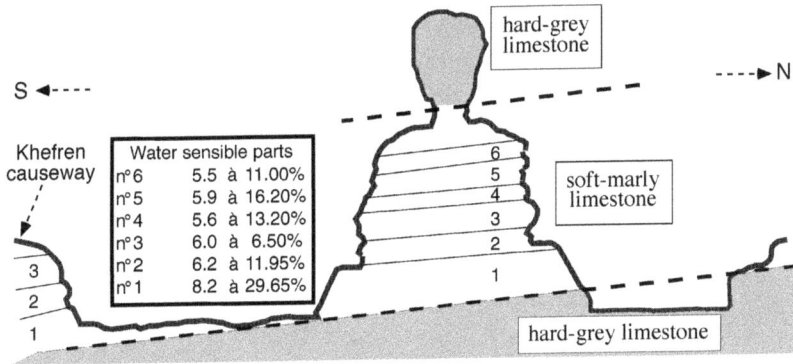

| Water sensible parts | |
| --- | --- |
| n° 6 | 5.5 à 11.00% |
| n° 5 | 5.9 à 16.20% |
| n° 4 | 5.6 à 13.20% |
| n° 3 | 6.0 à 6.50% |
| n° 2 | 6.2 à 11.95% |
| n° 1 | 8.2 à 29.65% |

**Figure 7.4:** A vertical north-south section above the front part of the Sphinx. Layers 1 to 6 analysed by L. Gauri for the proportion sensitive to water (salt + clastic material) for each stratum.

The Sphinx is severely eroded. According to some experts this damage is the result of *"erosion due to rain and flooding"*, i.e. disaggregation by water. The body of the Sphinx was continually restored during antiquity, and is today subject to a very considerable salvage operation. But this degradation is not the result of normal climatic erosion. For the body of the Sphinx was covered in sand for thousands of years and was thus protected from any damage by climatic erosion, wind and sand. Yet today it is highly degraded. In 1984, the American geologist K.L. Gauri carried out a petrographic study with mineralogical and chemical analyses of the various geological layers of the Sphinx (a total of seven layers) (see figure 7.4)[4]. He measured the quantity of water-soluble salts, and of non-carbonated clastic material (clay, silt and sand). These substances — water-soluble salts and clastics — are sensitive to the action of water. Either they are soluble (salts), or they increase in volume when they are wet (clay

[4]K.L. Gauri, Geological Study of the Sphinx, Newsletter American Research Center in Egypt, No 127, pp. 24-43, 1984.

and silt). In the figure, I name them "proportion sensitive to water". This water-sensitive percentage is very high; it can reach 29 % in layer number 1. This soft type of limestone marl, particularly with kaolin, is found in the quarries of the wadi.

Thus, the Egyptians chose a friable raw material, which disaggregated easily. In the raw state, the material is no use at all for building, because it is too fragile and is destroyed by water. They did not use the hard dense limestone, which would appear to be ideal for building monuments. Unfortunately, advocates of the theory of carving either keep quiet about this important information, which is actually well known, or are unaware of it.

# Chapter 8

# Analysis of stones

*Given that everything depends on the mineralogical constitution, it must be easy to prove the use of reagglomeration?*

Yes and no. The real problem is that if the geologist is unaware that the reagglomerated stone is artificial, he sees nothing; his analytical tools and his working method do not allow him to distinguish our geological glue. Either he takes it for an impurity, and therefore unworthy of study, or he genuinely considers it to be a natural glue. This expert really ought to be trained in geopolymer chemistry, otherwise he is likely to form an erroneous judgement based on incorrect knowledge of the system. As you will have understood, my detractors are not thus specialised, and so their criticisms are not scientifically valid.

*Have you analysed the pyramid stones with these experts?*

Yes, I have several, and all of them showed that the stone is artificial. But here we shall see that the application of science is not quite as fair as we might believe.

I knew that it would be impossible for me to prove the validity of my theory if I did not have official samples. So, in 1982, I requested a meeting with the French Egyptologist Jean-Philippe Lauer and visited him at his home in Paris. I had had several technical discussions with him during the Grenoble Congress in 1979. J.-P. Lauer was one of the most eminent European Egyptologists, and his attitude to my research was very reserved.

## 8.1 The analysis of the stones from the pyramid of Cheops

In a letter that I received before our interview (figure 8.1), he wrote: *"I defy any mineralogist worthy of the name to claim that the stones are agglomerated"*.

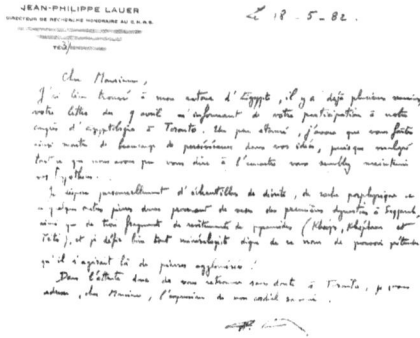

**Figure 8.1:** Copy of the letter from Jean-Philippe Lauer, 1982.

However, at the end of our interview, he gave me two samples, one from the pyramid of Cheops, the other from the pyramid of Teti. The piece from Teti came from an external casing block, and that from Cheops from the ascending passage of the pyramid (figure 8.2).

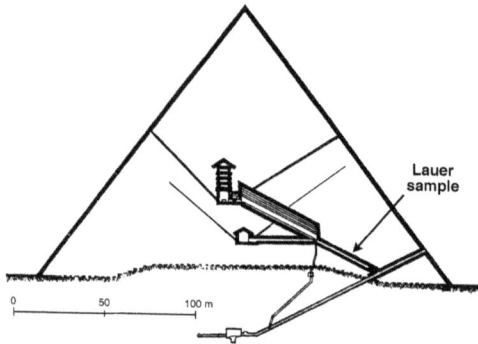

**Figure 8.2:** North-South cross section showing the inner rooms and the Lauer sample location

X-ray analysis showed with certainty that Lauer's samples were synthetic. I presented the results of the tests in a talk given at the third international Congress of Egyptologists the same year at Toronto, Canada. The title of my talk was *"No More than 1,500*

*Workers to Build the Pyramid of Khufu with Agglomerated Man-Made Stone*[1]. We saw in the note at the end of chapter 1 how the Canadian press reported the debate. More complete analysis were given at the Symposium held at the Smithsonian Institution[2], Washington D.C., USA, in 1984, and then at the Science in Egyptology Symposium, organised by Manchester Museum[3], UK.

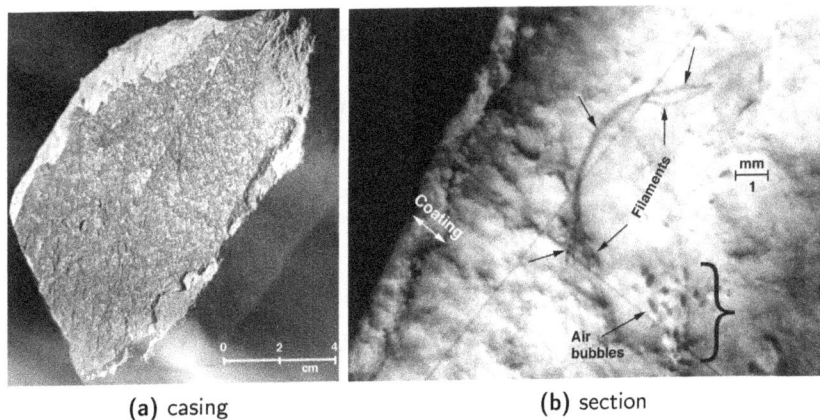

(a) casing     (b) section

**Figure 8.3:** The Lauer sample.

The stone of the pyramids has other features besides its chemical constitution and the disorientation of the fossil shells. Thus, the sample from Lauer (figure 8.3) is characterised by the presence of numerous oval air bubbles, like those produced when clay is kneaded. At one place in the sample from the great pyramid, I noticed a dark, narrow line situated just below the surface. This line is not the remains of a shell, but is actually a bundle of two or three organic fibres, perhaps hairs. Alternatively, these fibres may be of vegetable

---

[1] J. Davidovits, No More than 1,500 Workers to Build the Pyramid of Khufu with Agglomerated Man-Made Stone, 3rd International Congress of Egyptology, Toronto Canada, Abstracts, page 40, 1982.

[2] J. Davidovits, J. Thorez and M. H. Gaber, Pyramids of Egypt Made of Man-Made Stone, Myth or Fact?, 1984 Symposium on Archaeometry, Smithsonian Institution, Washington D.C., Abstracts, pp. 26-27, 1984.

[3] J. Davidovits, X-Ray Analysis and X-Ray Diffraction of Casing Stones from the Pyramids of Egypt, and the Limestone of the Associated Quarries, Science in Egyptology Symposia, R. David ed., Manchester University Press, U.K., pp. 511-520, 1984. Paper available at the Geopolymer Institute website www.geopolymer.org

origin. They may come from the ashes of plants, this being the source of several chemical ingredients making up the agglomeration cement.

## 8.2 The pitfalls of examining minerals with an optical microscope

My team gave samples of modern reagglomerated stone produced at the beginning of the year 2002 in the first phase of our experimentation (see chapter 10), to two leading geology laboratories for blind analysis. Using thin sections observed with an optical microscope, the geologists' preferred method of investigation, the scientists from both institutions stated that the sample was natural limestone.

In these tests, the geological glue is our modern geopolymer matrix. It represents 15 % of the limestone rock. This figure 8.4 is not negligible; it is even considerable for our system.

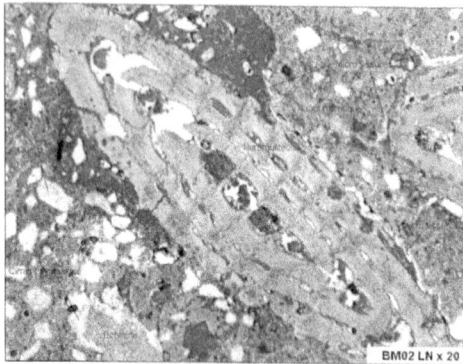

**Figure 8.4:** Thin section of geopolymer limestone examined by optical microscope. Photo BRGM, 2003.

Our glue was not detected, but simply confused with the micritic binder of the limestone! For, going back to the reaction discussed in chapter 6, the geopolymer geological glue also contains limestone, thus becoming a micritic binder. Only modern methods of analysis, such as nuclear magnetic resonance and electronic microscopy, used by chemists and physicists but rarely by geologists, allow a serious analysis of the geopolymer matrix. The "joke" devised 30 years earlier, with my colleagues from the Museum of natural history of Paris (see chapter 1), has now become a reality. An uninformed geologist sees nothing and genuinely thinks he has analysed a natural stone.

# 8.3 Recent analysis by independent teams

Now that more and more scientists agree and support the theory, some have decided to carry on researches without my help and without requesting any approval from egyptologists, so in total independence from both parties. Analysis carried out by geologists are used to *classify*, not to determine natural or artificial species. Indeed, the molecule of a mineral is by essence always the same, whether it is natural or synthetic, otherwise it would be another molecule, so another mineral. To determine the artificial nature of the material, they need to work with more powerful methods (analysis by synchrotron, transmission and electronic scan microscopy SEM TEM, Nuclear Magnetic Resonance, Paleomagnetism, Particle Induced Gamma-Ray Emission, Particle Induced X-Ray Emission, X-ray Fluorescence, X-ray Diffraction). These tools are seldom used in this situation. Studies have been made with modern and powerful equipment, and all show that the stones are artificial. Opponents prefer to ignore them.

## Electron microscopy

In 2002 a group of independent scientists was formed; these scientists are from the CNRS (Paris), Oakridge Laboratory (USA), the University of Drexel in Philadelphia (USA) and the University of Namur (Belgium) (Photo: figure 10.15, chapter 10). Because geologists, when examining a piece of modern reagglomerated limestone with an optical microscope, confuse it with natural limestone, our team of specialists decided to come up with an analytical method capable of detecting artificial specimens. They chose to use two electron microscopy techniques, SEM (scanning electron microscopy) and TEM (transmission electron microscopy).

They compared six pieces of natural limestone from the Giza plateau and five pieces of pyramid: the pyramid of Cheops and satellite pyramid number 2 of the Mykerinos pyramid (see figure 8.5 for the location of the samples and also in Appendix A at Stage 12, figure A.27). All the pyramid samples are made of the same limestone ingredient (calcite) as the pieces from the quarries. But they can be distinguished from the latter because in addition they contain micro-ingredients (only visible under the electron microscope) containing silicon in combination with other calcium, magnesium and chlorine atoms, combinations that do not exist in nature.

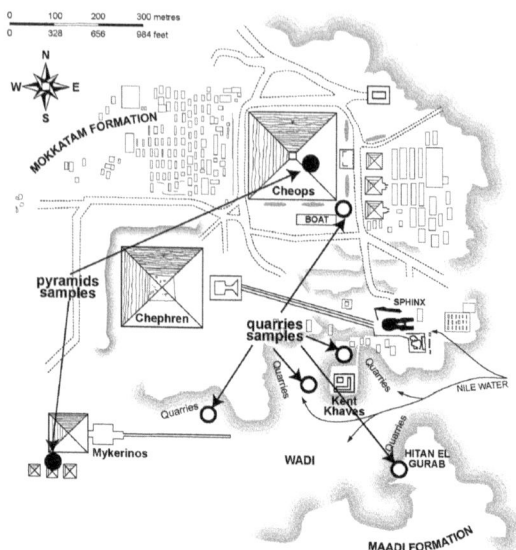

**Figure 8.5:** Locality of the samples examined under electron microscope

The amounts of silicon, in the form of silica, found in the pyramids are very large and have the texture of nano-spheres, visible only under the electron microscope. Our scientists took this as evidence that:

a) the starting medium was strongly basic (like the caustic soda referred to above);

b) the samples were formed very rapidly, within the space of a few days, unlike those formed in geological times of tens of thousands of years.

The scientific groups concluded that, since these features were not found in the six samples of natural limestone, they could not be ascribed to any normal geological mechanism. They had therefore found a reliable method of scientific analysis proving that the pyramid stones were the product of reagglomeration. The first scientific article was published in november 2006[4]. The scientific proof is thus in our hands. The pyramid stones are artificial. The analysis that provided the proof required ultra-sophisticated modern tools that geologists only rarely use; that is why they saw nothing. The reader will find further details in chapter 6 section 6.2 and in the

---

[4]Barsoum M.W., Ganguly A. and Hug G., (2006), Microstructural Evidence of Reconstituted Limestone Blocks in the Great Pyramids of Egypt, *J. Am. Ceram. Soc.* 89[12], 3788–3796.

book *Geopolymer Chemistry and Applications*[5].

## Nuclear Magnetic Resonance

A scientific analysis published in 2011 demonstrates the artificial nature of Egyptian Pyramid stone. The article titled: "Were the casing stones of Snefru's Bent Pyramid in Dahshour cast or carved? Multinuclear NMR evidence"[6] was published by an international team of scientists from New Zealand, UK and USA.

The abstract reads:

A comparison was made of the solid-state $^{29}$Si, $^{27}$Al and $^{43}$Ca MAS NMR spectra of the outer casing stone from Senefru's Bent Pyramid in Dahshour, Egypt, with two quarry limestones from the area. The NMR results suggest that the casing stones consist of limestone grains from the Tura quarry, cemented with an amorphous calcium-silicate gel formed by human intervention, by the addition of extra silica, possibly diatomaceous earth, from the Fayium area.

## Paleomagnetism

A scientific study published in 2012 in the renown "Europhysics News"[7], described how paleomagnetism study on several pyramid stones demonstrates the validity of Davidovits' theory on the artificial nature of Egyptian pyramid stones. Two scientists, Dr. Igor Túnyi from Geophysical Institute SAS – Bratislava (Slovak Republic) and Ibrahim A. El-hemaly from National Research Institute of Astronomy and Geophysics – Cairo, Egypt, made the following assumption (quote from their scientific paper):

Our paleomagnetic investigation of the two great Egyptian pyramids, Kufu and Khafre, is based on the assumption that if the blocks were made in situ by the geopolymer concrete technique described above, then their

[5] J. Davidovits, *Geopolymer Chemistry and Applications*, 2015, Fourth edition, Geopolymer Institute, ISBN: 97829514820982

[6] Kenneth J. D. MacKenzie, M. E. Smith, A. Wong, J. V. Hanna, B. Barryand M. W. Barsoum, Were the casing stones of Senefru's Bent Pyramid in Dahshour cast or carved? Multinuclear NMR evidence, *Materials Letters*, 2011, 65, 350.

[7] Igor Túnyi and Ibrahim A. El-hemaly, (2012), *Paleomagnetic investigation of the Great Egyptian Pyramids*, Europhysics News, 2012, 43/6, 28–31.

magnetic moments would all have been parallel, oriented approximately in the north-south direction. However, if the pyramids were constructed from blocks transported from the nearby quarries, having been rotated randomly during transport and construction, then the directions of their magnetic moments would be oriented randomly.

They conclude:

The aim of paleomagnetic investigation of the rock material of the great Egyptian pyramids, Khufu and Khafre, was to find out the directions of the magnetic polarization vectors of their building blocks. This is one of the possible ways to verify the hypothesis according to which the blocks were produced in situ by a concrete technique. The analysis of a limited set of paleomagnetic samples provided the following results. The paleodirections of three sampling locations (2 from Khafre and 1 from Khufu pyramid) exhibit the common north-south orientation, suggesting that they may have been produced in situ by a concrete technique. The block from one sampling location of the Khafre pyramid is of natural limestone and evidently comes from the adjacent quarry. It is likely that the block from one sampling position of the Khufu pyramid comes also from the same quarry. Finally, we conclude that even if the geopolymer concrete technique was used, the pyramids were constructed from a mixture of natural and artificial limestone blocks.

I have clearly shown in this book the location of the natural limestone blocks and terraces (see essentially in Appendix A the Circuit of the Giza Plateau). For example, we know that in the pyramid of Chephren, more than a quarter of the volume of the pyramid is natural stone, namely the terraces carved in the inclined limestone plateau and which constitute the first 5 layers of the pyramid.

This last study is the ultimate proof that the pyramids blocks are not natural. You may find various papers or opinions challenging the theory, but all prefer ignoring these independent analysis. **Believing in the artificial stone theory, or countering it, is simply no longer relevant. It has become a fact, a truth that is still fought by some people for irrational purposes.**

# Chapter 9

# The Egyptians' geological cement

*Modern analysis shows the stones not to be natural. Doesn't this then imply that the Ancient Egyptians had chemical knowledge pre-dating their architecture?*

Many people have a false idea of a chemical laboratory where a white-coated assistant is busy manipulating test-tubes filled with coloured liquids, while somewhere in a corner a flask of coloured liquid bubbles away, filling the air with trails of white vapour. But chemistry, like physics, is everywhere in the world around us, without our realising it.

*But don't you think that chemistry is rather a modern science?*

History teaches us that the ancient erudite priests of Heliopolis encouraged the development of the techniques of engineering, mathematics and astronomy, and this all had a primordial role in the construction of the pyramids. However, one of these sciences has been neglected by historians. This mysterious knowledge has nothing to do with the classical disciplines such as physics, electricity, heat, optics or mechanics, and nothing in common with the quantum physics, the atomic physics, and the nuclear physics of the solid state. What enabled the pyramids to be built was chemistry, or to be more exact, its ancestor, Alchemy.

# 9.1 The birth of Alchemy

One of the roles of the historian is to explain why events took place when they did. Similarly, the historian of science must throw light on the way society evolves under the influence of technical progress. The theory of the reagglomeration of stone is in agreement with the technical knowledge of the Egyptians of the Old Kingdom. They had mastered metallurgy, ceramics, alkalis, glass (in the form of enamel), binders (lime, plaster) and the disaggregation of geological substances. All of this enables us to validate our hypothesis.

First of all, we must understand the process by which man invented mineral cements and binders. This technology was invented between the Stone Age and the beginning of the Copper Age; man's knowledge of the resources around him, coupled with a certain understanding of his environment, set him on two paths: the development of metallurgy, and the production of synthetic stone and ceramic. Let us try to understand just what led a man to extract a rock of blue-green colour, of non-metallic appearance, to melt it at over 1000°C, and after a lot of patient manipulations to end up with copper. Before achieving this fabulous result, he must have gone through numerous intermediate stages, heating a piece of rock either in a reactive chemical powder (lime, plaster, alkalis), or in ceramic or in enamel. He owed his achievements to improvements in heating techniques (the bread kiln, the lime furnace, the ceramic furnace, and finally metallurgy), and hence to a better and better mastery of high temperatures. The processes of stone making and metallurgy complemented each other.

"Classical" alchemy brings to mind, images of a mixture of mediaeval research, mysticism and magic. Books on alchemy describe the vain quest for the philosopher's stone, which was supposed to be able to transform base metals into gold, and to provide the elixir of eternal youth. This legendary stone was one of the misunderstood vestiges of the alchemical science that had flourished during the age of the pyramids and that was known and used some 6000 years ago.

Why use the term "alchemy"? Because this term is generally used in a religious or spiritual context. In Egypt all technical skills were associated with a divinity. Egyptian chemists owed their knowledge to the god Khnum, whom we shall be meeting again in the next chapter. Thus, the term "alchemy" was applied to the chemical knowledge associated with the worship of an Egyptian divinity.

In the New Kingdom, when Egyptian alchemists developed the technology of glass they were merely continuing the ancient religious tradition devoted to the synthesis of stone and enamel. It is this ancient tradition on which is based the solution to the mystery of how the pyramids were built: the priests of Khnum had for a long time been experts in the art of making extraordinary cements. Indeed, the verb *Khnum* itself means to bind, to join, to unite, to cement. At several places in the Great Pyramid, 4500-year old cements are found; they are still in excellent condition. This ancient mortar is far superior to the cement used in our modern buildings, and modern cement of the "Portland" type when used for the restoration of ancient Egyptian monuments, has already degraded and cracked after 50 years.

So, if the Egyptians knew how to make such a high-quality cement for vases and statues, what was there to stop them adding aggregates such as fossil shells to produce a high-performance reagglomerated limestone? Clearly, nothing.

Moreover, in a block of reagglomerated limestone, most of the shells are intact, but instead of being oriented in a parallel way (horizontal segmentation), they are oriented at random (see figure 9.1).

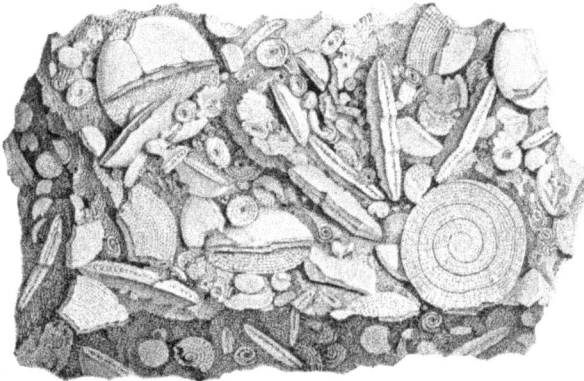

**Figure 9.1:** Fossil shells, nummilites, randomly oriented (Description de l'Égypte)

All the blocks of the Great Pyramids have this feature, whereas the limestone outcrop on which they were built was formed by horizontal segmentation of shells, as is generally the rule in limestone, with few exceptions (see chapter 2 figure 2.5).

A person in antiquity should have been able to produce this reagglomerated stone by conscientiously applying the knowledge acquired by intelligent and continuous observation of his environment, and then by experimenting with whatever mineral resources he found; this is all that would have been required. Of course, he had to have some knowledge of minerals, he had to know how to distinguish between them, how to react them chemically. Mediaeval alchemy went back to a time when science and religion were united and when the esoteric formed part of its teaching. But it was this same alchemy which gave rise to the prodigious development of modern chemistry around 250 years ago. By then, however, alchemy was far from its origins, and far removed from its astonishing performance in antiquity. The so-called advanced technologies played no role in the alchemical fabrication of stones. We must accept this if our theory is to be realistic.

## 9.2   The recipe

The composition of the blocks was as follows:
- 93 % to 97 % natural limestone as aggregates (fossil shells),
- 3 % to 7 % of geological glue (so-called "geopolymeric" cement), to bind the aggregates from the chemical reactions, which took place according to reaction schemes, given in chapter 6, figure 6.2).

We now know that the ingredients necessary for these chemical reactions were available in Egypt in enormous quantities (millions of tonnes). One of the ingredients, the salt *natron*, more commonly known as sodium carbonate, was extraordinarily abundant in the deserts and in the salt lakes. As we have seen, natron reacts with lime in the presence of water to give caustic soda, the main reagent in the (alchemical), fabrication of stone. Natron was a sacred product, used not only as a flux in metallurgy, but also for mummifying and for deification rites. Pyramid texts found on the walls of the funerary chamber of the fifth dynasty pyramid of the Pharaoh Ounas show the sacred value of natron:

You are purified, Horus is purified: one tablet of natron; you are purified, Seth is purified: one tablet of natron; you are purified, Thot is purified: one tablet of natron.

You are purified, God is purified: one tablet of natron.

You are purified, you rest among them: one tablet of natron.

Your mouth is like the mouth of the sucking calf at the moment of birth: five tablets of naturon from the North, at Stpt.

The place where natron was extracted for purification, called Stpt, is known today by the name of Wadi-el-Natron. However, the natron used for the enamels in mummifying rites was not so pure: it came from other much larger sources that were spread throughout the land. Thus, numerous ingredients used in the alchemical fabrication of stone later played a role in the manufacture of glass. From my study of ecology and of ancient products, together with Egyptian documents, I was able to trace the evolution of the alchemical discoveries which led to the development of the pyramid stones.

One important material, lime, could easily be obtained by the calcination of limestone in simple furnaces. But it was also possible to get it from the ashes of ovens that had been used to cook bread. In the time of ancient Egypt, the mines of Sinai contained considerable outcrops of turquoise and chrysocolla, which play a role in the production of synthetic geopolymers. These outcrops also contain minerals including arsenic, as olivine, and scorodite, which induce rapid setting and hardening of the stone.

But the most vital ingredient of all was the geological limestone of Giza. It had to provide practically the totality of the material. At Giza, the ancient Egyptians found a soft limestone, easy to extract (not carved), i.e. easy to disaggregate into loose aggregates (not crushed), and which could be hardened (reconstituted) to form blocks. But above all, this particular limestone had to contain a certain quantity of natural geopolymeric ingredients and reagents, such as kaolinitic clay, which are required in the geopolymeric reaction in which the binding cement (the geological glue) is produced *in-situ* within the stone. The geology of Giza shows that this material does indeed exist (see chapter 7, and the strip cartoon in chapter 5).

As we have seen, the blocks contained 93 % to 97 % by weight of limestone and fossil shells (the aggregates) and from 3 % to 7 % by weight of geological glue. We know that the Giza limestone has a natural content of 5 % to 10 % by weight of kaolinitic clay, so that, to obtain the geological glue chemically, only a very small amount of chemical reagents such as natron and lime need be added. Laboratory tests show that we need:
  - 0.5 % to 1 % natron and 1 % to 2 % lime
  - Equivalent to 5 kg of natron and 10 kg of lime for 1 tonne of stone.

If the Giza limestone did not actually contain this kaolinitic clay, between 50 kg and 100 kg per tonne of stone would have to be added.

By comparison, traditional lime or gypsum-based mortar needed between 15 % and 20 % by weight of binder, i.e. between 150 and 200 kg per tonne of stone. This is precisely the type of technology presented by Joel Bertho in a sensational article published in 2001 in the French periodical *Science et Vie*, under the title: *Les pyramides en fausses pierres* (The pyramids made of false stones). But though the author's intuition is interesting, the proportions are enormous, and it was therefore perfectly understandable that this should have been severely criticised by the community of Egyptologists and by scientists. With knowledge of geopolymeric reactions, on the other hand, these quantities of chemical reagents can be divided by 20! This important piece of information has now been successfully applied to the reagglomeration of the pyramid stones.

There also exist other alchemical reactions which at first sight appear more complicated than those given above, but which were used by the ancient Egyptians. There are, for example, those involving magnesium salts (magnesium chloride, magnesium sulphate, magnesia, MgO) (see chapter 6, figure 6.2).

## 9.3 You need water

Without water, the disaggregation, the mixing and the reagglomeration cannot take place. The wadi must be flooded, the reaction pools must be prepared — these essential stages in the process are described in the strip cartoon (chapter 5, figure 5.5). Emphasis has always traditionally been placed on this annual period, especially in the text of Herodotus, during which the entire valley is covered by the overflow from the Nile. It was in this season that, according to the official theory, a multitude of barges were supposed to have ferried enormous blocks of limestone and granite along the waterway. The waters must then have come up to the foot of the construction sites, but archaeological science has not up to the present given any proof of this.

According to the American Egyptologist Mark Lehner, research carried out over the past 20 years by Archaeological surveyors "... *provides information, most of which contradicts a large amount of what is taken for granted*". Thus, as far as the intensive use of navigation mentioned above is concerned, archaeological results show that the water was much too shallow for heavy barges. If the ancient

Egyptians dug canals across the flood plain, no archaeological trace remains today. Nevertheless, although the flooding can no longer be given its role in transporting the stone blocks, it still plays a major part in the agglomeration scenario.

At the beginning of Egyptian civilisation, in the pyramid region from Dashur to Giza, and in particular in the Memphis region, the course of the Nile was much closer to the western side of the valley. During the millennia, its course gradually moved eastward. Under the Old Kingdom there were lakes all along the western stretch bordering the pyramid plateau, and these lakes retained water long after the flood had receded[1] . We should note that, contrary to what is generally thought, a cross section of the Nile valley shows that the ground has a convex form; the highest regions are in the centre, where there is the greatest amount of alluvium from the Nile, while the lowest are near the slopes of the desert and the pyramid plateau.

These lakes existed directly at the feet of the sites of Abu Sir, Saqqarah, and Dashur and probably also at Giza. A few remained at Dashur, Abu Sir and Saqqarah until the Aswan High Dam was built, putting an end to the flooding. The pyramid builders probably also dug and widened numerous alluvial ponds, thereby creating several artificial lakes where water could collect during the flooding. They also used the wadis which penetrate quite deeply into the interior of the plateau towards the western desert. It was these which, once built, connected the flood valley, the geological outcrops and the construction site. These wadis are found in the main locations at Saqqarah, Dashur and Giza. They are at present completely covered with sand. At the Meidum site no such works were necessary because, even today, the arable zone subject to natural flooding comes right up to the foot of the pyramid complex.

---

[1]M. Lehner, Loaves and Fishes, in The Complete Pyramids, Thames and Hudson Ltd, London, 1997.

# Chapter 10

# Experiments

*No experiment is likely to be meaningful unless it is carried out on quantities of several tonnes.*

The scientific method is indeed based on theory verified by practice. The best approach is to carry out full-scale experiments and not to rely on small-scale models or computer simulations. Our team's aim was to make, not pyramids, but blocks weighing several tonnes.

*I'm sure the Egyptian authorities wouldn't let you extract such amounts from the Giza quarries. How did you proceed?*

Fortunately, we have in France limestone of a very similar nature to that found in Giza, i.e. friable and containing fossil shells (nummulites). This is from the quarry of Tracy-le-Val, in Picardie to the south of Saint-Quentin (figure 10.2).

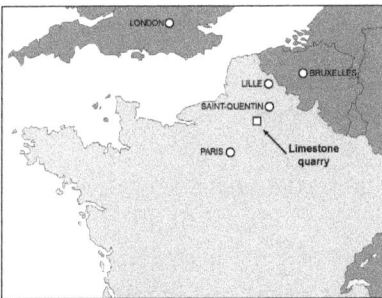

**Figure 10.1:** Nummulitic limestone outcrop in France.

**Figure 10.2:** Extraction of nummulitic limestone.

As at Giza, the Picardie limestone is naturally disaggregated and is extracted with a mechanical shovel (figure 10.1). There is no need to crush it, but unlike that of Giza it contains no kaolinitic clay. The latter therefore has to be added to the mixture so as to imitate the soft outcrop at Giza — because it is this that is the basis of the geological glue.

## 10.1   Laboratory experiments (figure 10.3)

These were carried out at the Cordi-Geopolymer laboratory in Saint-Quentin (Picardie).

**Figure 10.3:** Preliminary laboratory tests. 1. To 5 kg of limestone containing 250 g of kaolinitic clay are added 100 g of sodium carbonate (natron) and 200g of lime, followed by 900 g of water. 2. The ingredients are mixed with a trowel. 3. The wet material is put into a wooden mould. 4. It is packed with a wooden pestle. 5. The block is covered with a coating of plaster to prevent evaporation of the water and ensure the hardening of the geological glue. 6. The block is released and the plaster coating, which does not stick to the limestone, is removed.

We measured the compression strength two months after casting: the value was of the order of 150 kg/cm$^2$, i.e. 15 MPa. A one cubic metre limestone block with an area of 1 m$^2$ is therefore able to support a load of 1 500 000 kg. This means that one limestone block can support the weight of 700 similar blocks stood on it — three times the height of the great pyramids — without collapsing. We thus have a safety factor of three, enough to cope with errors due to faulty mixtures. A piece of this reagglomerated limestone was sent for blind analysis to two geological institutions (cf. chapter 8).

## 10.2   Full-scale experiments

During the summer of 2002, the team from the Geopolymer Institute experimented with the fabrication of five blocks totalling 12 tonnes resembling those of the pyramids of Giza. We used only those tools that have been found by archaeologists: a hoe to collect the aggregate, a basket to transport it, a wooden mould, a trough, a ladder, a square, a plumb line, a level, a float etc. (figure 10.4, 10.5). 14 tonnes of limestone were used to make these pyramid blocks.

**Figure 10.4:** Fabrication stages : 1. the bulk of 14 tonnes of limestone. 2. transport with basket. 3. the packing with a rammer.

**Figure 10.5:** Mould made from small reusable wooden planks.

In the experiments we made five blocks of differing sizes and composition. This enabled us to investigate the influence of various parameters. The shape of the blocks was chosen in such a way as to find out when it was possible to walk and work on the stone surface without damaging it. This turned out to be after one to two weeks (figure 10.6).

Each block was given a name; these names have the following meanings:

*Iri-kat*: a hieroglyphic word meaning synthesised, man-made (cf. chapter 11)

*Inr-nn*: a hieroglyphic word meaning wet stone (this was the dampest of all the blocks)

*Khusi*: a hieroglyphic word meaning to build, to construct (cf. chapter 5)

*Krossai*: the first Greek word used by Herodotus for the stone of the pyramid of Cheops. (see the conference of Frédéric Davidovits at the 9th Int. Cong. of Egyptologists, Grenoble, 2004[1])

*Bomos*: the second Greek word used by Herodotus for the stone of the pyramid of Cheops.

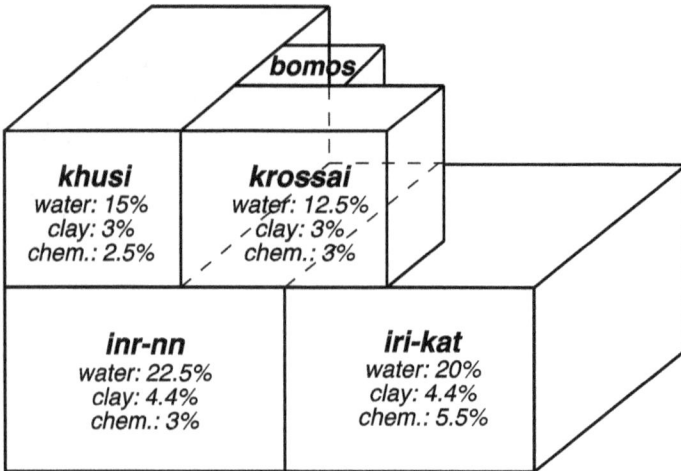

**Figure 10.6:** The various experimental stages and the variations parameters: water, clay, chemicals (chem.), natron and lime.

---

[1]F. Davidovits, Étude lexicographique des termes grecs Krossai et bomides dans Hérodotes (II, 125): étymologie égyptienne ou grecques?, Proceedings of the ninth international congress of egyptologists, Uitgeverij Peeters en Departement oosterse Studies, Leuven – Paris – Dudley MA, 2007, numb. 10, p. 361.

## 10.2.1 First block: *iri-kat* (28 July 2002)

For the first reagglomerated stone mixture, 2000 litres of water were poured into the pool. The geological glue was made by first of all mixing sodium carbonate (Egyptian natron) and lime. Kaolin — which would already have been contained in Giza limestone — was then added and the mixture was stirred with a wooden paddle. On the following day, four tonnes of limestone were poured in and mixed with the geological glue (figure 10.7). The block contains 95 % limestone and only 5 % Binder, after evaporation of water.

**Figure 10.7:** From the quarries to the mixture in the pool to form the geological glue. **1.** Nummulitic limestone outcrop (fossil shells), naturally friable, at Tracy-le-Val south of Saint-Quentin. It resembles that of Giza but does not contain kaolinitic clay, which has to be added. **2.** Into the pool containing 2 m$^3$ of water are poured 160 kg of kaolinitic clay to imitate the Giza limestone, followed by 60 kg of sodium carbonate (natron) and 80 kg of slaked lime. **3.** The geological glue is mixed with 4500 kg of limestone using a simple wooden paddle.

The next stage was to make a wooden mould and grease it so as to be able to release the block without it sticking to the wood. The mould was made with small wooden planks that we used several times to make more blocks. Because of the cool weather, the water only evaporated slowly from the pool (more than a week and a half); the limestone mortar was now ready to be used to make the first block, leaving the pool empty and ready for the next mixing operation. In the presence of water the shells have decanted down and the fine particles have floated up (figure 10.8).

The muddy limestone mixture is spread out on the ground for the water to continue evaporating. The limestone concrete, which still contains 20 % of water, is poured into the first mould and packed using a pestle. This packing gives cohesion, increasing the density, and the product becomes very hard during the initial setting.

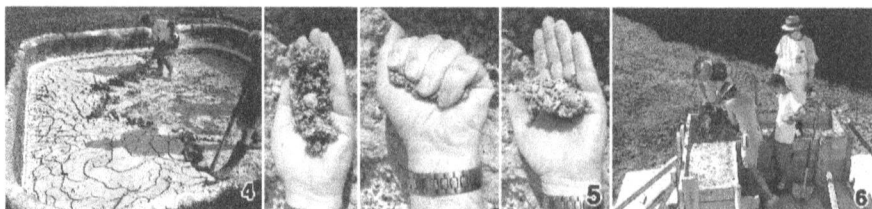

**Figure 10.8:** After water has evaporated, the still wet material is ready to be moulded. **4.** In Egypt, the water needs one or two days to evaporate, whereas it takes three or four days in northern France. The material, which has the consistency of wet sand, is collected and heaped up. **5.** With a residual water content of 15 to 20 % in the limestone, the shells are coated with a plastic, flexible geological glue that is readily compactable. **6.** By a chain of buckets or baskets the limestone mixture is transported from the heaps in the pool to the mould where it is packed.

## 10.2.2  Second block: *Inr-nn* (30 July 2002)

The same operations were carried out for the second of the largest 4.5 tonne blocks. We reduced the quantity of sodium carbonate from 1.5 % to 1 %, i.e. 45 kg, but kept the lime at 2 %, i.e. 90 kg. On the 2 August, we found that the water from the mixture for the first, four tonne block had not evaporated sufficiently on account of the rainy weather. We nevertheless attempted to shovel the material into the mould; but it was thixotropic, becoming more and more liquid as it was pressed down. It was out of the question to carry on, we had to get the sticky mortar out of the mould and spread it out on a plastic sheet to dry. But then the weather worsened, and we covered the whole lot with a plastic tarpaulin. During the night, there were heavy storms with driving rain until the following morning. It was not until 5 August that we filled the second mould. Part of the outside of the first stone crumbled after releasing, and we repaired it. The cool rainy weather also affected the second stone. The water did not evaporate as quickly as we wanted, and the mixture still contained 22 % water. The reagglomerated stone paste was so muddy that we sank down in it! The pressure of water on the mould was too great, partially breaking it (figure 10.9). We anticipated disaster.

The water started to drip out of the mixture in the mould. We solved this problem by reinforcing the mould with straps. By acting quickly we were able to save the stone. But we were concerned because, unlike the hot dry climate in Egypt, cool wet weather does not favour good setting.

**Figure 10.9:** Failure. **7.** The mixture containing too much water becomes muddy and a man sinks down. **8.** The pressure on the liquid paste is transmitted to the mould whose sides pull apart at the ends. Excess water drips out. **9.** This produces curved edges identical to those found on the large blocks of the pyramid of Chephren. The Egyptians had to deal with the same problems as us.

### 10.2.3 The third block: *Krossai* (9 August 2002)

The third mixture was ready to be removed from the pool by a mechanical shovel, and spread on the ground to aid evaporation. The week had been rainy and cool, at 20°C. Hoping for finer weather, the team built the last 2 moulds for the 1 tonne and 1.3 tonne stones (figure 10.10). We got the site ready for the last of our experimental pyramid blocks. The final dimensions of the mould were: length: 2.5 metres, width: 2.25 metres, height 1.6 metres. To work! We greased the inside of the mould and got ready to pack the smallest block of one tonne. After a week, the weather got warmer, and there was sufficient evaporation from our stone mixture. On 17 August, we began the block *Krossai*, doing everything by hand, forming a human bucket brigade from the mixing area to the mould. Thanks to the fine dry weather, the texture was ideal. We poured the mixture into the mould and packed it well down so that the stone would be hard and dense.

Very little effort was needed to pack down the material. After releasing a freshly moulded stone, no trace of any imprint from the board could be seen.

### 10.2.4 Fourth block: *Khusi* (17 Aug 2002)

The fourth block is just as perfect. The top of our stone structure is levelled. With a fair weather forecast, a team of only five people were able rapidly to produce a hard, dense reagglomerated limestone, with the required size and shape (figure 10.11). We were smiling again.

**Figure 10.10:** From packing to releasing: five blocks totalling 12.2 tonnes of natural limestone. **10.** Like adobe, the material is packed with a pestle. **11.** The surface is smoothed and levelled with a length of plank. **12.** After three weeks, the limestone of the two 4.5-tonne blocks forming the base is strong enough to support the next layer, comprising two blocks of 1.5 tonnes and 1 tonne. The fifth block of 750 kg (in the centre of the second tier) is packed into the mould made from small planks supported by "Egyptian" stays.

We used the mechanical shovel to pour the remaining one tonne of material.

**Figure 10.11:** A team of five to make several blocks at day.

I examined the material: 94.8 % limestone aggregate, 5.2 % geological glue, composed of 3 % clay, 0.7 % sodium carbonate and 1.5 % lime with a water content of 12 % to 17 %; it had the consistency of wet sand. I squeezed it in my hand: it kept its shape (figure 10.8). The stone would harden. With perfect weather, the process is so simple.

12 days later, we removed the mould. The synthetic limestone

looked just like natural stone. The two large blocks *Iri-kat* and *Inr-nn* weighing up to 4.5 tonnes, damper than the others, had a smooth finish. The two small blocks *Krossai* and *Khusi* weighing up to 1.3 tonnes, less damp, had a rougher finish. After releasing, there was no trace of any imprint from the wooden planks on the two large blocks of 4.5 tonnes (figure 10.12).

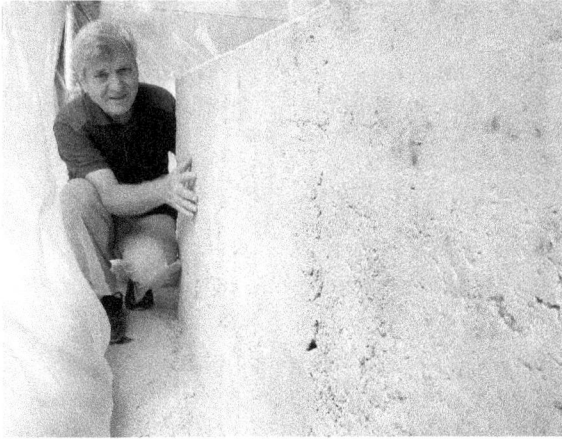

Figure 10.12: The author examining the blocks hardening in the tent.

To protect the stones from the rain and to allow them to harden, we built a tent. This would create a favourable greenhouse effect and give a warm climate closer to that of Egypt.

A white film started to cover the released stones; this is a by-product of the chemical reaction, and is simply bicarbonate of soda, as used in baking.

## 10.2.5  The fifth block: *Bomos* (24 September 2002)

The fabrication of the fifth block weighing 700 kg was made for the launching of my first French book *"Ils ont bâti les Pyramides"*. Our friends from the association *Loisirs et Traditions* were clad in Egyptian costume (figure 10.13). A small video commemorates the event and may be downloaded at the Geopolymer Institute website[2].

Three months later, in the climate of northern France, the stones would be completely hardened. In 4000 years, would future archae-

---

[2]See the video at www.geopolymer.org/category/archaeology/pyramids

**Figure 10.13:** The fifth block, which was made in front of the media, with the members of the Saint-Quentin association Loisirs et Traditions, clad in Egyptian costume, around the block Bomos.

**Figure 10.14:** Shooting of a TV documentary by the Relevant Television team. Geologist B. Manigault states that the reconstituted limestone is identical to natural limestone.

ologists declare that these imitations of pyramid stones are natural limestone?

In the autumn of 2002, we covered our work with a plastic sheet to protect it from the rain but not from frost. The winter turned out to be quite hard during the whole of the month of January 2003, with the temperature below zero every day (minimum -8°C.). In the spring we built a corrugated iron shelter so that the stones could aerate.

## 10.3 One year later

On 10 July 2003, the scientific team engaged to analyse the pyramid stones (see chapter 8) assembled (figures 10.15, 10.14). We examined the blocks and discussed the results of the various analyses, and then we removed the shelter. Some of the surfaces had suffered from frost, but on the whole everything appeared undamaged. The stones were hard, the best ones being impossible to damage, in the order *Inr-nn*, followed by *Iri-kat*. These were in fact the ones which had the most water.

Because the blocks had been made one directly against the other, no joints could be seen on releasing. One year later, because of the slight shrinking that accompanied hardening, very fine joints became apparent between the blocks (figures 10.16 and 10.17a). The joints were sharp and identical to those separating the majority of the pyramid blocks; the stone Krossai had been moulded above the two blocks

**Figure 10.15:** The scientific team : Prof. G. Demortier (Namur), Prof. J. Davidovits, Prof. M. Barsoum (USA), Dr. G. Hug (CNRS France), geologist B. Manigault, and architect F. Waendendries.

*Iri-kat* and *Inr-nn*. The separation between the upper block *Krossai* and the blocks underneath was hardly visible (figure 10.17b), leading us to assume that the surfaces had welded together.

In October 2003, the construction had to be demolished. This was done with a pneumatic drill (figure 10.18).

During the demolition, the stone Krossai separated easily from the two other blocks, displaying extremely precise jointing (figure 10.19). Such perfect horizontal joints are another of the characteristics shown by the stones at the Great Pyramids.

## 10.4 Recent experiments

The famous Massachusetts Institute of Technology MIT, Boston, USA, is supporting the re-agglomerated stone pyramid theory. Materials scientist Professor L. Hobbs and two colleagues and students are experimenting the construction of a small scale pyramid, according to an article published by the Boston Globe, April 22, 2008, titled *"A new angle on pyramids, Scientists explore whether Egyptians used concrete"*.

Figure 10.16: The author examining the large blocks *Iri-kat* and *Inr-nn*.

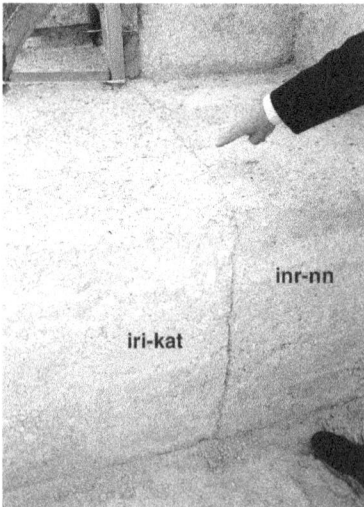

(a) between *Iri-kat* and *Inr-nn*

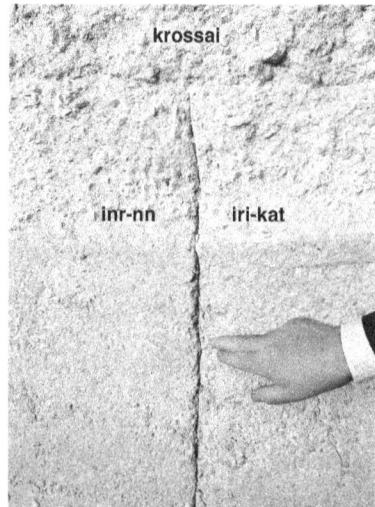

(b) not *Krossai*?

Figure 10.17: The formation of sharp joints.

**Figure 10.18:** The construction being demolished with a pneumatic drill one year later.

**Figure 10.19:** The horizontal joint is perfect.

At MIT, L. Hobbs teaches a course called Materials in Human Experience. Its scale-model pyramid contains only about 280 blocks, compared with 2.3 million in the grandest of the Great Pyramids. It is made of concrete-like blocks cast from disaggregated limestone sludge fortified with dollops of kaolinite clay, silica, and natural desert salts – called natron. The writer of the Boston Globe article, Colin Nickerson, further mentioned: *"And no whips cracked overhead last week as Myat-Noe-Zin Myint, Rachel Martin, and three other undergraduates stuffed quivering just-mixed "Egyptian" concrete into cobblestone-sized wooden molds marked 'King Tut Plywood Co.'"*

# Chapter 11

# Proofs by the religion of the god Khnum

*Your experiments were convincing. But does this all fit in with Egyptian civilisation?*

Yes, perfectly. But explaining and demonstrating the way in which the pyramids were built through science and archaeology is not enough. Egyptian culture with its beliefs and its religion must be in harmony with this alchemical technique. Otherwise, as for the head of Egyptology, Dr. Zahi Hawas, Cairo, this approach is *"stupid"*. More, the chemist and materials scientists that carry out these invistigations and experiments are *"idiots and insultant"*[1].

## 11.1  Stone: its religious significance

Through our research, the god Khnum, little known today, is restored to the place he deserves in the history of Egypt. For the ancient Egyptians, stone had a sacred value and could not be used for secular buildings. On the one hand were the pyramids and temples, and on the other hand the houses, palaces and fortresses built with such vulgar materials as silt bricks, dried clay and wood. Up to now, none of the Pharaohs' palaces and none of the houses that have been found are built of stone. The palaces were all built of clay bricks and wood, which time has destroyed. Only religious edifices remain: temples and tombs. This astonishing fact leads us to believe that the use of

---

[1] Colin Nickerson, article titled *"A new angle on pyramids, Scientists explore whether Egyptians used concrete"*, Boston Globe, April 22, 2008.

hewn or reagglomerated stone had a religious significance linking it to a divinity. It was only under the reign of the Ptolomies, some 2000 years after the pyramids, that stone became a banal building material, used indifferently for temples, palaces, garrisons and houses, just as it is today.

The reasons for this very clear distinction between stone and other building materials are to be sought in the founding myths of the Egyptian pantheon. And here, a surprising fact comes to light: there is not one, but two sources, each one exclusive of the other; two distinct divinities lay claim to the creation of man: Khnum and Amon.

## 11.2 The god Khnum

The god Khnum is the oldest of the gods. Worshipped during the Old and Middle Kingdoms (3000 to 1800 BC), he is represented in the form of a man with a ram's head and horizontal horns (*Ovis longipes palaeoaegyptus*) (figure 11.1). He personified the Nile, bringer of nourishment, and at Elephantine, Thebes, Heracleopolis and Memphis, he was the creator god.

In his act of creation, he KNEADS humanity on his potter's wheel with silt from the Nile and other minerals including *mafkat* and *natron*, just as in the genesis of the Bible and the Qur'an! This is no ordinary clay, but a stone called *Ka*, i.e. the soul is not of spiritual matter, but of eternal stone.

The Egyptians would indeed have seen, on observing their environment, that the only material that did not decompose was stone. This was therefore an inalterable material. Since it was eternal, it must be sacred and should only be used for religious purposes. Thus it was heresy to use sacred stone, symbol of eternity, to built palaces and houses. If stone lasts forever, the human soul must also be in stone.

One of the greatest achievements of the Egyptian civilisation was to make from stone a building material which to this day has found no equal. The choice of this hard material was based directly on religion. In the minds of the Egyptians, the need for a durable substance was ever present. Since stone was linked to durability, it is not surprising that it should be used above all in tombs and temples which had to last forever.

**Figure 11.1:** The god Khnum

According to Fernand Schwartz: *"the beginnings of stone archi-tecture are inseparable from the concept of Ka, which played such a great role for Egyptians, expressing their desire for eternal existence. Ka is a practical manifestation of vital energy, not of the physical kind, but rather, psychic; which explains its role of life bringer. Ka in his manifestation is the role of creator and preserver. Ka can thus designate not only the power of creation possessed by the divin-ity or Nether, but also the supporting forces that gave life to Maat, the Universal Order".*

Remember that Khnum does not only model the body in clay, but above all the *Ka* of the newly born, his stone soul, for nothing can be alive without *Ka* (figure 11.2).

The creation verb used for Khnum is iri-kat or ari-kat (literally, to make the *Ka*), the noun being either a seated man or a seated man with a bucket on his head. (figure 11.3). This is also found on the Famine Stele.

The desire for eternal existence finds its tangible expression in

**Figure 11.2:** Khnum modelling the body and the Ka of the pharaoh.

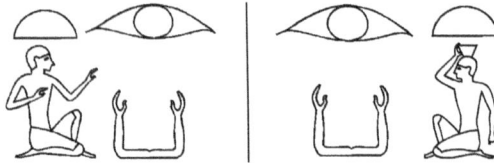

**Figure 11.3:** The verb to create, ari-kat / iri-kat.

stone architecture, for that alone is capable of providing an inde-
structible symbol to the invisible reality of *Ka*. Unlike the buildings
in mud bricks, which last only the limited span of a man's life, stone
buildings could withstand the ravages of time.

The importance of Khnum under the Old Kingdom around 2700BC
is not made clear in books on Egyptology. The name of Cheops is
*Khnum-Khufu*, may the god Khnum protect Cheops (figure 11.4).
Khnum has not the aura of the gods that we find the texts of the
New Kingdom 1500 years later.

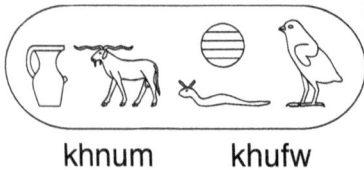

khnum        khufw

**Figure 11.4:** The cartouche of King Cheops, Khnum-Khufu.

But why should the pharaoh Cheops have chosen to add to his

royal cartouche the name of any "second-rank" god, as numerous Egyptologists would have it? And yet it was under the auspices of Khnum that the greatest of all the pyramids was built, that of Cheops. (figure 11.5). If Khnum personifies divine incarnation in reagglomerated stone, it is perfectly understandable that Cheops should place himself under his protection. Cheops would not seek the protection of a second-rate god!

Khnum is one of the most ancient of the prehistoric gods of Egypt. Since the most distant times, many functions had been attributed to him. Like all the other Egyptian gods, he was identified with the Sun god, but he was in general regarded as the creator of the bodies of the gods and of man. He was above all the potter god, who creates from clay. Khnum was also worshipped as god of the Nile and his outstretched arms made the waters rise or fall during the floods. The origin of the Nile floods was attributed to the presence of a sacred cavern on the Isle of Abu (the first town), known today as Elephantine, the main place of worship of Khnum.

Figure 11.5: View of the pyramids of Giza, Royal Air Force, 1924.

Over the generations, the annual overflowing of the Nile has gradually converted this narrow strip of desert into a rich area 1000 km long, ideal for agriculture.

The influence of Khnum increased steadily during the first dynasties, then diminished after the twelfth, reappearing again during the eighteenth. Khnum, normally represented in human form having a ram's head with horizontal forms, later acquired four ram's heads on the human form. According to Egyptologist Karl H. Brugsch[2] , this designated the four elements: earth, air, fire and water.

## 11.3 Creation is divine incarnation by the agglomeration of stone

The earliest of the mythologies of the Old Kingdom tells how the divine potter created the other gods, the kings and the other mortals on his wheel. But Khnum used different materials according to whether a divine being or a mortal being was being created. For deities, he used materials associated with the eternal kingdom. The gods were of gold with lapis-lazuli hair. The funeral statue of the pharaoh, representing his KA, (his eternal body) was of stone. The divine spirit was also incarnated in the everlasting material that is stone; this was divine incarnation in reagglomerated stone. Mortal man was made of dark silt from the Nile, and on frescoes and bas-reliefs, Egyptian man was always painted in a red-brown colour. The perishable, temporal body was destroyed by age and death. Only an offering made with an alchemical product sacred to Khnum, the salt natron, could confer immortality on the deceased. This is the rite of mummification; eternal life was acquired through a bath of natron, after 70 days.

Natron has never lost its liturgical value for the religions of the middle east. In the Talmud, natron symbolises the Torah (the law). In the Bible, Leviticus 2,13, natron is the salt sealing the alliance between God and his people:

*"And every oblation of thy meat offering shalt thou season with salt; neither shalt thou suffer the salt of the covenant of thy god to be lacking from thy meat offering: with all thine offerings thou shalt offer salt."*

In this verse, the salt in question is not sodium chloride, the salt used in cooking, nor is it potash (potassium nitrate); it is natron. To be convinced, read Proverbs 25,20:

*"As he that taketh away a garment in cold weather, and as vinegar upon nitre, so is he that singeth songs to an heavy heart."*

When vinegar is poured on to natron (sodium carbonate), the natron disintegrates and dissolves to give a solution of sodium acetate.

---

[2]H. Brugsch, Die biblischen sieben Jahre der Hungersnoth, Leipzig 1891.

If, on the other hand, vinegar is poured onto potassium nitrate or sodium chloride, nothing happens. The authors of Genesis in the Bible described the creation in terms of their span of knowledge and of the information that had been passed on since the earliest times. While the Old Testament has often been related to Assyriology, the influence of Egypt has been thoroughly neglected.

The ancestral traditions underlying Khnum are significant in history. Several thousand years after the building of the pyramids, Khnum was worshipped by the gnostics, a semi-Christian sect. And Egyptian creation legend involves Khnum in the following way: *"The mud of the Nile (Khnum), heated to excess by the sun, will fragment and, without any seed, generate the races of man and of animals"*.

Similarly, certain passages in the Bible leave no doubt as to belief in a potter god. In Genesis, the creation occurs with the aid of a substance similar to that used by Khnum: clay, mud. Genesis 2,8: *"And the Lord God formed man of the dust of the ground, and breathed into his nostrils the breath of life; and man became a living soul"*. The Hebrew verb used for God in this verse is YSR, from the same route as the word which means "potter". We also read in Isaiah 64,8: *"But now, oh Lord, Thou art our father; we are the clay, and thou our Potter; and we all are the work of thy hand."*

In the Qur'an, too: Surah 7 (creation from clay):

*11. And certainly We created you, then We fashioned you, then We said to the angels: "Make obeisance to Adam". So they did obeisance except Iblis; he was not of those who did obeisance.*

*12. [Allah] said: "What hindered you so that you did not make obeisance when I commanded you?" He said: "I am better than he: Thou hast created me of fire, while him Thou didst create of clay."*

In Surah 28 we find also:

*38. Pharaoh said: "O chiefs! I do not know of any god for you besides myself; therefore, O Haman, light me (materials) out of clay, and build me a lofty tower, that I may mount up to the god of Moses: but as far as I am concerned I think (Moses) is a liar!"*

According to the tradition, the tower, that Pharaoh asks scientist Haman to build, would be a pyramid, as there is no other tower in Egypt. The fire is needed to produce, among others, calcined clay as the metakaolin MK-750, one of the components needed to start a geopolymer reaction in making the stones.

# Chapter 12

# Hewn in stone for the god Amun

*By now the reader has the basically well founded impression that the whole of Egyptian civilisation was busy agglomerating stone for more than 3000 years, for religious purposes. But this doesn't fit in with the monuments of the New Kingdom, which are clearly built of hewn stone. Was stone made sacred in another, new way?*

Indeed it was. And it is incarnated in the role of the second, more recent demigod, the god Amun, the omnipotent God of the New Kingdom of Ramses II.

Of uncertain origin (Hermopolis or Thebes), Amun was at first an insignificant divinity, with ill-defined functions. He became a dynastic god during the twelfth dynasty with Amenemhaat (1800 BC). But he was still not the creator of life, a role still reserved for Khnum if we rely on texts from the time of the pharaoh Amenemhaat III. After expelling the Hyksos from Egypt at the beginning of the New Kingdom (1560 BC), the Theban Princes made him into the supreme god of liberated Egypt. (figure 12.1).

Amun's priests gave him the attributes of the other gods: of the sun god Ra, of the god Min, of the warrior god Montu. Then, under Ramses III, he became "King of the gods" and eventually the priests gave him the power of the creation of the world.

Figure 12.1: The god Amun.

## 12.1 Creation is the divine incarnation of hewn stone

In the book of Thot, the creation by Amun is described as follows:

*"In the beginning of the world, there was only an abyss with shadowy waters. There was only darkness of the water and over the water reigned the shadows, and there was no sign of life. A mountain of mud began to rise up from the shadowy waters, the mountain of mud swelled, bubbled and took the form of the first god: Amun. And Amun pulled out (carved) the limbs and all the parts of his body, and the parts of the body of Amun were transformed into men, animals and the whole of creation and all living things on earth. Amun signifies he who comes out of darkness. He is the creation and is everything that exists eternally in all things... "*

When he is kneading humanity, Khnum is represented on frescoes by a turquoise-blue colour, the colour of mafkat, a mineral essential to agglomeration, a symbol of creation and of the beginning. According to Egyptologist Monique Dolinska[1], the original colouring of Amun

---

[1]M. Dolinska, Red and Blue figures of Amun, Abstract of Papers, 66-67, E.A.O. Press, Fifth International Congress of Egyptology, Cairo, Egypt, Oct.

on the frescoes was red. The turquoise-blue colour symbolising the quality of demigod only became characteristic at the end of the 18th dynasty (1300 BC), probably by analogy. Only two divinities have their bodies entirely painted in this turquoise-blue colour: Khnum and Amun. Other divinities only have parts of their body in blue, in general the head, including the goddess Hathor, goddess of the mafkat mines of Sinai. Amun has now become the creator, thus replacing Khnum. But he does not use the same methods.

In the myth of the genesis, Amun is identified with a mountain and he CARVES each being in a part of himself. Amun and all the divine incarnations of Amun-Ra were therefore materialised by the act of carving in stone, and are at the origin of the monuments of the New Kingdom, such as those of Ramses II, 1300 years after the pyramids. We can now understand why tombs were no longer under the pyramids, symbols of agglomeration, but under a mountain, the Valley of the Kings, symbol of Amun. Similarly, temples were built in stone carved with the utmost care, and the granite obelisks are known as "the Fingers of Amun". As in the Old Kingdom, where the name of Khnum (he who binds) can be found in the complete name of Cheops (Khnum Khufu), the kings of the New Kingdom associated Amun (he who is hidden) with their ancestors such as in Amenhotep.

## 12.2   The rise to power of Amun

Around 1750 BC, the Hyksos invaded the north of Egypt, but in the south they let the pharaohs at Thebes exercise phantom power, keeping up the cult of Amun. In the Middle Kingdom, the local god of Thebes was assimilated to Ra under the name of Amun-Ra. Around 1600 BC, an emancipation movement spread out from Thebes, and the god Amun personified national resistance to the invader. A Theban King known as Kamose broke the truce under whose terms the monarch of the Hyksos shared Egypt with him. In the name of the fatherland, he announced his intention of marching northward. In doing this he was carrying out "Amun's orders" and he attacked an Egyptian collaborator who was a vassal of the Hyksos. He thus took back from the Hyksos the 15th, 16th and 17th nomes (regions) of Upper Egypt.

---

29-Nov. 3, (1988).

During this re-conquest, the god Amun gained national status. His prestige grew with the epithet "liberating god" under the leadership of King Kamose and above all under the reigns of the first sovereigns of the 18th dynasty: Amosis, 1550–1525 BC, Amenhotep I, 1525–1504 BC, Tutmosis I, 1504–1492 BC and Tutmosis II, 1492–1479 BC.

From being a liberating god under Amosis, Amun became transformed into a god who subjugated foreign peoples, delivering them to the domination of his sons, the pharaohs Amenhotep I, II and III. Amun's priests took advantage of this situation, making hitherto unequalled profits and becoming richer than the kings themselves. Each victory brought them the bounty captured on the battlefield, the taxes levied on the vassals and the enemy prisoner slaves. When, after conquering Meggido, Tutmosis III organised the pillage of the country, it was to the profit of the god Amun-Ra that he had the wheat harvested and sent to Egypt. Any useful plants or rare animals taken during these campaigns were added to others already acquired to embellish the woods and gardens of the temples of Amun and his own property. The pharaoh never kept for himself all the bounty taken by armed force. A portion was always put by for the treasure of Amun. His successors kept up the practice, and under Amenhotep II, Tutmosis I and Amenhotep III, the clergy of Thebes saw their wealth grow unceasingly.

To resist the Hyksos they needed the protection of a warrior god — Amun — and of a god of the new bronze weapons. This was Memphis Ptah, the god of blacksmiths and stone carvers, and now of users of bronze tools and weapons. The first act of peace of the Pharaoh Amosis was to open the soft limestone quarries of Tura. The bas-relief illustrating this act is the first among the documents that give evidence of the use of the technique of carving. In reopening the Tura quarries, Amosis obtained a good quality white stone for the temple of Amun at Thebes and of Ptah at Memphis. The picture sculpted on the stele of Amosis shows us that a block has been detached from the mountain and is being squared up with a chisel before being taken away by an ox-drawn sledge (figure 24.6 in chapter 24).

## 12.3 Amun becomes the demigod

When they were at the height of their power, the priests of Amun added the act of creation to the powers of their god. Beforehand, on painted frescoes, Amun had been painted in red-brown. Now he was represented by blue, the symbol of genesis.

The colour turquoise blue is the colour of the *mafkat* of Khnum, the first god. Amun has become the demigod, the creator taking the place of Khnum. But he does not use the same methods as Khnum.

Khnum agglomerates, he kneads humanity with his Nile silt and other minerals such as mafkat and natron. Amun was a mountain and he carved each being out of a part of himself, in this mountain. It is easier to understand this obscure page in the history of Egypt if we recall the hypothesis according to which Khnum and all the divine incarnations of Ra (Ra-Harakhtes) were materialised by the act of agglomeration in stone. Stone was a sacred constituent of tombs, of temples, and statues. Then think of the principal by which Amun and all the divine incarnations of Amun-Ra were materialised by the act of carving stone, leading to the monuments of the New Kingdom. Under this hypothesis, the carving must be done in the mountain, directly in Amun's body. It is therefore perfectly understandable that the burial places should no longer be under the pyramids, symbols of agglomeration. Tombs are now carved in caves, in the mountain, on the side of the setting sun. It is in the mountain of Deir el-Bahari that we find the tombs of the pharaohs of the 18th dynasty, Tutmosis I, II, and III, Hatshepsout, Amenhotep I and II. Those of Amenhotep III and the Ramses pharaohs are found in the Valley of the Kings.

During New Kingdom, the most widely used building material for the temples and tombs was monumental sandstone, or so-called psammite. In chapter 24, we mention the study undertaken by the team of D.D. Klemm to date the various sandstone quarries of Silsilis. This enabled the various marks of chisels and tools that were visible in the quarries to be attributed to each period. In one area of the quarry, the stones had been cut leaving extremely thin regular chisel marks (carving in the body of the god Amun) in closely spaced parallel lines or in a herringbone pattern. In another part of the quarry, on the other hand, were found traces of wedges and wooden dowels. The wooden dowels had being pushed into notches made in the stone, and then soaked with water when they would have swollen, causing the rock to crack open. The technique of wooden wedges and dowels is very rudimentary and appears primitive, and therefore archaic; several archaeologists have used this as a proof of the use of carving and stone working in the building of the pyramids. But we know that this rough method of extracting the stone was in fact used by the Romans during the Roman occupation of Egypt, from the first century BC up to the third century AD. On the other hand, the technique involving fine parallel cuts made with bronze chisels had been introduced 1400 years earlier by the Egyptians of the 18th dynasty; cf. figure 24.4 of chapter 24.

**Figure 12.2:** The carved stones of the Karnac and Luxor temples, and Amon's fingers (2000).

It is easy to understand why each block, large or small, was cut directly in the mountain (the quarry). To have reduced the large stone to several smaller ones, outside the quarry, could have been considered as sacrilege to the body of Amun (figure 12.2). This explains why the obelisks were carved in one piece on the spot in the mountain, just as it was perfectly normal for colossal statues representing the Ka of the Pharaoh during the New Kingdom, erected in front of and within their funeral temples, to have been sculpted directly in the rock. The exact origin of every obelisk and every colossus has been found, because their imprints are visible in the granite and the monumental sandstone quarries worked during the New Kingdom. All the monuments of that period can be associated with the precise location where they were extracted, except — and it is the exception that confirms the rule — the two gigantic colosses of Memnon.

If the Egyptians cut stone with such precision, such finesse and such beauty, as illustrated by the traces left by their tools, this was because their stone had religious significance. Now we understand why Ramses II built his magnificent temple of Abu Simbel directly in the hillside of soft sandstone (figure 12.3), actually in the body of Amun. The quarrying of rock with wedges and dowels, an extremely rough technique which injures the body of Amun, was the practice of the Greeks and Romans who did not consider stone in the same metaphysical way as the Egyptians.

**Figure 12.3:** The temple of Abu Simbel carved in the body of Amun (2000).

# Chapter 13

# Two civilisations, two distinct lands

*In ancient Egypt, religion seems to have played the same role as politics does in our modern civilisations.*

It is often the case that priests play an important role in civilisations, by exerting a power in competition with that of the King. One is continually seeking to have influence on the other.

*Divine incarnation in agglomerated stone belongs rather to the religion of Memphis, that of the Pyramids, in the North. What about the south, where religion was based on hewn stone?*

The fact of there being two antagonistic religions, a source of rivalry, of competition and conflicts in society, had serious consequences. The opposition between north and south has always existed in Egyptian civilisation. The country was never unified. It was like a federation between two adjacent states where the pharaoh alone represented the link between the two different cultures.

There was a vizier at Thebes and a vizier at Memphis. In the King's title, the southern state is represented by the sign *s-nw*, ⚶ a kind of bulrush, while that of the North is a bee, *biit* 🐝 .

The Pharaoh was King of the Two Earths, *s-nw-biit* ⚶🐝 . He wore the white crown of the south and the red crown of the North (figure 13.1), and sometimes the double crown.

Egyptian history is the history of the domination of one state over the other, the northern part and the southern part together forming the Two Earths. The dominant state imposed its religion and its places of worship on the other land, together with its economic and

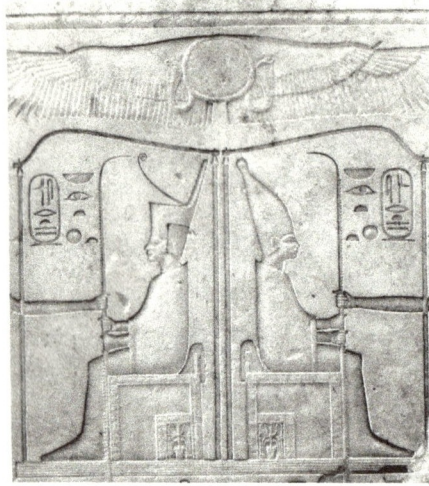

**Figure 13.1:** The two crowns, the northern on the left and the southern on the right, being worn separately by the pharaoh Sesostris III, 12th dynasty.

military power.

We find that the two Egyptian societies not only had their own special existence through their respective cultures, but also that they had precise geographical locations (figure 13.2). During the Old Kingdom, at the time of the pyramids and of the God Khnum, the centre of gravity was situated in the north. In the New Kingdom, 1200 years later, at the time of the Valley of the Kings and the worship of Amun, the seat of power was in the south.

Over its 3500 years, Egyptian civilisation did not stay completely unchanged. During these three millennia, it went through three great periods that were quite distinct, even opposing: the Old Kingdom of Cheops protected by the God Khnum, followed 1500 years later by the New Kingdom of Ramses II under the protection of the God Amun. Finally 900 years later, came the Ptolemaic period with Cleopatra and Greek domination. These three great periods were symbolised by three different capitals, Memphis, Thebes and Alexandria. The heretic Pharaoh Akhenaton tried to put an end to this bivalence between North and South by setting up a new capital, el Amarna right in the centre to bring the two peoples together. He failed. The map magnificently shows this geopolitical difference of which the public and some Egyptologists are often unaware.

Khnum did not disappear from the Egyptian pantheon and kept

a minor role afterwards. But the memory of him as the God of the Pyramids remained wreathed in glory for several pharaohs of the New Kingdom, who restored his worship and his temples, pharaohs such as Hatshepsout, Amenhotep III and the Ptolemies.

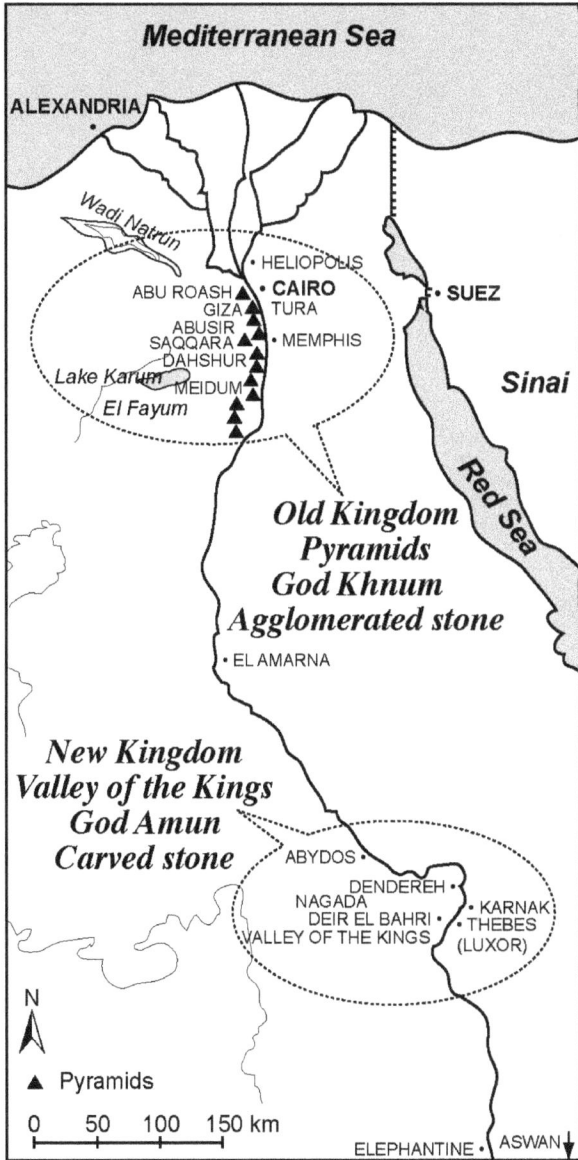

Figure 13.2: Two Egyptian civilizations.

# Chapter 14

# Hieroglyphic texts discovered

*A singular fact: you have discovered hieroglyphic texts describing the building of the pyramids and the use of this technology. We saw earlier in figure 5.3 that the hieroglyphic sign for the action of building shows a worker packing material in a mould. In which text is this found and why has this remained unknown up to now?*

This is the so-called Famine Stele. Translating the key words in question was no easy task. It should be pointed out however that the translation was shown officially to Egyptologists specialised in linguistics, who expressed no objection. It is obvious, almost trivially so, that texts explaining the building of the pyramids must have existed.

The building of these monuments and the events marking their consecration and use over the centuries are too momentous for no written trace to have been left. It is important to realise that the number of documents dating back to the Old Kingdom and surviving to this day is very limited. All the experts agree on the absence of any steles, frescoes or bas-reliefs describing how the pyramids were built. But what they have looked for is representations of the various stages that they assume were used such as extraction, hewing, transport, positioning and ramps — and they don't find them. Were these documents written or engraved and, if so, were they destroyed afterwards? If there are texts, moreover, why have Egyptologists been incapable of decoding them?

In an interview published in the French magazine *Historia* of

February 2003, following a feature on the building of the pyramids by agglomeration, the eminent French Egyptologist Jean Leclant explaining why the documents do not exist, speaks of a state secret:

*"No text about their construction has been found, nor any architectural treaty, whereas treaties on medicine have been found. There is not a single example. The reason is that the method of construction had to remain a state secret. There is therefore little chance of one day solving the mystery".*

To evoke a state secret is to admit one's ignorance. But the texts do actually exist. Among others, I shall quote the Sehel stele — the so-called Famine Stele — the stele of the Irtysen sculptor in the Louvre Museum and the fresco of Ti. In this chapter we shall deal with the Sehel stele, the Famine Stele, and in a later chapter we shall talk about the stele of the Irtysen sculptor. Other texts are being studied, including those concerning the building by agglomeration of the colosses of Memnon.

The interview with J. Leclant, moreover, is rife with statements that are all in the same vein. Thus for example the question about how the Egyptians of the predynastic period could have made vases in a stone that is harder than iron using their rudimentary tools:

*"These vases exist, so there must have been carved by the Egyptians... The same thing goes for the colosses of Memnon, which the author [J. Davidovits] claims to have been made in a stone that is almost impossible to carve. But they must have been carved, because they exist".*

The corollary is: if they were not carved, they don't exist; if they were agglomerated, they don't exist. Further on, J. Leclant adds:

*"In comparison with Egyptian civilisation, our behaviour is in total opposition to the great lesson of humility that the Egyptians have given. They managed to achieve all this in the greatest secrecy and as for us, we are trying to break the secret".*

This is quite a remarkable statement when we consider that Egyptologists have no scruples in opening tombs, unearthing mummies, unclothing them and exhibiting them in museums, thereby violating the sacred and secret character of the sepulchre.

# 14.1 The Famine Stele

This is a document that is well known to Egyptologists, engraved on a rock and called the *Famine Stele*, discovered in the island of Sehel near Elephantine by Charles Wilbour in 1889 (figure 14.1). This stele refers to the reign of the Pharaoh Djoser, builder of the first pyramid, the Step Pyramid of Saqqarah, more than 2500 years earlier. In these documents, Egyptologists recognise a copy of ancestral texts from the Old Kingdom, emanating from the architect scribe Imhotep and reproduced by the priests of Khnum around 200 BC.

**Figure 14.1:** The Famine Stele, Khnum brings minerals to the Pharaoh Djoser (first pyramid) (1988).

The Famine Stele was engraved during the reign of king Ptolemy V Epiphany (205–182 BC). This Pharaoh is known above all for having had the famous Rosetta Stone sculpted, in 196 BC. This Rosetta Stone is linked to the Famine Stele, because they were both engraved in the reign of that same Pharaoh, and both relate the same event, a famine followed by exceptional floods. Just as the Rosetta Stone gave Champollion the key to decipher the hieroglyphs, so the Famine Stele enabled me to describe how the pyramids were built.

According to the Rosetta Stone, in the eighth year of the reign of Ptolemy V, the flooding of the Nile was so great that it covered all the plains, and the water stayed longer than usual. The result was a food shortage. Khnum symbolised the Nile and his clergy were able to correct the aberrations of its course. There still exists at Elephantine a nilometer, the device for measuring the water level and enabling the progress of the flooding to be followed step-by-step.

The priests made a visit to the library of Hermopolis in 197 BC. There, they found ancient texts showing that, in the past, they knew how to cope with the random nature of the flooding. Although there had been several famines in Egyptian history, they were looking in particular for the account of one going back to the time of the Pharaoh Djoser and of Imhotep. According to this document, to put an end to the food shortage, generous offerings had to be made to the god Khnum. Armed with this text, the priests were able to show how, 2500 years earlier, their predecessors had been able to control the abnormal flooding of the Nile.

The advice given to the sovereign by the priests had a beneficial effect. Again according to the Rosetta Stone, king Ptolemy V built a dam to divert the excess water from the Nile into new canals. Having done this, he organised the irrigation of new land, enabling agriculture and abundant harvests. He received the title of Saviour of Egypt. The King issued decrees, restoring to the temples of Khnum their previous rights. They once again obtained sovereignty over territories stretching up to 35 km from Elephantine, including several lost domains of Nubia. In this territory, all fishermen and hunters had to pay dues. The quarries of Sehel and Aswan could only be exploited with the permission of the priests of Khnum. They also exacted duty on goods transported by boats arriving in Egypt by the Nile from the south.

On the Famine Stele, although the main part reproduces authentic documents dating from the reign of the Pharaoh Djoser, the priests of Khnum in the Ptolemaic epoque may have added some stylistic elements. The Famine Stele also contains information unconnected to territorial rights or the famine. The stele should actually have been called the Alchemical stele of Khnum, for it includes a large amount of information on the fabrication of artificial Stone.

Out of a total of 2600 hieroglyphs, around 650, about a quarter, refer to descriptions of rocks and mineral products and of their processing. This alchemical list is found in columns 10 to 22. Figures 14.5, 14.6 show columns 11 to 19.

In my work, I referred to earlier translations and research carried out by the Egyptologists Karl Brugsch (1891), W. Pleyte (1891), Jacques Morgan (1894), Kurt Sethe (1905), Paul Barguet (1953), D. Wildung and Lichtheim (1973)[1] .

The study carried out by P. Barguet served as a guide in our own investigation, because it is the most recent version in French.

This list does not mention building stones such as limestone (hieroglyphic name *ainr-hedj*), the stone used for the pyramids, nor materials used to build the temples from 1600 BC up to the Roman period, such as monumental sandstone (*ainr-rwdt*) or Aswan granite (*mat*), both abundantly used during the Ptolemaic period. If we rely strictly on the contents of the stele, it is true that pyramids and temples cannot be built just with minerals, unless these minerals are used to make a binder for reconstituting stone.

In this list, the names of several minerals have never been translated. Others have been interpreted, and these interpretations must be used cautiously. Understanding these words, which I call key words, is vital to the accurate translation of the text. These key words designate either rocks, minerals or transformation processes. I have tried to understand a large number of these terms which have been misunderstood, on the basis of my archaeological mineralogical and chemical knowledge.

I presented the results of my work in 1988 during the International Conference of Egyptologists, in Cairo, Egypt[2]. My translation of these key words attracted no negative criticism on the part of specialists, experts in hieroglyphs. Here I have selected a few of the key

---

[1]Famine Stele list of authors: H. Barguet. La Stele de la Famine à Sehel, Institut Français d'Archéologie Orientale, Bibl. d'Etude, 24, Cairo. 1953. H. Brugsch, Die biblischen sieben Jahre der Hungersnoth, Leipzig 1891. M. Lichtheim, Ancient Egyptian Literature, A Book of Readings, Vol.III, University of California Press, Berkeley 1973. J. de Morgan, In Catalogue des Monuments et Inscriptions de l'Egypte Antique, 1 série, Tome 1, Ed. Adolphe Holzhausen, Vienne, Austria; pp. 78–83, 1894. W. Pleyte, Schenkingsoorkonde van Sehele; Letterkunde, 3 Reeks, Deel VIII; Royal Academy of Sciences, Amsterdam, Netherlands, 1891. K. Sethe, Dodekaschoinos; Ed: J.C. Hinrisch, Leipzig; pp.19–26, 1901. S. Aufrère, Remarques sur les termes servant à désigner l'émeraude, le béryl, l'olivine, Revue d'Egyptologie, Paris 1984, 35, pp. 23–30.
[2]J. Davidovits, Pyramid Man Made Stone, Myths of Facts, III. The Famine Stele Provides the Hieroglyphic Names of Chemicals and Minerals involved in the Construction, 5th International Congress of Egyptology, Cairo, 1988, Abstract, pp. 57–58. Paper available at the Geopolymer Institute Website, Library section, www.geopolymer.org.

**Figure 14.2:** The key words of the Famine Stele.

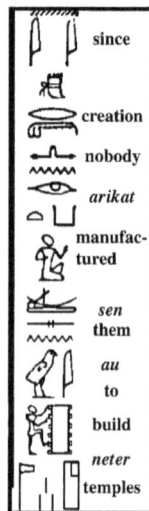

**Figure 14.3:** The verb iri-kat in column 19.

words from the list reproduced in figure 14.2. For a complete list the reader is referred to the paper presented above.

### 14.1.1   *khusi*: build, construct

This verb has already been mention in figure 5.3. It contains the hieroglyphic sign showing a worker packing material in a mould. Here, in column 12 of figure 14.5, we read:

*"... with these products that we seek to build the temples... and the royal tomb (the pyramid)... "*

### 14.1.2   *iri-kat (ari-kat)*: create, fashion the KA (the soul), in eternal stone, manufacture

This is a compound verb made up of the two words *iri* and *kat*. The word *iri* or *irit* (the eye) on its own is a verb meaning to work with, fashion, make, do. The second term, *kat* (the two raised arms) means the work of man (the Ka); the group *iri-kat*: do work by man, the determinative being a squatting man with or without a basket on his head (see figure 11.3, chapter 11). In other words, *iri-kat* is an adjective meaning artificial (man made), created, fabricated, synthetic. We find it for example in the expression meaning an imitation of the natural stone lapis-lazuli. This verb appears in column 13, 19 and 20. In columns 13 and 19 it is used in the process for making the material necessary for the pyramids, figure 14.3.

*"... Since the creation thou art the first to manufacture them for building the temples..."*

In column 20, it qualifies the act of the creation of humanity by the god Khnum.

### 14.1.3   *rwdt*

This key word is found in column 11. According to Barguet, it designates the notion of hard stone. It has been particularly well studied by the Egyptologist and mineralogical specialist J. R. Harris[3] . According to Harris: *"in fact, there is some doubt as to the notion indicating a hard stone in general, and it would be very difficult to say what sort of stone belongs to this category, especially if in reference to the fact that alabaster is here mentioned as rwdt".*

Egyptian alabaster is a very soft stone. Furthermore, *rwdt* is very often associated with the monumental sandstone of Egypt. This is a very soft stone used for the construction of the temples of Karnak, Luxor, Edfu, Dendera and Abu Simbel, a material so soft that it can be scratched with a fingernail. This stone is eight times softer than Aswan granite; this shows clearly that *rwdt* cannot designate a hard stone.

On the other hand, the verb *rwdt* has the meaning of to germinate, to grow (for a plant). A causative forms of the verb, *s-rwdt*, signifies strengthen or bind strongly; *rwdt* is also associated with aggregates, with the small stones found in sandstone, quartzite and granite. We can extrapolate by saying that these stones are the result of the natural solidification of aggregates. Sand for example gives sandstone. *Rwdt* may thus be the word designating the aggregates which are naturally bound together to make up stone; it may also be the determinative for agglomerated stone (natural sedimentary or metamorphic stone, or artificial stone).

---

[3]J. R. Harris, Lexicographical Studies in Ancient Egyptian Minerals, Akademie-Verlag, Berlin, *aat* and *rwdt*, p. 21–24 (1961)

### 14.1.4   *ain*

This expression designates natural, solid stone. Building stones are expressed by *ainr*. When the "r" is removed from *ainr* to give *ain*, the word becomes a generic term for stone, distinguishing it from other materials such as wood or metal. The generic term *ain* appears in column 15 at the top of the list giving the rocks and certain mineral varieties. On the other hand, the term for building stones *ainr*, for example *ainr-hedj* (limestone) or *ainr-rwdt* (monumental sandstone) is not found at all in the Famine Stele.

### 14.1.5   *aat*

This word appears in column 11, 16 19. According to K. Brugsch, it designates stones (Steinen); for Sethe, it means precious stones (kostbare Mineralien), for Barguet, precious stones, and for Lichtheim, precious stones. J.R. Harris, in his study of Egyptian minerals, has this to say:

*"... It appears obvious that aat actually covers a wide variety of materials, mainly mineral... If we regard aat as being a mineral having perhaps a certain value due to its rarity, then we can make a very clear distinction between aat and ain, because the latter refers essentially to stones extracted in large amounts... In this way we can understand what the attitude of the ancient Egyptians was to the concept of raw material as a whole and that of mineral substances in particular... It appears that in general there was a very sharp distinction between natural mineral resources on the one hand, and those having an animal or vegetable origin on the other hand, the former being called aat and the latter shmw".*

It is thus clear that *aat* is a mineral found in the form of small lumps in the mountains and was probably extracted in galleries, as opposed to the large blocks of the construction stones; *aat* may under these conditions designate an ore. 16 begins with the injunction *"Learn the names of the rare aat"*, followed by a list of hieroglyphic names of mineral and metal substances, of semiprecious stones (*mafkat*), of minerals (red ochre) and other substances that are not translated. The metal and mineral ores are found in the same list. Most of the metals are obtained by processing ores, suggesting that *aat* may designate all the metal and mineral ores, the mineral ores having to undergo similar processing to the metal ores. It is in this column that we also find turquoise (*mafkat*) and chrysocolla. Egyptologists very often assimilate *aat* to the hard stone vases. Yet a large number of the minerals given in columns 16–17 are friable or even powdery. Column 19 shows the exceptional importance of this text: we read there that the mineral substance must, for the first time in Egyptian history, be transformed, used to build the pyramids in the temples. Thus, Khnum declares: *"I give thee quantity after quantity of aat... Nobody before thee has transformed them (to make stones) to build the temples of the gods... "*

## 14.1.6  *khnem, khem* (a bladder with liquid)

This hieroglyphic sign opens several avenues of discussion. The ideogram has not been translated by the various authors and, according to the dictionary, it is pronounced *khnem* or *khem*. As an ideogram it is always associated with the notion of smell, but not with a pleasant smell or perfume. It is found in combination with substances that give off smells, vapours or emanations which are not dangerous; but it does not mean stink or smell bad. It is sometimes found in the concept of pleasure or pride.

According to Brugsch, this ideogram has the meaning of unguent, while neither Barguet nor Lichtheim translate it. In fact, Barguet remains very cautious, commenting: *"products related to those which are quoted in column 11 "*, i.e. mineral substances.

The sign *khnem* (a bladder with a liquid coming out) may be the key enabling the names of some of the minerals found in the stele to be deciphered; I suggest that the symbol shows a bladder containing urine, giving off a certain smell that is not pleasant as perfume is. Urine is often involved in alchemical formulas; I deduce that this ideogram represents the smell given off by certain chemicals. Most chemicals have a characteristic smell that chemists can recognise. According to columns 11 and 12, and according to Barguet, these smelly substances emanate from minerals, and precisely those ones which were used to build the pyramids and the temples.

In modern times, identifying the composition of a mineral is done from its colour, its taste and its smell. Up to now, no one has suggested that the ancient Egyptians could have used the same practical methods both to classify and to determine the chemical composition of mineral substances. We know that since prehistoric times, the Egyptians heated minerals to obtain enamels. Today in geology and mineralogy, we use the flame of a blowpipe to analyse the emanations produced during heating. Some rocks melt, others produce a coloured flame, for example violet for potassium and yellow for sodium. Some minerals crepitate, others swell, producing bubbles. Some such as the arsenic minerals and sulphides produce pungent fumes.

In Latin, the name of a stone is generally derived from its colour and general appearance. For example, the word ruby comes from the Latin *rebus* which itself contains the root of the Latin term *ruber* meaning red. But it is not certain that in ancient Egypt the same process was used to name the rocks and minerals. In fact, most of the hieroglyphic names of rocks and minerals found in the Famine Stele have not been translated, because they do not correspond to any known colour. The Egyptians therefore used another approach for characterising their minerals.

## 14.1.7  Relation to the text of Herodotus

Mineralogical investigation methods where never used in deciphering the Famine Stele, perhaps through ignorance or underestimation of the industrial use of these ores. Some of the minerals used by the Egyptians, such as *mafkat*, olivenite (copper arsenate) and scorodite (iron arsenate), do feature in guides to rocks and minerals, but are of no interest except to mineralogists and collectors. In ancient Egypt, these minerals mixed with copper ores gave a harder cuprous material, a sort of bronze with a high arsenic content.

When they are heated with a flame, these arsenic containing ores give off a strong odour of onion or garlic. There are historic accounts which could prove that these arseneous rocks were used in the building of the pyramids. The great historian Herodotus (485 to 425 BC), relates what the Egyptian guides told him at the time when he saw the Great Pyramid. This text of Herodotus is discussed in considerable detail in the book Ils ont bâti les pyramides; here, I will mention a few special observations. Thus, we read:

*"On the pyramids, there is an inscription in Egyptian characters indicating the amount spent on radish, onions and garlic for the workers. The person who interpreted this inscription for me, and I remember this very well, told me that the sum was 1600 talents of silver".*

Today, 1600 talents of silver are equivalent to around 100 million euros, a colossal sum, much too great simply to pay for radish, onions and garlic, which presumably were used to feed the workers. Herodotus himself is very surprised at the size of this sum, considering the type of food in question. On the other hand, in the light of the chemistry invoked for Khnum, this legendary inscription makes complete sense: the sum of 100 million euros represents the expenses for the extraction of arseneous minerals used in the building — minerals that smell of garlic, onion or radish when they are heated. And moreover, the physicist Guy Demortier, a member of our scientific team, discovered arsenic in the casing stone of the Cheops' pyramid in 2003.

Now let us look at the list of rocks whose names are related to the words onion, garlic and radish. The Famine Stele helps us to understand the text of Herodotus and the involvement of minerals in the building of the pyramid. The ore that smells of onion when it is heated is here written *hedsh*. So onion stone must refer to a mineral which, when it is heated, gives off white fumes smelling of onion (i.e. one of the ores containing arsenic). Similarly, the expressions *tutem* and *taam* contain the root *tem*, are associated with garlic. In column 16 we find the ore *tem-ikr*; this could be a mineral giving off a smell of garlic. The last two letters *kr* mean "weak". Here, then, we have a mineral giving off a weak smell of garlic (another of the ores containing arsenic). The word *gau* (also *ga-t*) means "radish". In column 16, we find the mineral *ga-y*; this could be a mineral smelling of radish when it is heated.

The ideogram *khnem*, *khem*, has raised further discussion and etymological reasoning. Many hieroglyphic terms vocalised as *khem*, *schemm*, *shem*, contain this ideogram. These words may mean products characterised by their smell. For some etymologists, the origin of the word alchemy may come from the Egyptian "kemit" meaning black earth. Others suggest a Hebrew root: the word for the Sun, *chemesh*. I suggest that the root of the word alchemy is *khem*, which during the Old Kingdom was written as *shnem*. Over time, the corruption of this word in the Greek language could have led to *khemi* or *chemi*; other instances of this word evolution exist. For example, the builder of the great pyramids, whose Egyptian name is Khnumu-Khufu, in Greek is called Cheops and also Chemis. The symbol *khnem*, *khem* may thus have become the root of the word alchemy through corruption of the language: in Greek, chymia, in Arab alkimya, in Latin alchemia, in old French alchimie and in English alchemy.

113

## 14.2 The new translation

Here is the new translation of the Famine Stele, still based on Bar-guet's text, but now including all the key technical words. There are still many minerals and ores whose representations remain unknown (they are written in italics). My transcription suggests that the use of a technology in which the minerals undergo various treatments (with chemicals) enabled the stones for the pyramids and temples to be manufactured. Words having a meaning different from that given by Barguet are underlined in the text.

### 14.2.1 The revelation of Imhotep

(Col. 11)... There is a group of mountains in a western location, with all kinds of minerals (ores) and loose (disaggregated, weathered, split apart, ground) stones (aggregates) suitable for agglomeration and everything

(Col. 12) what is needed to build any temple in upper and lower Egypt, sacred animal stables, royal tombs (pyramids), and all the statues that are erected in temples and shrines. Their chemicals are brought together and placed in front of Khnum and around him, at the same time as

(Col. 13) large green plants and all kinds of flowers which are found from Elephantine to Bigeh, both to the east end to the West. There is, in the middle of the river, covered in water at its annual rejuvenation, a place of relaxation for all; minerals are worked to make stones on both banks of the river...

(Col. 14)... Learn the names of the gods that are in the temple of Khnum:...

(Col. 15) learn the names of the stone materials that are there in the middle of the frontier zone (that is to say those) that are to the east and to the west, that are (on both banks) of the canal of Elephantine, that are in the eastern and the western centre, that are in the middle of the river: *bekhen, mthay* (dead or weathered granite), *mhtbtb, rags, wtshy hedsh* (disaggregated stone smelling of onion), at the eastern end, *prdn* to the West, *teshi* (disaggregated stone) to the West and in the river.

(Col. 16) learn the names of the rare minerals (ores) from the quarries upstream, some of them at a distance of 4 nautical miles: gold, silver, copper, iron, lapis-lazuli, turquoise, thnt, red jasper, *gay* (radish stone), *mnw*, emerald, *tem-ikr* (garlic stone); in addition *nshmt, taamhy, hmaagt,*

(Col. 17) *ibht, bks-anḥ,* green make-up, black collyrium, red ochre of *shrt, mimi,* Nubian white earth, in this region..."

## 14.2.2 The dream of Djoser

"(Col. 18)... While sleeping peacefully, I discovered the god standing in front of me; I worshipped him and supplicated him in front of him to appease him; he said: "I am Khnum, your creator; my arms are around you to embrace your body

(Col. 19) so that your limbs become strong. I give you mineral (ores) after mineral (ores),... nobody before you has transformed them (to make stone) — to build temples, to repair what is in ruins, to garnish with incrustations the eyes of their teacher. For I am the Lord who creates, I am the one who created himself, the very great Noun, the one who has existed since the origin of time, Happy who runs

(Col. 20) as he wishes, the one who works with men, the one who guides each in his time, Ta-Tenen father of the gods, Chou the great, the master bringer of gifts".

Figure 14.4: The first pyramid of all, the Step pyramid of Djoser (1988).

Which pyramid (the royal tomb, col. 12) and which funeral complex (the temples, col. 19) is being referred to in the Famine Stele? Obviously the magnificent site of the Step Pyramid at Saqqarah, the first pyramid of all, built by Imhotep for his Pharaoh Djoser, around 2700 BC (figure 14.4).

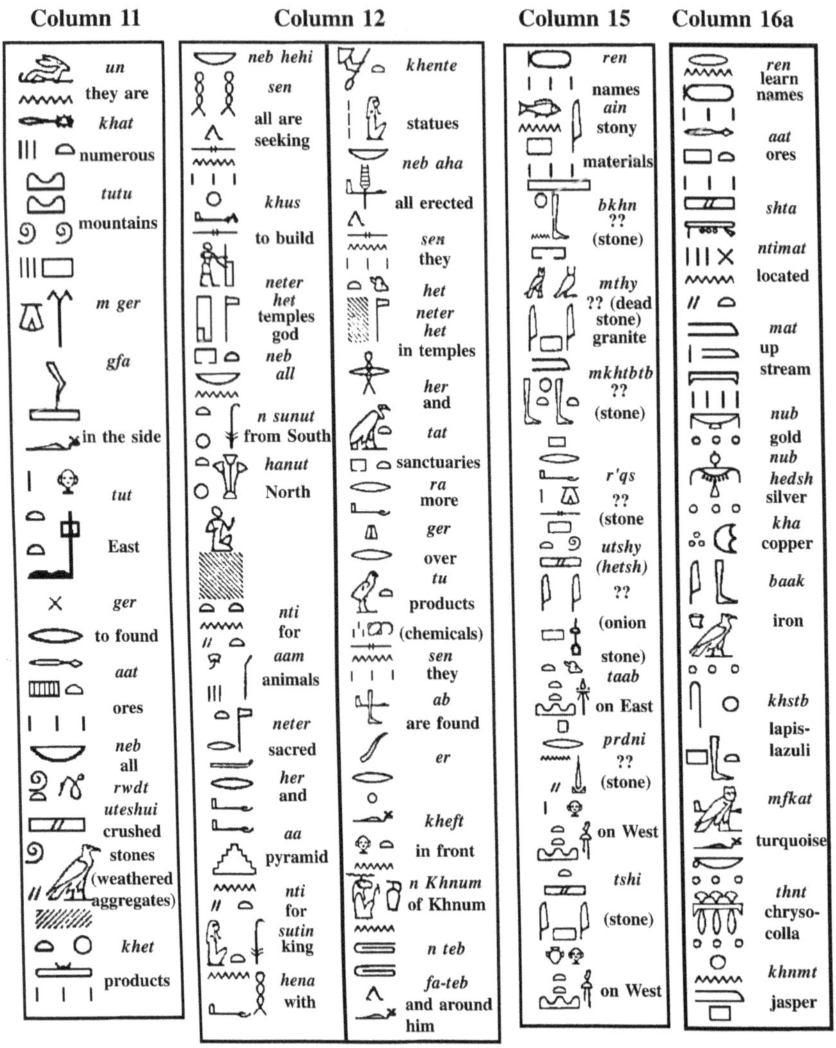

| Column 11 | Column 12 | Column 15 | Column 16a |
|---|---|---|---|
| un | neb hehi | ren | ren |
| they are | sen | names | learn |
| khat | all are | ain | names |
| numerous | seeking | stony | aat |
| tutu | khus | materials | ores |
| mountains | to build | bkhn ?? (stone) | shta |
| m ger | neter het temples god | mthy ?? (dead stone) granite | ntimat |
| gfa | neb all | mkhtbtb ?? (stone) | located |
| in the side | n sunut from South | r'qs ?? (stone | mat |
| tut | hanut North | utshy (hetsh) ?? | up stream |
| East | nti for | (onion stone) | nub gold |
| ger | aam animals | taab on East | nub hedsh silver |
| to found | neter sacred | prdni ?? (stone) | kha copper |
| aat | her and | on West | baak iron |
| ores | aa pyramid | tshi (stone) | khstb lapis-lazuli |
| neb all | nti for | on West | mfkat turquoise |
| rwdt uteshui crushed stones (weathered aggregates) | sutin king | | thnt chryso-colla |
| khet | hena with | | khnmt jasper |
| products | | | |
| khente statues neb aha all erected | sen they | | |
| het neter het in temples | her and | | |
| tat sanctuaries | ra more | | |
| ger over tu products | (chemicals) | | |
| sen they | ab are found | | |
| er | kheft in front | | |
| n Khnum of Khnum | n teb | | |
| fa-teb and around him | | | |

Figure 14.5: Columns 11 to 16a of the Famine Stele with the translation.

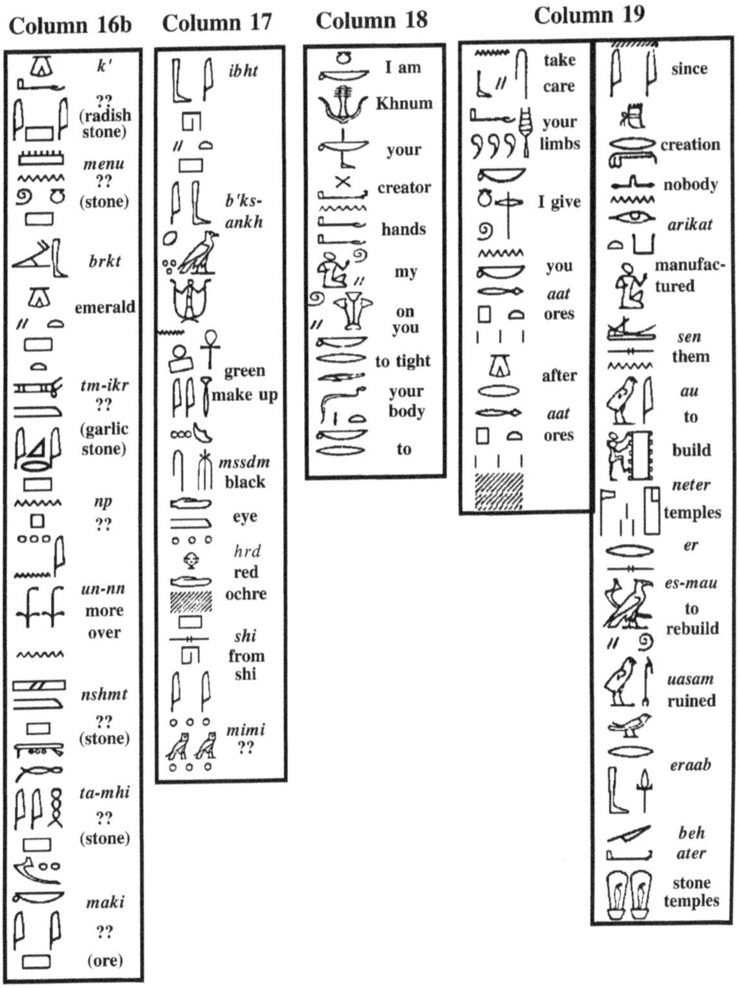

**Figure 14.6:** Columns 16b-19 of the Famine Stele with the translation.

# Chapter 15

# The stele of Irtysen, sculptor and moulder

*You said you had found the second hieroglyphic stele dating from a period much earlier than the Famine Stele?*

Yes, I did. Any tourist visiting the Louvre Museum in Paris can see this marvel in room seven of the thematic tour. It is called the stele of Irtysen and is more than 4000 years old (figure 15.1).

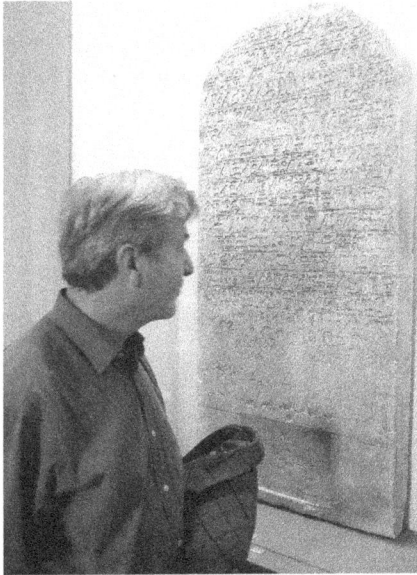

Figure 15.1: The author in front of the stele of Irtysen, Louvre Museum (2002).

## 15.1 Incomprehension

The stele (C14 in the Louvre nomenclature) is an autobiography of the scribe and sculptor Irtysen who lived around 2000 BC, under one of the pharaohs Mentouhotep, 11th dynasty. At the bottom of the stele, we can read the following note, as it appears in the Louvre translation (the question marks correspond to the hesitations of the translator):

*"Stele of the chief craftsman, scribe and sculptor Irtysen, reign of Nebhepetre Mentuhotep, 2033–1982 BC, 11th dynasty, limestone. I know the techniques of moulding (?). (. . . ) I know how to make materials (encrustation?, porcelain) that fire cannot consume nor water dissolve. (. . . ) I shall reveal the process to nobody, except my eldest son. . . "*

The stele of Irtysen has been studied by many authors. However, as it contains several expressions belonging to the technological domain, the translators have given a wide range of different translations.

Among the 14 transcriptions published since 1877, I selected five for study which, I believe, are representative of all the publications.

The translation of the ancient Egyptian into English by A. Badawy in 1961 seems to me to be the most adequate. This is the one I have chosen as a guide in a discussion on the main body of the stele (lines 6 to 15).

According to Badawy's interpretation, Irtysen was a sculptor who made both bas-reliefs and high-reliefs, but he sculpted no statues. I shall show that Irtysen possessed secret knowledge on the making of statues which were not carved, but cast (agglomerated stone) in the same way as plaster casting.

## 15.2 The new translation

We shall carefully examine the various technical terms and compare the five versions (I shall exclude certain sections including the general introduction, the style and the eulogy of the eldest son, which do not contain any scientific formulas that may be difficult to understand). The translations selected are those of G. Maspero, M. Baud, J.A.

Wilson, A. Badawy and W. Barta[1].

All of these translators agree on the exceptional knowledge of Irtysen presented in lines 8 to 9 (figure 15.2). However, their various transcriptions differ from one to the other and remain obscure. Thus:

G. Maspero: "... I know what belongs to it, the sinking waters, the weighings done for the reckoning of accounts, how to produce the form of issuing forth and coming in, so that a member go to its place..."

M. Baud: (translated from French) "... I know how to mix the cements, to weigh the parts according to the rules, to dig out the bottom, go in and dig in so that the member (the flesh) (remains or) goes to its place" (in French : "Je savais malaxer (gacher) les ciments, doser suivant les regles, creuser les fonds, introduire sans que cela dépasse ou creuse de facon que le membre (la chair) (reste ou) vienne a sa place").

J.A. Wilson: "... I know (how to reckon) the levels of the flood, how to weigh according to rule, how to withdraw or introduce when it goes out or comes in, in order that a body may come in its place."

A. Badawy: "... I know the parts of *baagw*; the weighings of the norm; bringing forth (or) letting in as it comes out (projects) (or) goes in (recedes), so that a member come in its place."

W. Barta: (translated from German) "... I know the parts of transformation, how to determine the right calculation...". (in German: "Ich kenne die Teile der Umwandelbarkeit und die Abschätzungen der richtige Berechnung...")

A very important technical word *baagw* is found just after the expression "I know..." (figure 15.3). It is written with three "n" signs for water. This explains why many translators associate it with the measurement of the level of water in the Nile, a skill difficult to explain for a sculptor. Badawy does not translate it and Barta ignores these water signs (which actually express fluidity), reducing the meaning to a simple graphic. Baud supplies an interesting idea. She translates the word *baagw* by cement, in reference to another

---

[1] G. Maspero, TSBA 5, pp. 559–560, (1877). M. Baud, Le métier d'Iritisen, Chronique d'Égypte, Bruxelles, Tome XXV, pp. 21–34, (1938). J. A. Wilson, The Artist of the Egyptian Old Kingdom. Journal of Near Eastern Studies, VI, Chicago, P. 245, (1947). A. Badawy, The Stela of Irtysen, Chronique d'Egypte, Bruxelles, Tome XXXVI, pp. 269–276, (1961). W. Barta, Das Selbstzeugnis eines altägyptischen Künstlers (Stele Louvre C 14), Münchner Ägyptologische Studien, Verlag Bruno Hessling, Berlin, (1970).

**Figure 15.3:** The hieroglyphic word *baagw*.

verb *baag*, to thicken. Badawy compares this word with a Semitic root, *megwn*, which in Arabic means paste. The following is our interpretation of lines 8 to 9:

The action of casting a fluid stone paste mixture in a mould to make a statue corresponds exactly to Irtysen's technique. To do this, we take a fluid (the water signs *nou*); this is a cement, a binder which thickens (it hardens, sets, the verb *baagw*). Thus we make a moulding with a liquid raw material. The various reactive components must be weighed (*faat*) according to a precise recipe (*hesb*). The casting and releasing of the statue are tricky. When the statue contains undercuts, it is very difficult to release it without breaking either the mould, or the object. To avoid breakage, use is made of movable mould components. Casting and releasing thus require the use of multiple moulding parts that must be introduced into the moulds (*shdjt saqt*) (during casting and hardening) and then removed (*prj aqt.f*) to make releasing easier "... so that a member goes to its place...".

In the technical section, lines 11 to 12, Irtysen sets out the technology:

G. Maspero: "... I know the making of amulets, that we may go without any fire giving its flame, or without our being washed away by water".

M. Baud: (translated from French) "... I know the making of embellishments (literally pretty items) that are inlaid, not melted by fire, and not washed away by water..." (in French: "Je savais faire des enjolivures (exactement de jolis objets) qui s'incrustent, qui ne sont pas fondues au feu, et qui ne sont pas delavables non plus à l'eau").

J.A. Wilson: "I know how to make (things of paste and inlaid things), without letting the fire melt them, nor do they wash off in water either".

A. Badawy: "I know how to make baked (objects), things cast without letting the fire burn them, nor that they be washed by water, either".

W. Barta: (translated from German) "I know the making of the outward appearance (literally: the things that belong to it), without letting a fire melting them; they also cannot be washed out by water". (in German: "Ich kenne die Herstellung des Äusseren und der Bestanteile (wörtlich: der Dinge, die dazu hineingehen), ohne zuzulassen, dass ein Feuer sie verbrennen könnte; sie können auch nicht vom Wasser fortgewaschen werden").

Another important keyword *irit ymyt* is found just behind the expression "I know" (figure 15.4). It includes the verb *irit* (make) and complements *ymyt*, translated by amulets (Maspero), adornments (Baud), objects in paste (Wilson), baked objects (Badawy), and external appearance (Barta).

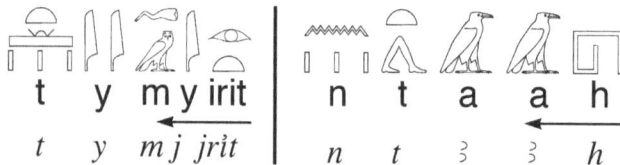

| t | y | m y irit | n | t | a | a | h |
|---|---|---|---|---|---|---|---|
| *t* | *y* | *m j jrit* | *n* | *t* | *ꜣ* | *ꜣ* | *h* |

**Figure 15.4:** The hieroglyphic words irit ymit and haatn.

In the plural complement *ymyt* there is the sign F23 in Gardiner's list, the thigh of an ox, found also in the word *khepesh*, the blacksmith's forge, the foundry, a place with fire. Only Badawy accounts for the sign, translating *ymyt* by baked objects. However, the foundry is a place where metallic objects are found, or clay objects (*ammit*) which are cast in moulds. Irtysen therefore uses moulds to cast, make and reproduce objects several times (Badawy's cast objects). The word *haat-n* (figure 15.4) is very close to the word hawt meaning the descendant, the offspring. Thus, with a single mould, Irtysen is capable of producing several reproductions (*haat-n*) (descendants) in a material that cannot be burned by fire and which is stable in water.

It is important to note that Irtysen does not use wax or natural resins to reproduce the statues. Although these materials are in general stable to water, they burn. Irtysen's reproductions are made in a material that cannot be destroyed by fire, which is not the case for wax and resins. It is both a mineral (resistant to fire), and water-resistant, and cannot therefore be plaster. Irtysen's materials are thus like those obtained by the geopolymeric reactions already mentioned in this book.

The last paragraph (The eulogy of the eldest son), line 13, is very interesting, because it explains how the function of Irtysen, master in the arts and sculptor, will be transmitted to his son. We learn there that the passing of professional secrets must be authorised by the pharaoh Mentuhotep himself. The eldest son of Irtysen can inherit the secret, on condition that he proves himself sufficiently skilled in the profession. The recipe is thus highly confidential and is a part of the initiation ritual (the fabrication of the statue of the *ka*, the stone doppelganger, according to the technology of the god Khnum).

The stele in the Louvre Museum describes the secret and religious technique of making statues in agglomerated stone (cast stone, synthetic stone). My interpretation of Irtysen's stele and his knowledge is thus as follows (the new translations of key words are underlined).

(...) (*Craft*) (lines 8–9)

"I know the parts belonging to the technique of moulding (with castable) a fluid that hardens (cast stone), namely: (line 9) the weighing (of the ingredients) according to the exact recipe; (make) the parts of the moulds which must be introduced inside (during the casting and the hardening) and removed before demolding so that a member come in its place.

(...) (*Technique*) (lines 11–12)

I know how to make moulds (for a foundry) to make reproductions of objects (line 12) cast in a material that is not burned by fire and that does not dissolve in water. (...)"

Other hieroglyphic words demonstrating the use of this technology of reconstituted, artificial stone, exist. The interested reader should consult the French book *Ils ont bâti les pyramides*. It is comforting to find authentic texts that bear out my interpretation. The theory of building in reagglomerated stone is thus the only one whose description has been found in hieroglyphic texts describing the recipe and the use of this knowledge.

# Chapter 16

# The sculptors and fashioners of the fresco of Ti

*You claim that Egyptian statues were largely made in reagglomerated stone. In other words, numerous statues were not carved, but cast in a mould. Yet in frescoes of the Old Kingdom there is clear evidence of carving. What is your explanation?*

You must be referring to the fresco of Ti, which illustrates sculptors working on wooden statues, making a stone statue and hollowing out hard stone vases. There too, a reading of the hieroglyphic designs and a minute examination of the various features of this fresco show the use of geosynthesis, in other words, of chemistry. The craftsmen used it to create a stone paste and to cast statues in this material. But to understand the situation better, let us first look at the hard stone vases.

## 16.1   The hard stone vases

For Egyptologists, the hard stone vases of the Old Kingdom (3500 BC) (figure 16.1) were hollowed out with a sort of instrument very often shown in frescoes in the tombs. This tool comprised a straight stem and a curved inclined handle. On this handle are hooked two stones or two bags of sand, to facilitate a movement of rotation or twisting back and forth (figure 16.2).

And yet up to now no archaeological survey has come up with a tool of this sort. On the other hand, discoveries are often made of the remains of boring devices that are rotated by means of a bow,

**Figure 16.1:** Hard stone vases, 3500 BC, Louvre Museum (2003).

**Figure 16.2:** Are they hollowing out stone vases?

the technology commonly described for drilling through all sorts of materials such as wood and metal. The device is shown on the right of each of the two vases. Its lower end appears to hold a horizontal drill, either in metal or hard stone.

By turning the tool, the craftsman was supposed to have hollowed out the vase, a process that would have left marks such as the grooves that can be seen on the inside of the vase in figure 16.3. This reasoning would appear perfectly accurate — but not so. Why?

Figure 16.3: The interior of a vase showing markings, Louvre Museum (2003).

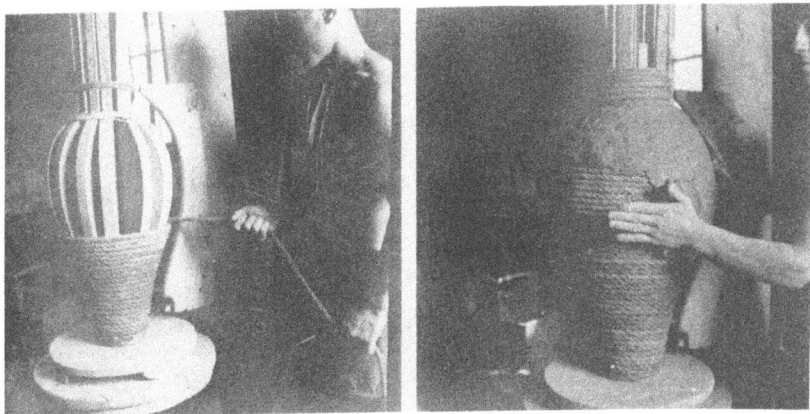

Figure 16.4: The method of the removable string core. a) The string is wound around the removable wooden core; b) The ceramic paste is applied to the string.

Quite simply because there exists an ancestral ceramic technique involving the use of a temporary internal core around which a cord or string is wound. A ceramic paste is then coated over this. Roman amphorae were made in this way, using cord. They were not turned on a wheel. This method, still used today, is illustrated in figures 16.4a, b. After drying, the core is easily removed by pulling on the cord. The interior of the ceramic vase made in this way bears traces of the cord. These are identical to the marks inside the hard stone vases. We can therefore safely say that these hard stone vases were made using this technique, simply replacing the clay by a stone paste.

## 16.2 The fresco of Ti

The bas-reliefs of the tomb of Ti, fifth dynasty, provide additional and very interesting information.

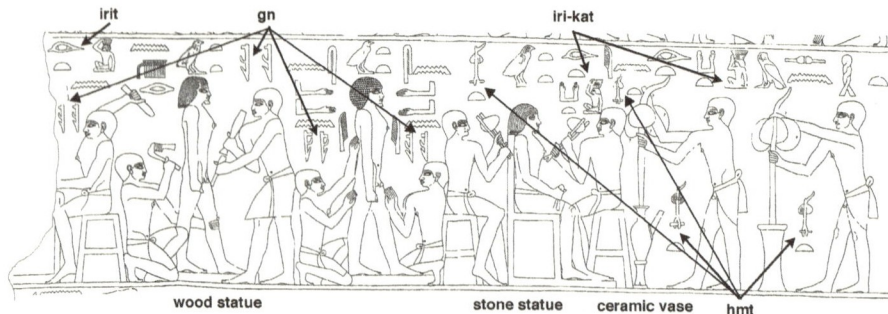

**Figure 16.5:** The fresco of the tomb of Ti, fifth dynasty, 2450 BC.

### 16.2.1 Sculpting and carving wooden statues

On the left of the bas-reliefs, the sculptors can be seen carving statues in wood and not in stone! These artists used tools identical to those used by carpenters; above the head of each craftsman we find the double hieroglyphic sign *gn* ⸙⸙ , the determinative for the word sculptor (cutting, carving). For the carving of wooden statues, the hieroglyphic verb is simply *jrt* (irit): to make. It can be seen in the upper left of the figure.

### 16.2.2 Mixing the material in the vases

On the right, two standing men are working on vases. It is claimed that these men are hollowing out the hard stone vases. This is not so. The first vase from the right is an Egyptian alabaster vase; this is a limestone vase that is translucent, very soft and very easy to hollow out, especially if a solution of vinegar, which readily dissolves this mineral, is used. The details of this technique, which was well known to the Egyptians, are explained in these notes[1]. On the other hand, the second vase is, without any doubt, a ceramic vase, because it has a spout. Now, stone vases do not have one, and for a very good reason. It is not possible to carve a spout sufficiently accurately in hard rock with primitive stone or soft copper tools. The evidence is thus that the craftsman is not hollowing out the ceramic vase, but simply working on it. The two artists are indicated by the same hieroglyphic sign *hmt* ⚒, which, according to the dictionary and to grammar is the determinative for: master craftsman, artist. It also designates workers with specialised technical knowledge.

To a chemist such as myself, this device represents rather a hand mixer, used to mix corrosive products contained in the stone or ceramic vase. In Gardiner's list, this sign expresses the boring tool for stone (U25), which is wrong. In 1986 the archaeologist D. Stock[2] showed that drilling with this tool is ten times less efficient than with the bow drill, a technique in use at the time. Why ever use a tool that is ten times less efficient when the craftsman had at his disposal a much more suitable and well known device?

## 16.2.3 Making a statue in agglomerated stone

In the middle of the bas-relief, two craftsmen are finishing a stone statue: the men are seated. Each has in his hand a stone mallet. Evidently, they are finishing the stone statue by hammering its surface. To deduce from this that this statue was carved in a block of natural

---

[1] J. Davidovits, A. Bonett and A.M. Mariotte, The Disaggregation of Stone Materials with Organic Acids from Plant Extracts, an Ancient and Universal Technique, Proc. 22nd Symposium on Archaeometry, A. Aspinal and S.E. Warren eds., University of Bradford, U.K., pp. 205–212, 1982. J. Davidovits, Fabrication of Stone Vessels, Bio-tooling and Plant Extracts, 3rd International Congress of Egyptoloy, paper AA.121, Abstracts p. 39, Toronto, Canada, 5–11 Sept. 1982. See also: J. Davidovits and F. Aliaga, Fabrication of Stone Objects by Geopolymeric Synthesis in the Pre-Incan Huanka Civilization (Peru), 21st Symposium on Archaeometry, Brookhaven N.Y., Abstracts, p. 21, 1981. The last two papers are available at the Geopolymer Institute website www.geopolymer.org

[2] D. Stocks, Stone Vessel Manufacture, Popular Archaeology, May 1986, pp. 14–18.

stone is unsafe, to say the least, for when a statue is obtained by agglomeration, it is very often necessary to applying finishing work — for example, the removal of flash that has oozed from the joints of the mould, the removal of a hard layer from the surface of the mould that has adhered to the stone, by hammering and polishing. Even for a statue made with reagglomerated stone, hammering tools must be use for the final finishing.

The remainder of the fresco finally tips the balance in favour of a statue in artificial, reagglomerated stone. The two craftsmen are not sculptors or stone carvers. Logic implies that they should be called *gn* like their colleagues the wood sculptors. But no, they are called *hmt*, like their colleagues who are doing the mixing in the vases.

There is therefore an obvious connection between the two parts of the fresco on the right, the mixers prepare the alchemical products in vases, and these products are then used to make a stone statue. In addition, there is another very revealing feature: The hieroglyphic caption at the top on the right of the bas-relief states: a statue made by the hand of man (*twt jrt kt*).the verb *jrt kt* (pronounced irit-kat) appears twice in this sentence and as we now know, it means artificial, man-made, created. On the other hand, on the left of the fresco with the carving of a wooden statue, the verb used is *irit*; the sculptor is making an object from wood (*jrt*), and is not creating his material (*jrt kt*).

Why did they not use the same expression for both the sculptor in wood and the sculptor in stone? Quite simply because the latter is not a sculptor but a fashioner of stone paste, a creator of stone.

# Chapter 17

# The invention of building in stone by Imhotep

*Hieroglyphic texts tell us that this technology exists; so is it possible to put a date to the innovation?*

Yes, it is, and we have even done better than this, because we know the name of the inventor of reagglomerated stone. It is Imhotep. It was this scribe of genius who made it possible for the Pharaoh Djoser, around 2710 BC, to build the first pyramid in Egyptian history.

Before the first stone pyramid, the Step Pyramid of Saqqarah, the ancient Egyptians built very imposing monuments and fortresses using a much commoner material, mud bricks. These constructions include the great funeral temple in places of the second dynasty, the finest example of which was that of Khasekhemwy, figure 17.1.

Khasekhemwy (ca. 2730 BC), the last monarch of the 2nd dynasty, left no male successor to the throne. The first Pharaoh of the 3rd dynasty was named Zanakht. His successor was Neterikhet, better known by the name of Djoser. Imhotep, King Djoser's architect, was charged with the building of the first pyramid. We have very little information about Imhotep, one of the most intriguing and venerated of the Egyptian personalities. It is very rare to see a man remaining famous for more than 3000 years, as did Imhotep, from 2700 BC up to the Greco-Roman period. Imhotep was so renowned for his art, his medicine and his wisdom, that he was considered as a god. He was indeed deified in Egypt, 2000 years after his death when the Greeks started to worship him, calling him Imhotès and

Figure 17.1: The funerary temple enclosure of Khasekhemwy, Abydos.

identifying him with a god Asclepios, the son of Apollo, the god to whom legend attributes the discovery of medicine. Around 250 BC, Ptolemy II made Imhotep a divinity and built him a centre of worship on the upper part of the temple at Deir el-Bahari, that of Queen Hatshepsut, on the west bank of the Nile opposite Karnak. There still exist vestiges of the temple dedicated to Imhotep on the island of Sehel, built by Ptolemy V around 186 BC.

Imhotep wrote the earliest "writings on wisdom", a venerated work which unfortunately did not survive. The Egyptians considered him as one of their greatest scribes. This genius was the first prestigious national hero of Egypt. Under the Pharaoh Djoser, Imhotep was the second most important person in the country if we are to believe texts engraved in stone (figure 17.2). This title is chiselled into the base of the statue of Djoser discovered in the Step Pyramid, next to the titles of the King. He had many functions such as King's Chancellor of Lower Egypt, First after the King in Upper Egypt, Administrator of the Great Palace, doctor, noble inheritor, Grand Priest of Anu (Heliopolis, or On in Coptic), Architect in Chief for the Pharaoh Djoser. In addition, and this is very interesting, he was a sculptor and made stone vases. This suggests that he was initiated into the alchemical secrets of Khnum.

**Figure 17.2:** Statue of Imhotep from the Lower Period, Louvre Museum (2003).

## 17.1 The invention of stone by Imhotep: the Manethon text

The titles found at Saqqarah confirmed the statements of the Greco-Egyptian historian Manethon. His writings, set down during the Ptolemaic period in the third century BC, tell of Imhotep, 2400 years after his death. Manethon was one of the last great priests of Heliopolis. A part of his texts (reported by Sextus Julius Africanus) was translated in 340 AD by the ecclesiastical historian Eusèbe de Césaré whose modern translation is *"Imhotep... was the inventor of the art of building with hewn stone..."*.

In fact, this translation of the work of Eusèbe is not correct. The Greek words used by Manethon, *"xeston lithon"*, do not mean "carved stone"; rather, they indicate the action of polishing a stone or scraping the material to make chips. These words designate either a stone with a smooth surface, a characteristic of agglomerated stone, or a stone made with chips, i.e. aggregates, in other words agglomerated stone. If *"xeston lithon"* expresses the invention of "carved stone" or "carving stone", the expression is strange. In Manethon's

135

text, to designate carved stone or carving stone, i.e. a crude block extracted from a quarry then roughed out and then finished, Greek architectural vocabulary is rich in more suitable expressions.

Thus, the crude block is designated by *lithos argos*. The carving stone, most often quadrangular, corresponds to *lithos eggônios, lithos orthos, plinthos*; we also find the adjective *eutenès* for carved stone, and *katamitta*, which could have the same meaning. Now, in the passage in which we are interested, none of these expressions is used by Manethon to designate the idea of "carved stone" in general. If Manethon had wanted to glorify the invention of the concept of "carved stone", he would have chosen an expression other than *xestos lithos*, one that comes from the vocabulary of Greek architecture.

Here we have an error of translation. It seems reasonable to think that, for Manethon, Imhotep was "the inventor of the art of building with agglomerated stone". He was referring to the building of the first pyramid.

## 17.2   Bricks of varying dimensions

When King Djoser came to the throne in 2710 BC, he was probably already thinking about building his funeral edifice in the form of a mastaba of mud bricks surrounded by a superb eternal palace, as his predecessor Khasekhemwy had done. Khasekhemwy's eternal palace is a massive wall made of mud bricks formed in moulds. It contains a unique architectural feature ignored by Egyptologists. It is generally assumed that, since the bricks were made in moulds, there dimensions must be uniform from one layer to another. In the photo of the wall of Khasekhemwy and in the diagram representing the height of the bricks, it is very easy to see that this statement is wrong (figures 17.3a, b). Although they were made in the same moulds, the mud bricks are of different sizes, implying the use of several sizes of mould: a deliberate choice by the architect.

How can all the architectural Egyptologists be unaware of, ignore or simply dismiss a fact of this importance? This is a mystery, because the favourite argument of opponents of the theory of agglomeration is to say that if the stone blocks were moulded, their dimensions should therefore be strictly identical, just like mud bricks which were also moulded. Now, the wall of Khasekhemwy features five different heights of brick. In other words, the architect deliber-

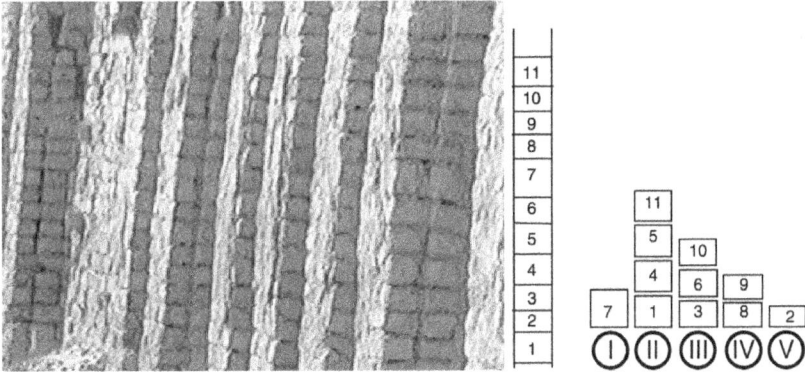

**Figure 17.3:** a) enclosure of Khasekhemwy, eternal palace, made of mud bricks of different sizes (1998); b) the five sizes of mud bricks in the enclosure of Khasekhemwy

ately asked that five moulds of different sizes be prepared to make the mud bricks.

This fundamental architectural feature appears again in the mastabas built of mud bricks. For example, the one beside the pyramid of Meidum has bricks with heights varying from 20 to 30 cm. This feature turns up again and again in large monuments built since that period, right up to the present-day, as evidenced by our cathedrals. Architects use the technique in order to stabilise buildings, protecting them from earthquake damage by scattering the seismic waves and ensuring that they do not resonate with the building. This also accounts for the variation in height of the layers of the pyramid of Cheops discussed in chapter 2.

## 17.3  Imhotep's invention

Shortly before or during the building of the mastaba, it is likely that Imhotep made an important discovery. He became aware of the properties of the yellow limestone that is found at Saqqarah: a flinty limestone and a clay limestone (marl). The plateau has a rather particular geology; the strata consist of an alternating series of alluvial deposits of very hard, flinty limestone and of very soft marl. This feature has obviously been created by erosion, as can be seen from the road leading from the valley to the top of the plateau (figure 17.4). The hard layers are between 20 and 30 cm thick, leading all the experts to believe they had discovered where the stone used for the pyramids of Saqqarah came from — and in particular that of Djoser.

**Figure 17.4:** Alternate hard and soft strata, Saqqarah (2003).

But this limestone is so hard (it contains a lot of silica) that it is very difficult to carve. More or less rectangular cobblestones can be made and used to fill gaps both in the mastaba and in the outer walls of the funerary complex.

The second soft clay limestone layer sometimes occurs as pockets several metres thick at the surface of the plateau (figure 17.5). It is this that was used as raw material. Some of these pockets are of sandy limestone with up to 30 % sand, 60 % limestone and 10 % clay. Other strata are composed of clay limestone containing 20 % to 60 % of clay and 40 % to 80 % of limestone, the majority of the clay being of the kaolinitic type, which is highly reactive in geopolymerisation.

These limestones are very susceptible to weathering and disaggregate very easily in water, giving a limestone slurry from which bricks can be made. We have observed this property in our laboratory. The clay component contains alumina and silica, and is chemically activated by caustic soda (formed by mixing natron with lime, $CaO$, calcined lime), forming an aluminosilicate of Na and Ca, the basic

**Figure 17.5:** The thick upper layer of soft clay limestone (2003).

ingredient of geological glue. The clay limestone paste is then packed in wooden moulds — the same as are used to make mud bricks. The bricks are then removed from the moulds, dried in the shade and taken to the pyramid building site.

**Figure 17.6:** To build pyramids of the third dynasty, the workers (a) packed limestone bricks in wooden moulds of various sizes, (b) carried the bricks to the construction site and built the pyramid in inclined layers made of bricks of various dimensions.

Imhotep had discovered how to produce a building material. There exist other "alchemical" reactions that can be applied to this material. Only a thorough scientific analysis of the pyramid blocks will enable the exact formulation to be determined.

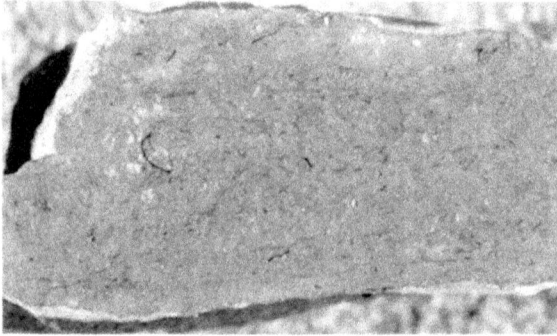

**Figure 17.7:** Limestone brick of the Step Pyramid (after D.D. Klemm).

The compression strength of mud bricks is very low, of the order of $10$ kg/cm$^2$, i.e. one MPa. With a material like this, high buildings cannot be made – only long, low buildings. It was perfect for mastabas and enclosures. With the invention of the limestone brick, Imhotep possessed a building material with a compression strength 10 times greater, 10 Mpa or $100$ kg/cm$^2$. He could then go up in height. The method remained exactly the same. They used the same tools as for mud bricks, merely replacing the clay with a limestone paste: a simple improvement in technique.

If we examine a limestone brick from the pyramid of Djoser, we do indeed see a structure similar to that a compacted clay brick, figure 17.7.

### 17.3.1 They needed water: the wadi at Saqqarah

To disaggregate the limestone and make a slurry needs a lot of water. The source of this water must be very close to the construction site. Even if we assume that the course of the Nile was much closer at that time to the western cliff that it is now, a supply of water remains the key point in the process.

Egyptologists have always wondered why the pyramids of Djoser and Sekhemkhet and others are located so far inside the desert and so far from the Nile. However, the American expert Mark Lehner[1] points out that if we look at the map of Saqqarah (figure 17.8) we see that the wadi of Abousir, just to the north, forms a natural

---

[1]M. Lehner, Loaves and Fishes, in The Complete Pyramids, p. 83, Thames and Hudson Ltd, London, 1997.

depression. This connects the Nile plane, with its floods, to the edge of the plateau at Saqqarah via the construction sites of Djoser and Sekhemkhet. It is possible that there was also a lake at the entrance to this wadi, and perhaps even a port. This was all connected to the Nile whose course at that time was much closer to the desert than it is now.

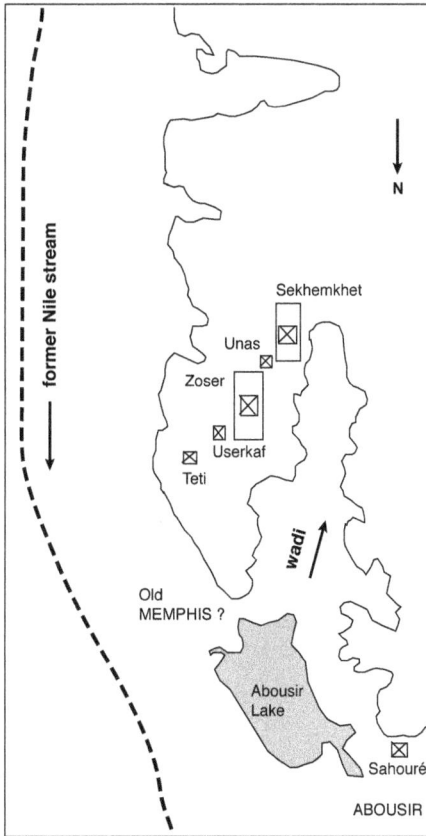

**Figure 17.8:** Map of the site of Saqqarah, the old course of the Nile and the wadi.

During the annual flooding the water came into the wadi, arriving close to the place where the limestone bricks were being made, and to the construction sites. Had the Egyptians dug out the wadi to transform it into a great artificial lake able to hold the water for several months? Today, this wadi is filled with sand and the only way to show its depth and suitability will be to take core samples.

The presence of these wadis in the immediate neighbourhood of the pyramids was to become a constant feature in choosing the construction sites for subsequent pyramids, notably the great pyramids of the 4th dynasty. We shall be coming back to this point in later chapters.

## 17.4 The Egyptian archaeology theorem: agglomeration

From a technical point of view, it was perfectly feasible. In the first place, methods for agglomerating stones, even the hardest, had been known in Egypt for a long time. The thriving stone vessel industry is evidence of this; it was at its height around the end of the Nagadien period just before the 1st dynasty. And then, by agglomerating limestone blocks of suitable dimensions, it was relatively easy to build by following the principles of building with mud bricks, i.e. by laying them in regular layers. Imhotep was thus able to make use of the progress brought with the mud brick building technique and to apply this to stone, dealing one by one with the difficulties involved in this change. The monuments of King Djoser are the preservation in stone of Thinite and predynastic architecture.

# Chapter 18

# The various stages in the building of the first pyramid

*Every innovation progress goes through various stages. From the initial invention, human genius seeks to improve and perfect the system, eventually to achieve extraordinary results. Can the same thing be seen here?*

We can follow the evolution of Imhotep's innovation like an open book. Three main stages can be distinguished: the mastaba, then the first pyramid P1, and finally pyramid P2 (figure 18.1). We can ask the legitimate question: was Imhotep in charge of the project from the start, or did he only come in after the first phase?

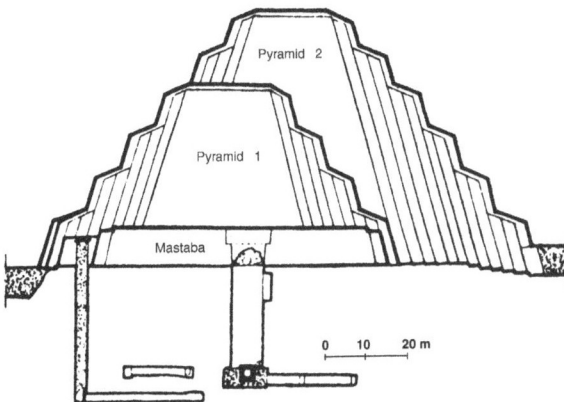

**Figure 18.1:** The various stages in their building of the pyramid of Djoser, North-South section after J.P. Lauer.

143

# 18.1   The mastaba in Roman concrete ashlars

After digging the funerary chamber, it was covered by a mastaba made of irregular stones extracted directly from the hard limestone layer. These more or less regular blocks were stabilised with mortar to ensure the cohesion and stability of the structure (figure 18.2, Mark A). The mortar was vital, to avoid any collapsing of the enormous access shafts to the underground chambers. It could be called a rough kind of concrete.

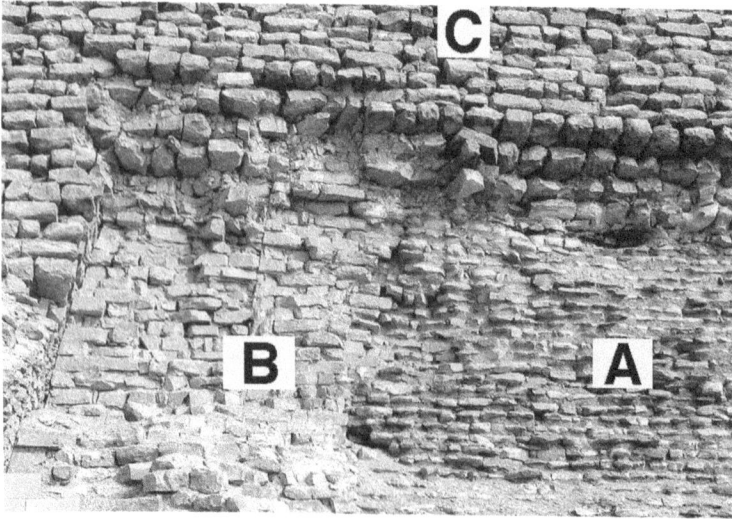

**Figure 18.2:** The evolution from the initial mastaba in irregular stones and mortar (A), then small bricks (B), followed by the pyramid P1 (C), southern face (2003).

The same material, the more or less rectangular ashlar, was used for the walls of the funerary enclosure. It is made of natural stone with thick mortar. In fact, to a layman this would look very much like the sort of work done by Roman engineers, who, 2600 years later, invented (or rediscovered) this method of construction, called in Latin, *opus caementicum*, or Roman concrete. This name is actually the origin of the word cement. Imhotep, as we can see, knew how to make excellent mortar and cement and thus had everything he needed to develop reagglomerated stone.

## 18.2 Imhotep's limestone bricks

Meanwhile, the tests that Imhotep undertook proved conclusive. The stone bricks remained intact, showing no sign of cracking. The Pharaoh therefore decided to use this new building material to enlarge his construction. Imhotep presented him with novel plans for the enlargement of the mastaba. First of all, each of the sides would be lengthened by around 3 metres, using reagglomerated limestone; this corresponds to part (B) in figure 18.2. The architecture then became audacious. The eastern face was lengthened by 11 metres, making the mastaba rectangular. Stone bricks, produced alchemically, entered into the construction of an imposing enclosure and a square mastaba with its sides oriented to the points of the compass. The limestone bricks of the temple were also of varying heights.

On inspection, the monument showed exceptional stability of the material used, with no apparent cracks. The Pharaoh Djoser and Imhotep decided to change their initial plans and to add two extra levels to the structure. At the same time, they would add underground chambers, a shaft and corridors.

## 18.3 Pyramid P1

The dimensions of the bricks increased as the structure grew, but were still restricted to five or six different values. Initially in the mastaba, the height of the limestone bricks varied between 20 and 26 cm, finally reaching 25 to 35 cm in thickness in pyramid P1 (figure 18.2, Mark C). Their architects were at the beginning of a learning curve, comparable to that accompanying revolutionary modern technological processes.

The more extraordinary and miraculous their architecture became, the more they expanded it. There seem to be no limit to the amount of reagglomerated stone they could produce.

## 18.4 Pyramid P2

To the four-sided structure was added another phase of construction, the pyramid P2 (figure 18.1), taking the construction to its final shape, with six tiers and measuring 60 metres in height, figure 18.4. It included internal walls, and successive layers of stone are inclined, to lend more stability to the work. With great skill and remarkable ingenuity, Imhotep incorporated all the arts and craft accumulated by the Egyptian nation over the decades with wood, reeds and mud bricks.

**Figure 18.3:** The author on the second tier of pyramid P2, western face (2003).

The result was an extraordinary funerary complex. According to James Henry Breasted (1886 to 1935), at the Oriental Institute of the University of Chicago, the pyramid was a representation of "ben-ben". Heliopolitan theology taught that at the creation, an original megalith called "ben ben" emerged from the churning waters. The *benben* represented the hill or mound on which the whole of creation started. Once the first Heliopolitan temple had been built on the site of the benben, the Egyptians assimilated the ideology of the *benben* stone to the symbol of the sun god. The theological themes are displayed in the underground chambers of the pyramid of the Pharaoh Djoser. Some rooms are covered with blue ceramic tiles in a representation of the original marshland with its reeds from which all plant life emerges. The colour blue symbolised the creator, the demigod, and the blue enamel covering the ceramic tiles imitated chrysocolla, the mineral *mafkat* that was a synonym of creation.

In a purpose-built room there stood a statue of Djoser seated on his throne, representing his eternal soul, the KA. When archi-

146

**Figure 18.4:** The author in front of the final pyramid P2, northeast face (2003).

tects found the statue, it was intact except for the eye sockets. The eyes were probably of semiprecious stone, before being pillaged during the looting of the tomb. Numerous stone statues dating from the Old Kingdom, now in the Louvre and in Cairo Museum, were endowed with admirable encrusted eyes, the fruit of a technique enabling extraordinary realism, easily obtained with the aid of artificial alchemical stone. Other underground chambers held the 38000 stone vases of Khnum, agglomerated using aggregates of siltstone, breccia (limestone rubble), granite, diorite and various types of stone.

The pyramid was surrounded by an enclosure of very simple architectural design, originally more than 10 metres high. The stones forming this wall appear to have been polished. To this day, the wall guards an elegant entry built of colonnades, large interior courtyards, large buildings, a mortuary temple, altars and chapels. The complex had the dimensions of an entire town. The style of the enclosure resembles today's architecture; in fact it greatly influenced the avant-garde movement in town planning in the 20th century. All the European architects who visited Saqqarah at the beginning of the 20th century were fired with enthusiasm by this architecture, so different from the pompous style of the Victorian age. They took their inspiration from it and developed a contemporary style. The funeral complex was delimited by a wall in *opus caementicum*, in rough limestone blocks and mortar.

The restoration work undertaken by Jean-Philippe Lauer has enabled the splendour of this site to be displayed once more. However, visitors will have to look very carefully if they are to distinguish the original work and the reconstitution using soft limestone or concrete. Similarly, the use of rectangular blocks in the repair of the southern part of the pyramid (to the left of figure 18.2) leads to great confusion between what is original and what has been restored.

These monuments were the pride of Egypt. The funeral complex of Djoser, with its pyramid reaching for the sky, represented unprecedented progress, unique in the annals of the world. During the whole of Egyptian history, the age of Imhotep was considered as the age of great wisdom. It was called the first step in the creation of the Egyptian nation, and was identified with its first Pharaoh, King Menes, so that eventually, the Step Pyramid of Djoser was regarded as one of the original events in this civilisation.

# Chapter 19

# From Djoser to Sneferu

*After the first pyramid, how did the successors of the Pharaoh Djoser build their monuments?*

Following the initial innovation, the building technology followed a similar course to that of the modern cement industry founded on the invention of Portland cement. In the nineteenth and twentieth centuries, with the increasing use of this type of cement came a steady increase in the size of the blocks and structures used in building, civil engineering and public works; and this is highly significant.

The same was true in Egypt. The blocks of the first pyramid are small and only weigh a few dozen kilograms. As the technology progressed, the size of the stones gradually increased, eventually reaching the enormous blocks and lintels weighing several dozen tonnes. Had the pyramid been made of hewn stone, this progression of size would have been in the opposite sense; carving small bricks requires more work than carving large blocks.

The pyramid of the Pharaoh Djoser served as a prototype for succeeding sovereigns of the third dynasty. However, the history of this dynasty is obscure and it is very difficult to assign the name of the King and his place in the chronology to each monument. After Djoser, the pyramid builders of the third dynasty were Sekhemkhet, Neb-ka and Kha-ba, figures 19.1, 19.2. None of these kings reigned sufficiently long to finish his work, and because of this all these pyramids have been destroyed; this is a very curious fact.

We also know of eight small step pyramids located in the provinces, a long way from Memphis. The southernmost is on the island of Elephantine. The others are spread along the Nile between Elephantine

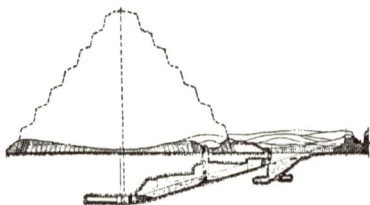

**Figure 19.1:** The remains of the Step Pyramid of Sekhemkhet.

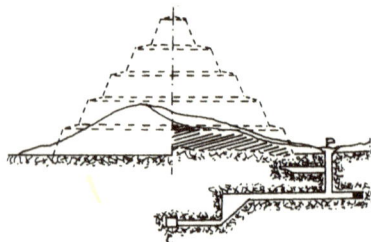

**Figure 19.2:** The remains of the pyramid of Kha-ba.

and Saqqarah (see the map, figure 19.3).

The last of these pyramids was discovered in 1985 by Nabil Swelim near Abu Roach. While the first seven of these pyramids are made of small limestone bricks, the last one uses mud bricks. It is agreed that these pyramids should all be attributed to the last Pharaoh of the third dynasty, Huni, but the purpose of these monuments is unknown, for they were evidently not intended as tombs. The pyramids of the third dynasty are all step pyramids and have underground tombs below them. The architecture is in general similar to that of the pyramid of the Pharaoh Djoser. These pyramids are of mediocre quality and have all been destroyed.

## 19.1 The three pyramids of Sneferu: fourth dynasty (2600 BC)

Sneferu was the most prolific of all the Egyptian builders. The combined volume of his three pyramids exceeds that of the Great Pyramid of Cheops. The architectural variations introduced by the various architects are the result of their attempts to improve building efficiency either by increasing the speed of hardening of the stone, or by making better quality blocks with larger dimensions.

As we know, the use of larger unit elements has numerous advantages. The builders quickly realised that large blocks, which are difficult to shift once they are in place, give extra protection to the funeral chamber. It is possible that the first pyramids were destroyed because they were used as quarries. It is very easy to transport small stones, whereas handling large blocks requires complicated logistics. Logically, then, the builders would have opted for fabricating large

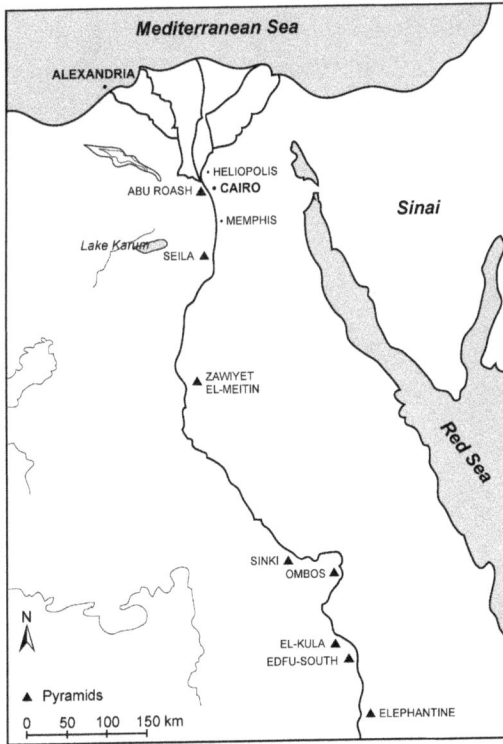

**Figure 19.3:** Map of the first pyramids of the third dynasty.

blocks on the spot, eliminating at a stroke the need to transport stones, this operation now being replaced by the transport of materials. In other words, the larger the blocks, the less work was required, and the more invulnerable the sepulchre became.

### 19.1.1 The first pyramid at Meidum

Until recently, it had been suggested that it was Huni, the last King of the third dynasty, who built this pyramid. But from the old name given to Meidum results the fact that it was the name of Sneferu which appeared in texts connected to this site. Most Egyptologists are convinced that it was under the Pharaoh Sneferu that the building of Meidum began, 60 km south of Memphis, in the northeast of Fayum.

Of all the great pyramids, this is one of the most mysterious (figure 19.4). Like the Step Pyramid of Djoser, the pyramid at Meidum was built in several phases (see figure 19.5). First of all there is a step pyramid made up of seven tiers with a total height of 92 metres (tier E1). Then, before finishing the fourth or fifth levels, the pharaoh decided to expand the project to a pyramid with eight tiers, which appears to have been achieved during the first 14 years of the reign of Sneferu (tier E2).

Figure 19.4: The pyramid of Sneferu at Meidum (2003).

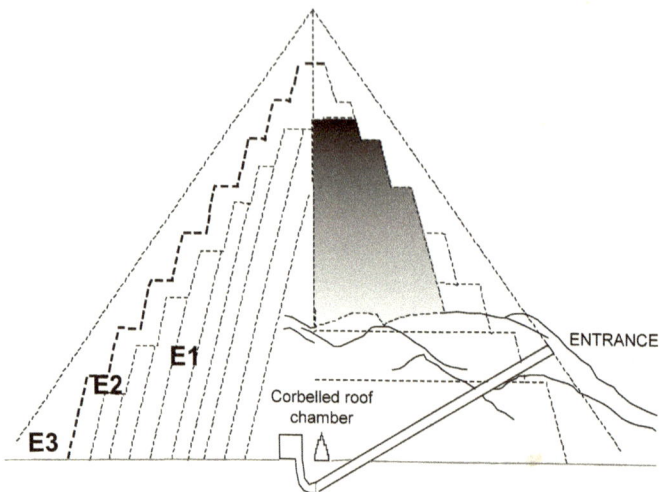

Figure 19.5: Cross-section of the pyramid of Meidum, tiers E1, E2, E3.

In the 15th year of his reign, Sneferu left Meidum with his court to settle around Dashur. Then, about 15 years later according to the German Egyptologist Rainer Stadelman, he sent his workers back to Meidum to finish work on the pyramid, transforming it into a proper smooth pyramid (tier E3). Sneferu's building programme thus began and ended at Meidum.

When you are standing near the pyramid, you are struck by the fact that it overlooks an area still cultivated in the 21st century. The water needed to make the bricks and limestone blocks is right and alongside. This situation is different from that of the other great pyramids. But this elegant superstructure was to vanish in a cataclysm as sudden as it was unexpected. A large part of Sneferu's recently added masonry, together with part of the original building, collapsed in a thunderous crash. The debris formed a hill from whose summit protrudes from the remains of the Step Pyramid.

The causes of the accident have been the subject of much speculation. Initially, it was thought that some of the base blocks were deliberately removed. If this proves to be the case, the guilty party could have been the pharaoh Ramses II, who is known to have deliberately dismantled some pyramids in order to obtain stone blocks to use in his own monument. Another theory involves an earthquake, demonstrating the incompatibility between the original building and the new structure. In modern Egyptology, the accepted theory is that the pyramid collapsed shortly after work was completed, this also demonstrating the incompatibility of the two parts of the pyramid.

### 19.1.2 The two pyramids of Dashur: the Bent Pyramid and the Red Pyramid

Sneferu was the most important builder in Egyptian history. He built two gigantic pyramids on the Libyan plateau, 10 km south of Saqqarah, at Dashur. The first one he named Bright Pyramid of the South, and the second, in the north, the Bright Pyramid. Today we know them as the Bent Pyramid and the Red Pyramid (figures 19.8, 19.10). Together, these two pyramids contain more stones than the famous Great Pyramid of Cheops. According to Rainer Stadelman, Sneferu's workers built their monuments between the fourteenth and thirtieth years of his reign. This amount of labour does not fit the traditional theory of hewing and transporting stone, which would have encountered numerous logistical problems, especially if we include the work on the pyramid of Meidum that was carried out afterwards.

But this is not all. Texts teach us that Sneferu built numerous temples throughout Egypt. The activity of this pharaoh surpassed anything that was subsequently undertaken in Egypt. According to the texts, he sent an expedition to bring back cedars from Lebanon. We have historic confirmation that he created a fleet of a hundred boats to ship the enormous tree trunks from the Lebanese coast. In our scenario of reagglomeration, this was to supply the wood needed to make the moulds and containers. We also find the name of Sneferu engraved on many steles in the Sinai mines. Naturally, as we would expect, he exploited these mines intensively. For more than a thousand years the Sinai mines that were opened during his reign were called "the Mines of Sneferu".

Like the Step Pyramid of Djoser, the two pyramids of Sneferu are built inside the plateau and are relatively far from the valley. Here too, the builders took advantage of the presence of wadis, which had two purposes (figures 19.6, 19.7):

a) to bring water near to the centre of the building site;
b) to make it easy to localise soft clay limestone outcrops susceptible to weathering and disaggregate very easily in water, and could be attacked directly in the sides of the plateau. In modern times, the site at Dashur was closed for a long period, because it was within a military area. Today, these wadis are completely filled with sand, and nobody has yet undertaken to dig them out.

### 19.1.3 The Bent Pyramid (figure 19.8)

This is the first of the colossal pyramids, 180 metres along the side of the base and 105 metres in height. What distinguishes this pyramid from all the others is the state of conservation of large areas of casing on each face; the casing stone is smooth and well jointed. The summit has kept its pointed shape. The general appearance of the monument is of having a profile in two different slopes: the large lower part has an angle of 54° and the other part of 44° to the horizontal. The upper pyramid appears to be standing on top of a truncated pyramid. In the lower section, the casing seatings are not horizontal, but perpendicular to the inclined face, whereas in the three other parts, the seatings are horizontal. The pyramid is made of blocks of thickness varying from 0.50 metres to 0.80 metres. Tiers

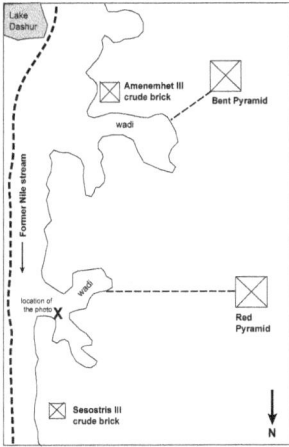

**Figure 19.7:** The author standing in front of the wadi leading to the red Pyramid (x on the map) (2003).

**Figure 19.6:** Map of Dashur.

of lesser heights are found between a succession of two to four tiers of greater heights, a feature that is also found in the pyramid of Djoser and of Cheops (figure 19.9). Inside, within the bulk of the pyramid, the stones are not laid in any regular way; there are often spaces between them, filled with stone rubble. Evidently, the blocks here were made in moulds of various dimensions, and then manipulated into place on the pyramid. It can be seen that they are not perfectly arranged. The blocks were made nearby or on the spot, then laid into the required position.

### 19.1.4   The Red Pyramid (figure 19.10 to 19.13)

The base of the northern pyramid (the Red Pyramid) is a square of 220 metres along a side; its 152 tiers rise to a height of 103 metres. The angle of the pyramid is 44°, like the upper part of the Bent Pyramid. The stone blocks are around 0.50 to 1.4 metres in height — quite large dimensions, so they must have been moulded on site. These dimensions are close to those of the great pyramids of Giza. Until 1995, the two pyramids of Sneferu were situated within a military area, and I was only able to visit them quite recently, in 2003. This new type of architecture is a real pyramid, enabling the funerary chamber to be brought to above ground level.

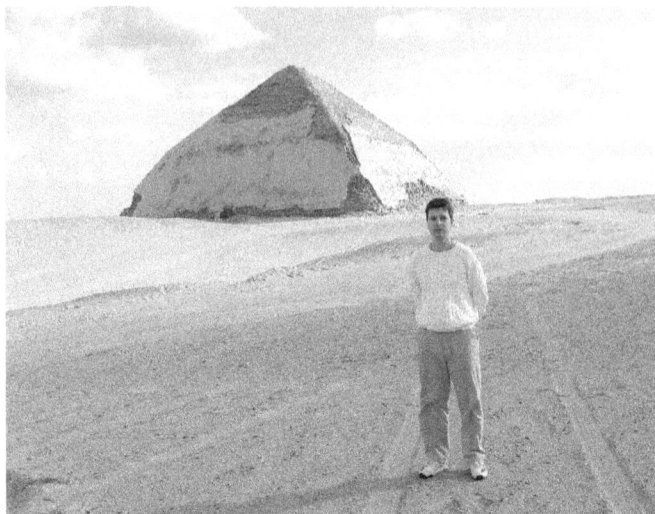

**Figure 19.8:** Ralph Davidovits in front of the Bent Pyramid at Dashur (2003).

**Figure 19.9:** Bent Pyramid, succession of thickness from 0.50 metres (scale) to 0.80 metres (2003).

**Figure 19.10**: The Red Pyramid at Dashur (2003).

## 19.1.5 The pyramid casing

Excavation work carried out in the 1980s by the German Egyptologist Rainer Stadelman on the eastern face of the Red Pyramid brought to light its still intact casing at the base of the pyramid (figures 19.11, 19.12). The three lower rows in particular were left completely untouched by the demolition parties. They are in their original state, apart from surface erosion by the action of sand, wind and sun.

On closer examination, these casing blocks show the following features:

- the vertical faces are perfectly jointed, as are the horizontal faces;

- the oblique faces protrude by 1 to 2 cm over the lower row.

These same features are found in the casings of the Bent Pyramid and in those of Chephren at Giza. Another feature discovered in a number of casings (at Saqqarah, Meidum and Dashur) is a vein 1 mm thick (perhaps silica) in the vertical plane of the block. These features taken together exclude any building method involving on-the-spot moulding, with no further moving of the block. It rather suggests that material was packed into initially horizontal or vertical moulds, and then removed and laid into its final position next to its neighbour. This accounts for the inclined rows observed in the lower part of the Bent Pyramid. It also explains the protrusion of one layer

**Figure 19.11:** The author on the ninth level of the Red Pyramid, in the background, the Bent Pyramid (2003).

(a)                                                             (b)

**Figure 19.12:** Remains of the Red pyramid casing blocks.

over the layer beneath. The vein is a sign that the filling of the mould was temporarily interrupted.

## 19.2 The different stone qualities in the three pyramids of Sneferu

Unlike those casings which appear to have been made to a single alchemical recipe, the core blocks of the three pyramids of Sneferu are of different qualities. The pyramid of Meidum is quite far from Dashur, so it is not surprising that the stones in the two sites should differ geologically. But this should not be the case for the Bent and Red Pyramids of Dashur. Yet the stone in the Bent Pyramid is the hardest of all the pyramid stones in Egypt, while that in the bulk of the Red Pyramid is a conglomerate of crustacean limestone of very mediocre quality. Why?

At Saqqarah, the material for the Step Pyramid came from the immediate surroundings; but this was not the case for the small blocks of phases E1 and E2 of Meidum (figure 19.13). There, evidence of local geology is only found in phase E3 (figure 19.5). If we assume that the Meidum catastrophe occurred in the distant past, just after construction, i.e. 4600 years ago, it is surprising to observe that the blocks of E1 and E2 have withstood climatic erosion, even though exposed for all that time. On the other hand, the part E3 is highly degraded.

**Figure 19.13:** The small intact blocks of Meidum E1-E2 (1988).

In the Bent Pyramid, too, the casing stones are undamaged; indeed they look as though they have come straight out of the mould.

159

This is in stark contrast to the totally degraded limestone blocks at the Giza site, the result of local people using the casing as building material. Even on the most exposed western and south-western faces, there is no trace of damage. The surfaces of the blocks are beautifully smooth as though polished, with no tool marks, and of remarkable hardness (figure 19.14). Were they made according to the same alchemical recipe as the small blocks of Meidum E1-E2? This is more than likely, because some people identify them as a hard sandstone of which no nearby outcrop has been found. On the other hand, the material of the Red Pyramid is a rough crustacean limestone of similar geological nature to the plateau of Dashur (figure 19.15).

**Figure 19.14**: The smooth and hard blocks of the Bent Pyramid.

## 19.3 How the corbelled chambers evolved

The corbelled chamber appears for the first time at Meidum (figure 19.16). It is small, with the following dimensions: length 5.9 metres, width 2.65 metres, height 5.05 metres.

The system seemed to work, and it was improved in subsequent pyramids (figure 19.17). Inside the Bent Pyramid there are various types of chamber with corbelled vaults. For many of these pyramids, the change in slope on the upper part could have been to lessen the load on the vaults and inner chambers, some of whose walls were already showing alarming cracks and other signs at the time of construction. One thinks that this would have led Sneferu to abandon

Figure 19.15: The crustacean conglomerate of the Red Pyramid.

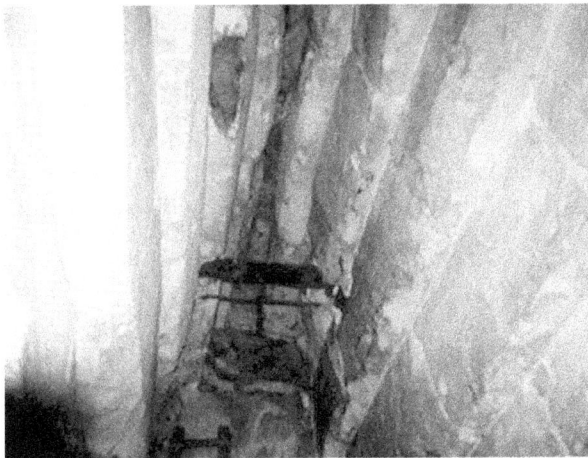

Figure 19.16: The corbelled chamber of Meidum, height 5.05 metres. (2003).

this monument and to build a second Pyramid to the north with a much larger base. None of this has been proved. These chambers are vast, more than three times the height of those of Meidum. The dimensions of the underground chamber (chamber 1) are as follows: length 6.3 metres, width for.96 metres, height 17 metres; and those of the chamber inside the pyramid (chamber 2): length 7.97 metres, width 5.26 metres, height 16.5 metres.

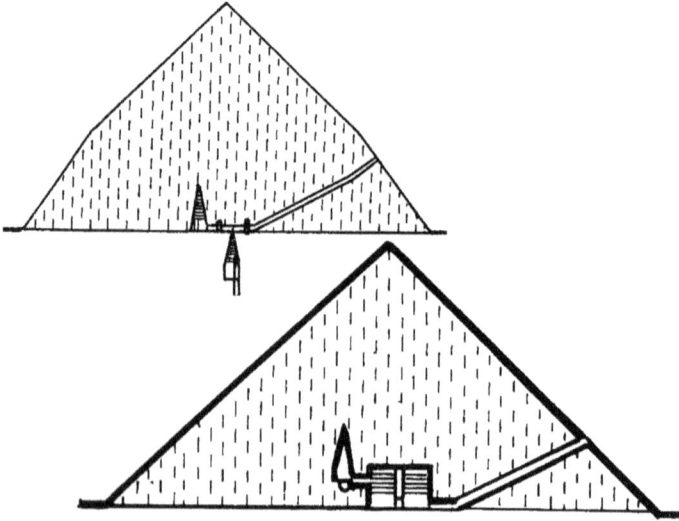

**Figure 19.17:** The chambers of the Bent Pyramid (left) and of the Red Pyramid (right).

The Red Pyramid had a new feature. The mortuary chamber was entirely situated above ground level, prefiguring the architecture of Cheops. The proportions of the chambers are similar to those of the Bent Pyramid: Chambers 1 and 2 on ground: length 8.36 metres, width 3.65 metres, height 12.31 metres; mortuary (above ground): length 8.55 metres, width 4.18 metres, height 14.67 metres.

The stones are very large and carefully assembled. Inside the early chambers is another feature. The surface of the stones in these chambers is covered with a viscous black substance exuding from within the stones themselves (figure 19.18a). Could this be a proof of agglomeration? In other pyramids such as that of Meidum or the Queen's chamber in the pyramid of Cheops, the stones are covered with a thick layer of salt. This large quantity of salt (several cm thick) is the result of the geochemical reaction occurring at the moment when the geological glue was made. This has now been confirmed by recent scientific analysis (see chapter 6 section 6.2.1).

Figure 19.18: a) the black substance exuding in the chamber; b) the mortuary chamber of the Red Pyramid (Manuel Delgado).

# Chapter 20

# The Giza plateau

## The two Great Pyramids of Cheops and Chephren, and the small pyramid of Mykerinos

*Now we're getting to the heart of the subject, the Great Pyramids of Giza. Can you explain why the pharaohs Cheops, Chephren and Mykerinos decided to build the seventh wonder of the world in that particular place?*

The architects who built the first of these pyramids, the Great Pyramid of Cheops, did not choose the location of the plateau of Giza arbitrarily. On the contrary, it is a perfect example of the conditions necessary for building by reagglomeration. It is the ideal site for the builders where they could find an appropriate geological outcrop and a generous supply of water in the same place. The geographical feature of the wadi, its length and its depth enabled Chephren and Mykerinos to build their pyramids with the application of their scientific, cosmogonic and astronomical knowledge. The alignment and positioning on the sites are the result of the unique technology of agglomeration.

From photographs and from the map it can be seen that the limestone would not have been extracted from a single continuous face; quarries are dispersed throughout the site, leaving some areas intact (see figures 20.1 to 20.3). In short, it is very easy to see that the Egyptians of the fourth dynasty were following an outcrop of soft limestone, abandoning any places where the limestone was harder and less suitable for disaggregation by water. Both the Sphinx and the area of Kent-Khaves bear witness to this.

**Figure 20.1:** The ideal vantage point from which to study the pyramid plateau is the Hitan el Gurab overlooking the wadi. Dromedaries can be seen at the bottom of the wadi (2003).

**Figure 20.2:** Panoramic view of the plateau of Giza, from the Hitan el Gurab; tourists walking in the sand give an idea of the scale. The trees show where the water comes up to in modern times inside the Wadi. In ancient times, this water would have penetrated further to the left (2003).

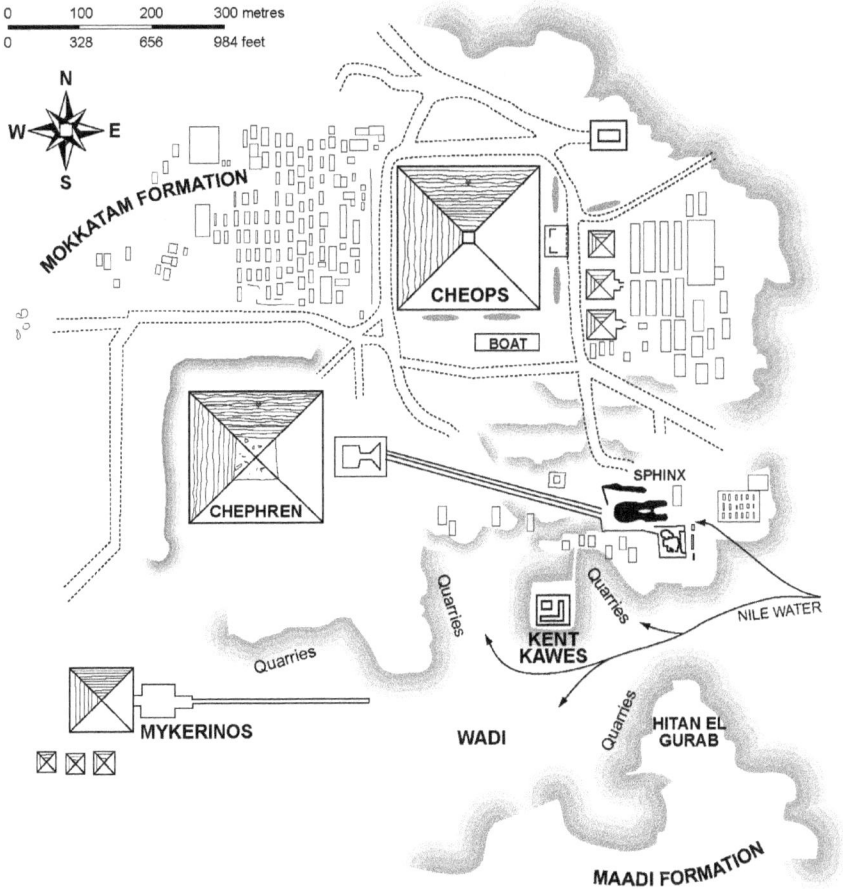

**Figure 20.3:** Map of the plateau of Giza showing the alignment of the Pyramids of Cheops, Chephren and Mykerinos, the Sphinx, the wadi, the quarries and the Hitan el Gurab.

## 20.1 The Wadi

According to the historian Herodotus, the Great Pyramids were linked to the Nile by canals:

*"10 years were spent working on this causeway, not counting the time spent on work on the hill where the Pyramids are built, and on the subterranean constructions that had to be made, to serve as a sepulchre, in an isle formed by the waters of the Nile, which were introduced by canal. The pyramid itself took 20 years to build: it is square..."*

167

Herodotus could never have observed the Pyramids as we see them now, with their stepped contour. He visited the site at Giza 1800 years ago before Cairo's inhabitants began helping themselves to the casings of all the Pyramids. Today on the pyramid of Cheops there remain a few casing blocks at the base. We also find mention of canals from the Nile up to the site. We know what these canals were for; they brought water to the Giza plateau, or at least to the quarries of the wadi, to supply the water used to disaggregate the limestone in order to produce vast quantities of agglomerated stone. This is what is being referred to in the account of Herodotus, which is thought to come from typically Egyptian sources[1]. The canals also have a significance in mythology: the pyramids were connected to the Nile by canals so that every night the spirit of the pharaoh could go on a voyage into the underworld.

The remains of this "cement works" appear to have vanished long since. The wadi is filled with sand. Some soundings have been made in the quarry of Cheops and have shown that the bottom was indeed at the level of the Nile flooding.

There does however exist an account in which it is supposed that the waters of the Nile were deviated to the site by means of canals, for the purpose of disaggregating limestone and natron by the processes described previously. Thus, Diodorus of Sicily (90 to 20 BC), another Greek historian, after visiting the pyramids, wrote in book 1 of the Historic Library:

*"7. And the most extraordinary thing is that, despite the enormity of the constructions and the fact that the entire surroundings are covered with sand, no trace exists either of terracing or of stone hewing, so that the construction appears not to be due to the prolonged labour of men, but to have been set into place in a single gesture by some divinity, in the middle of the encircling sand. 8. Some Egyptians have a strange way of explaining these facts, saying that these terraces were made of salt and nitre, and that the floods having reached them, dissolved them and effaced them without the intervention of human hand. 9. Such is surely not the truth;"*

Diodorus was writing four centuries after Herodotus, and we know that he stayed in Rome and in Egypt. He leaves us in no doubt that

---

[1] Alan B. Lloyd, Herodotus, Book II, tome 1, Introduction, Collection "Etudes préliminaires aux religions orientales de l'empire romain", E. J. Brill, Leiden, 1975, pp. 76-140.

he did see the pyramids. His admiration at their imposing architecture is manifest in this passage, and in any case, since he was in Egypt, it would have been incumbent upon him to visit this, one of the Seven Wonders of the World. Although Diodorus emphasises the lack of any evidence of the vestiges of any works (remains of terraces and stone hewing), this is not mentioned by Herodotus. The account of the terraces of natron and salt is related by the "Egyptians", and therefore comes from an Egyptian source that Herodotus would not or could not talk about. The apparently fantastic account is easily interpreted by the theory of reagglomeration: the terraces were heaps or hillocks containing a limestone/natron mixture that disaggregated when it was covered by the waters of the Nile, flowing in along the canals.

The water was brought in by canal leading directly into the wadi quarry, and the limestone could disaggregate very easily. The Egyptians also made artificial lakes that held water for much longer periods than the duration of the flood itself. This scenario, with men treading the muddy wetted limestone, is much more realistic than the scenario of labourers sweating blood in the heat of the desert, in the dust of the quarries. And moreover, with the reagglomeration of stone, a much stronger building material than natural limestone is obtained: by chemical reaction, the glue that binds the natural constituents and fossil shells is strengthened.

From another location, and in the same manner, muddy limestone rubble intended for the pyramid or temple building blocks was obtained. Then, when the soft limestone layer had been completely worked out, the workers would pack up and move off to another site. The harder, intact material that was left behind resembled an animal. And it was this that served as the base of the body of the great Sphinx. The head of the Sphinx is assumed to have been sculpted in a small isolated outcrop belonging to the upper, highly resistant hard grey limestone stratum of the Mokkatam formation. The head has perfectly withstood the ravages of time, whereas the body of the Sphinx, consisting of the remains of the extraction of stone from the softer, marly layer (figure 20.4) is severely eroded.

But this degradation is not the result of normal climatic erosion; for the body of the Sphinx was covered with sand thousands of years and was therefore protected. And yet here it is today, highly degraded.

**Figure 20.4:** The body of the Sphinx was sculpted in the soft severely eroded lime-stone layer (1988).

## 20.2   Solving the logistics problem

Agglomerating or casting blocks on the spot enormously simplifies logistic problems. In this scenario, it is easily calculated that 1000 to 3000 labourers working on site for three months, or from 400 to 1000 labourers for 10 months a year would have been sufficient to build the great pyramid in 15 or 20 years, if that is the time span we wished to allot. The architect Benoît Demortier[2] and the physicist Guy Demortier have carried out time and motion simulations for the pyramid of Cheops, basing their calculations on a distance of less than 5 km from the quarry. They conclude that the maximum number of men working at all levels of the pyramid was never more than 2300. Since the quarries are less than 1 km away, the actual number would have been smaller. This calculation is in complete agreement with what was discovered by the Egyptologist M. Lehner while excavating in the workers village at Giza: the village could not have housed more than about 2000 people[3] .

---

[2]B. Demortier, Regard critique sur la construction de la pyramide de Khéops ; le point de vue d'un futur architecte, Mémoire de diplôme d'architecte, Institut Supérieur d'Architecture Saint-Luc de Wallonie, Liège, Belgique, 1998.

[3]M. Lehner, Loaves and Fishes, in The Complete Pyramids, Thames and Hudson Ltd, London, 1997.

## 20.3   The great pyramid of Cheops

Sneferu's son, Khnumu-Khufu (May the God Khnum protect Cheops) built the great pyramid (figures 20.5, 20.6). He called his pyramid: The Pyramid That Is At The Place Where The Sun Rises And Sets. This name was inspired by the Heliopolitan myth in which the pyramid is the throne of Ra, the sun god, on whom it rests during its diurnal course.

Figure 20.5: The southern flank of the pyramid of Cheops (2003).

The Cheops pyramid complex was part of a royal establishment that was maintained for thousands of years. During the whole of this time, a cohort of Cheops' servant priests maintained the temples and the entire property, and perpetuated the worship of the god king with ritual libations. The altars were covered with offerings of flowers, incense and food. Several monuments refer to these priests; they show that their activities continued over several millennia. The tradition was still in force at the beginning of the Ptolemaic era; it was almost certainly these priests, the successors to Khnum, who guided Herodotus on his visit.

The other complexes, those of his Father Sneferu and Chephren, his son, were also the object of such worship. Like his father before him, Cheops commanded many building projects. His name appears on monuments throughout Egypt. He organised mining expeditions in the Arabian desert, in Nubia and Sinai and left his cartouche engraved on the cliffs at the entrance to the mines (cf. figure 21.2, chapter 21).

Almost the entire complex attached to the Great Pyramid is now destroyed. All that remain are the foundations of the enclosure at the mortuary temple. The great causeway described by Herodotus, whose volume was equivalent to that of the pyramid, was still intact in the 19th century. Today you can see a few very large blocks that give an idea of the scale and solidity of the undertaking. To the west of the Great Pyramid, mastabas of uncommon proportions were built in the area set aside for dignitaries.

The Great Pyramid is the seventh or eighth in the chronology; it is the bulkiest, and represents the zenith of Egyptian engineering. Egypt would never again build to such a scale. The pyramid remains one of the most famous monuments of all time and in all the world. Its base is 232 metres along a side, on an area of 5.3 hectares. Its original height is estimated at 147 metres including the summit. Today, it is only 138 metres high, having lost its summit and several tiers. It probably contains 2.6 million stone blocks — about 5.5 million tonnes. In the scenario of hewn stones, rubble and waste from the extraction and hewing of the stones would have increased the total tonnage to about 15 million, an enormous figure and difficult to conceive.

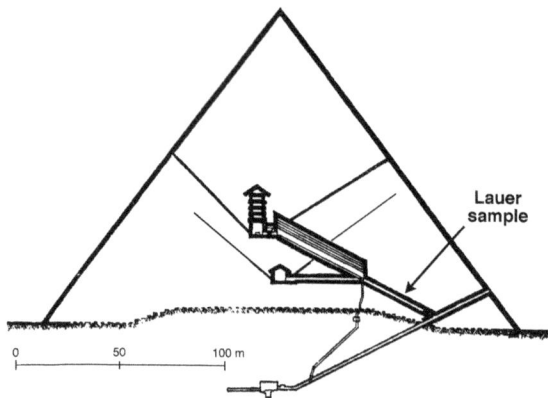

**Figure 20.6:** North-South section showing the inner chambers.

Everything connected to the Great Pyramid underlines the enormity of the project, and the many statistics can only give a small idea of the colossal nature of the undertaking.

In a talk given during the second international geopolymers conference on 30th of June 1999, the physicist Guy Demortier[4] reviewed some problematical facts, including the following:

"... An attentive examination of the surfaces of those block that are visible today, and which thus once underlay the casing blocks (which have completely disappeared from the pyramid of Cheops) shows that, although they are irregular in shape, they are remarkably well fitted together. Furthermore, the material is systematically more porous at the top than at the bottom. How is it to be imagined, then, that they were hewn to fit so perfectly? the excellent fit between the blocks would have been far easier if the blocks had been hewn into perfect parallelepipeds! And the care that would at first sight appear to have been exercised in the juxtaposition in the blocks would, in any case have been a waste of effort, since the blocks that are visible today would have been hidden under a layer of casing. How can we explain, furthermore, that hewn blocks should have variable porosity, but that wherever the blocks are situated, the maximum porosity is always at the top of the block? This topmost porosity feature cannot be explained by any natural limestone erosion; it is characteristic of a material that solidifies in a short time.

... The ducts of square section 20 cm × 20 cm issuing from the Queen's chamber, explored by the robot Upuant of R. Gantenbink (1996) clearly indicates that carving was not used; they are made in agglomerated stone. For there exist no gaps where the walls meet the ceiling of the duct; it is only at the floor of the duct that interstices can be seen. Moreover, following the robot in its progress, no vertical and horizontal joints that might suggest the laying of pre-hewn blocks can be observed.

... The irregularities in the blocks now visible on the pyramid of Cheops would be due to "accidents" during demoulding of the block. Any breakage and hence loss of material during releasing would have been corrected when the next adjacent block was cast, by partial overflow of material to the damaged area, ensuring at the same time perfect jointing between the two blocks in spite of any damage... "

In 1987, two French architects, Gilles Dormion and Jean-Patrice Goidin[5], became headline news when they received the authorisa-

[4]J. Davidovits et G. Demortier, Construction of the Great Pyramids (2500 BC) with Agglomerated Stone, Update of the Latest Research, Geopolymere '99 Proceedings, Institut Géopolymère, Session F 32, pp. 327-368.
[5]G. Dormion and J-P. Goidin, les Nouveaux Mystères de la Grande Pyramide,

tion to bore holes in the wall of the chamber of the Queen. They were looking for secret chambers. The presence of these mysterious chambers had been suggested to them by the results of measurements of the density of the pyramid. Using electromagnetic measurements, they had obtained a figure for the density of the pyramid that was 20 % lighter than the density of limestone. The article, published by the Associated Press in December 1986, was headed: *"480 000 stones missing from the pyramid"*. The two architects were reported as commenting: *"Holes, we have holes. Maybe the size of a fist; maybe the size of Notre Dame... the reason could be that the stones have lower density than the limestone forming the plateau or that spaces that were thought to be empty are actually filled with stone rubble"*.

They found neither any chamber nor any enormous holes; earlier, in 1974, another scientific team, the SRI International[6], had also shown that the density of the blocks was lighter than that of the limestone of the Mokkatam formation. The measurements carried out by SRI International on the density of the blocks of the pyramid of Chephren also give a 20 % difference compared with the local limestone, which is denser. A lower density is a consequence of agglomeration. Cast blocks always have a density that is 20 % lighter than the natural stone of which they are made because it is less compacted and has more holes or microscopic interstices.

## 20.4   The irregular blocks

One of the first criticisms that I met concerned the presence of blocks of irregular shape in the heart of the pyramid, where they have no structural function, but are simply fillers. These heaps of stone can be seen in various places where treasure seekers have dug passages towards the interior of the pyramids. Three tunnels of this type are known: the first is the entrance for tourists visiting the Great Pyramid of Cheops (attributed to Al Mamun), the second near the top of the pyramid of Chephren and the third in the yawning gap in the pyramid of Mykerinos. Only the first of these is easily accessible,

Albin Michel Ed., Paris, 1987, pp. 104-112.

[6]L. T. Dolphin et al., Electromagnetic Sounder Experiments at the Pyramids of Giza, Report prepared for the Office of International Programs, National Science Foundation, Washington D.C., NSF Grant No. GF-38767, by SRI International Memlo Park, CA, USA, and Ain Shams University, Cairo, Egypt (1974).

and we shall return to it in stage 20 of the *Giza Plateau Circuit*. We know that the stones visible on the outside of the pyramids and within the passages and chambers have a more or less right-angled parallelipipededal shape: this regular geometrical shape fits well with the use of wooden moulds. But the irregular appearance of the filler blocks appears at first sight to contradict the theory of reagglomeration. However, we also find misshapen blocks on the outside, which are attributed by some people to damage sustained during releasing, and by others to the deliberate production of oblique joints.

In fact these deformities have a logical explanation. Once we have set aside any damage caused by tunnel boring, we observe that the stones are perfectly jointed, some with no gap, others with a very thick layer of mortar, from 10 to 15 cm thick. Some joints are plaster incorporating stone lumps of various sizes, others are clay (tafla) and coarse rubble. These joints are probably the left-over walls of moulds that were left in place. These permanent moulds were necessary for the integrity of the construction while building was in progress and sometimes one of their walls was made of natural quarried stone of small dimensions (cf. Stage 12 in the *Giza Plateau Circuit*). The moulds of tafla, mortar and stone lumps have no intrinsic cohesion. While the tunnel was being dug, these remains readily disaggregated into dust in the tunnel, leaving visible voids. Early accounts by visitors all describe this dusty debris of stone rubble and tafla. The tunnels have since been entirely cleared of debris, particularly the current entrance to the Pyramid of Cheops, giving a misleading appearance of unsquared blocks assembled willy-nilly, which are in actual fact the remains of the rough imprints of the moulds.

One of the sons of Cheops, Djedfra, started building his monument at Abu Ruash, 9 km north-east of the Great Pyramid. Today practically nothing remains of it; we find a few granite casing blocks and a trench in the rock that must have served as a descent towards the mortuary chamber. Djedfra is thought to have lived for only a short time and his pyramid was never finished.

## 20.5   The pyramid of Chephren

Another son of Cheops, Chephren, built a pyramid 120 m south-west of the Great Pyramid. Today, it is usually called the Second Pyramid (figures 20.7, 20.8). In his own time, Chephren named it the Great Pyramid. It is slightly smaller than its neighbour, measuring 143 m high. It is 200 m along the side of the base; but from a distance, as it is built on high land and is therefore raised up compared with the first pyramid, the difference vanishes, many visitors assuming that the two monuments are of the same height. Inside, the pyramid is very simple, and, unlike Cheops or Sneferu, the galleries are not in the centre.

Figure 20.7: South-east side of the pyramid of Chephren.

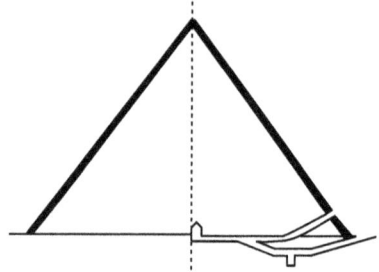

Figure 20.8: North-south section of Chephren.

Looking again at the system used by Sneferu for the first pyramid at Meidum, we see that the mortuary chamber was first of all hollowed out from the geological stratum; it was then covered with a roof, not a corbelled structure but enormous oblique beams like those used for the chamber of the king in the pyramid of Cheops.

Chephren, too, had a taste for the gigantic if we are to judge from the colossal blocks used to build the temples: the Mortuary Temple above, near to the pyramid (see figure 2.2 in chapter 2) and the Valley Temple near the Sphinx. During Bonaparte's Egyptian expedition, this was a revelation to Jomard. Describing the Mortuary Temple, he shares his excitement:

"... The walls are 2.4 metres thick, this being the width of the stones; their lengths vary from 3.5 to 7 metres. They are so big that at first I took them for the rock itself, worked and hewn, and would still think so had we not seen the cement in the joints. The eastern extension is formed from two enormous walls no less than 4.2 metres thick. We may well wonder why such extraordinary walls had to be built, since half the thickness would have been just as strong; and we can find no answer to this puzzle ... "

In modern books about the building of the pyramids according to the traditional theory, no mention is made of how these enormous blocks weighing at least 60 tonnes, and some more than 150 tonnes, may have been manipulated. Jomard found the problem insurmountable:

*"... But we wonder too what sort of men the Egyptians were to have playfully handled these colossal masses; for each of these stones is a kind of monolith, in the sense that it is a monument built in a single piece; hewing, hauling, hoisting, setting into place, assembling hundreds of these monoliths weighing 40, 50, 60 tonnes and more was, for them, a simple everyday job ... "*

In chapter 2, we noted that the strata in the mortuary temple blocks were not horizontal, unlike the geological stratification of the Giza plateau. Their undulation is the result of an interruption in the filling and packing of the moulds. The height of the strata in the blocks is smaller than those of the plateau strata. Moreover, these blocks exhibit the same erosion patterns due to variation in density as measured in the pyramid blocks.

The Valley Temple was not excavated until 1853, by A. Mariette. It does not feature in the drawings of Bonaparte's Egyptian expedition. There, Mariette discovered the famous anorthositic gneiss statue of Chephren. The temple walls were originally covered with granite blocks, most of which had been taken out, while those inside the temple remained intact (see Stage 17 in the *Giza Plateau Circuit*).

These and other descriptions from previous chapters unequivocally support the theory of agglomeration. Thus, figure 2.1 shows how some enormous blocks in the first tier of the pyramid of Chephren on the eastern side fit together with curved joints. This feature occurs commonly when, after making a first block, the second is cast directly against it, producing a joint characteristic of the technology. Like Cheops and all the other pyramids before, the heights of the tiers of the pyramid of Chephren vary according to a set pattern. Very large blocks are found at various tiers, some of them quite close to the summit.

Today, parts of the casing are visible at the summit. Some of the casing on the western face extends lower down than on the others. The various casing stones fit together in a special way: they overlap and interlock inseparably, forming a strong and stable bond.

## 20.6   The small pyramid of Mykerinos

However, a decline soon became evident.  The pharaoh Mykerinos
had a pyramid built which he called the Divine Pyramid, known
today as the third pyramid of Giza (figure 20.9).  Though built with
blocks of similar dimensions to those of the pyramids of Cheops and
Chephren, it is only 66.5 metres high and 108.5 metres along a side
of the base. Its volume is only 7 % that of the Great Pyramid.  The
mortuary chamber is once again underground, hollowed out in the
rock as for the pyramids of the third dynasty.   There are neither
corbelled chambers nor ceilings of inclined beams (figure 20.10).

**Figure 20.9:**  The pyramid of Mykerinos
and its satellites (2003)

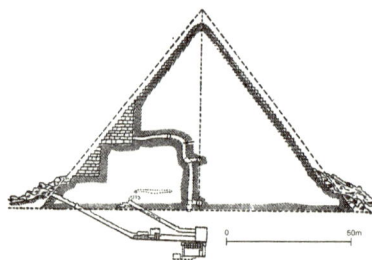

**Figure 20.10:** North-south section showing the excavation of Vyze-Peering.

The upper three quarters of its casing was limestone and has disappeared.  The lower quarter, still in place, is made of unsquared
granite. According to Egyptologists, Mykerinos began the casing using granite and then for some unknown reason continued with limestone as for the previous pyramids. But the scenario could well have
been very different. Examination of the pyramid complex of Mykerinos reveals that it was unfinished during the time of the pharaoh
and the pyramid may initially have been without a casing.

Later, another pharaoh undertook the restoration of the pyramid
of Mykerinos, first of all using hewn granite at the base and later,
limestone for the upper part. This scenario is not pure speculation
on my part, but is based on scientific data that came to light during
the dating survey carried out by the team of Mark Lehner[7] . While

---

[7]H. Haas, J. Devine, R. Wenke, M. Lehner, W. Wolfli and G. Bonani, Ra-
diocarbon Chronology and the Historical Calendar in Egypt, Chronologies in
the Near East, Aurenche O., Evin J. and Hours P. eds., British Archaeological
Report, International Series nr. 379, Part II, pp. 585-606, 1987.

west axis would have been very easy to determine. Every year at the summer and winter solstices it corresponds exactly to the rising and setting of the sun. This is an immutable constant, unlike the position of the stars which varies through the centuries. And we know that the Egyptians first and foremost venerated the sun god Ra. Finally, we should remember that Cheops called his pyramid *"The Pyramid which is the place where the Sun rises and sets"*. The east-west compass points form the foundation of the esoteric design and underscore the architectural obligations of the builders of the Great Pyramids. No extraordinary astronomical knowledge is necessary to determine absolute north. And even if such knowledge existed the north follows automatically from the east-west alignment.

# Chapter 21

# Alchemical substances in the making of stone

## Mafkat and ash

*Pyramid building is thus a whole industry requiring labour and a large amount of raw material. How did the Egyptians organise all this?*

To make stone we need not only a suitable geological raw material but also some reactive chemicals. These are as follows:

- Natron (a mixture of sodium carbonate and sodium sulphate),
- Carnallite and other magnesium salts,
- Lime-ash (a mixture of lime, silica and potash): ashes from a bread kiln (hardwood + reeds + papyrus etc.); Giza bakeries,
- Dolomitic lime (lime and magnesia),
- Baked gypsum (calcium sulphate)

The Mafkat minerals (from the Sinai mines) that improve the hardening are:

- Turquoise (aluminium and copper phosphate),
- Chrysocolla (copper silicate).

## 21.1 Lime-ash

How much lime-ash would have been needed, and how might it have been obtained? From experiments carried out in my laboratory, to agglomerate Giza limestone, you need around 2 % by weight of lime-ash. To build the great pyramid with its 2.5 million m$^3$ of stone

— a weight of 5 million tonnes — required 100 000 tonnes of lime-ash. With such a large quantity, it might seem worth looking for the remains of lime furnaces; but in fact, it could all have come from domestic sources. Bread was baked daily in Egyptian households and the fuel was probably palm wood and accacia, commonest trees in the Nile Valley. Now, these woods give ash that is rich in lime.

All they had to do was to arrange daily, weekly or fortnightly ash collection — very easy in such a well-organised and well-policed country as Egypt at the time of the great pyramids. The population at the time of Cheops is estimated at around 1.6 to 2 million people, i.e. 300 000 to 400 000 households. Let us assume that only 100 000 of these households were requisitioned for ash duty (a sort of tax). As the table below shows, the amount of lime required for the great pyramid could be collected in 5, 8 or 10 years according to whether the daily contribution was set at 1 kg, 500 g or 200 g. Since it is generally held that the pyramid of Cheops was built in 20 years, the lime-ash could have been collected at the rate of 200 g a day per household — not at all difficult to achieve.

**Table 21.1:** Capacity to produce and collect lime-ash per tonne for 100 000 households.

| Lime-ash production from household bakery ash | | | | | |
|---|---|---|---|---|---|
| Amount per day per household /kg | Total production/tonnes | | | | |
| | in 6 months | in 1 year | in 5 years | in 10 years | in 20 years |
| 0.2 | 3 600 | 7 200 | 36 000 | 72 000 | 144 000 |
| 0.5 | 9 000 | 18 000 | 90 000 | 180 000 | 360 000 |
| 1.0 | 18 000 | 36 000 | 180 000 | 360 000 | 720 000 |

## 21.2 The Sinai mines

To complete the stone mixture, certain geological materials must be added. These can be either silica, crushed rocks or clays together with other materials that aid geosynthesis. These materials occur in the ground, most often in mines. Thus, the purpose of the Sinai mines (figure 21.1) was to provide the blue minerals called *mafkat* in Egyptian, assimilated to turquoise, which are vital to certain geopolymerisation reactions and which improve the hardening.

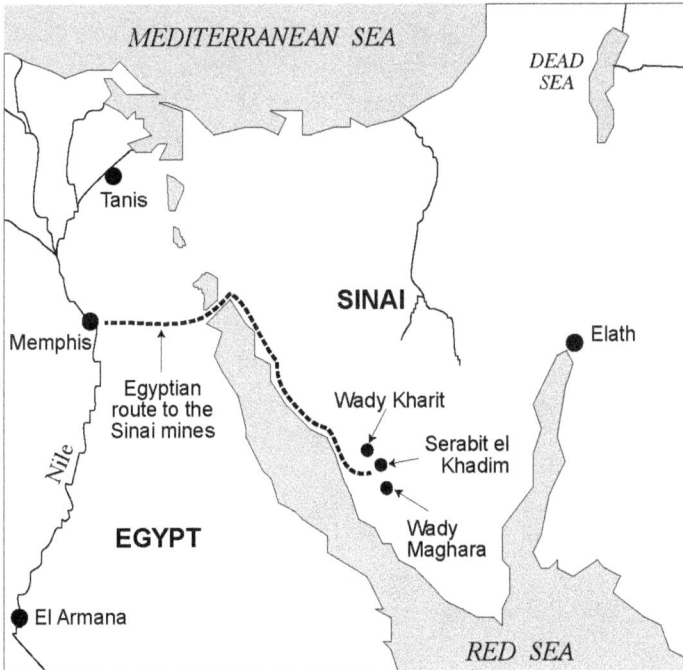

**Figure 21.1:** Map of the Sinai mines.

The Sinai mines are known as the turquoise mines. Turquoise is a semiprecious stone, and when it is well crystallised it has a certain value. When translations of the old texts started to appear in the 19th century, a number of speculators and adventurers were expecting a turquoise rush to Sinai, imagining that huge fortunes were to be made. But the turquoise from these mines turned out to be worthless, because it was insufficiently crystallised, and moreover rapidly lost its brilliance once extracted. In fact, some of this mafkat is not turquoise at all, but a mineral of the same light blue colour, chrysocolla, a hydrated copper silicate. *Mafkat* would have been the general name for all blue or green minerals containing copper.

Now, the Egyptians were able to distinguish between turquoise and chrysocolla. Texts dating from the time of the Pharaoh Amenemhaat III (12th dynasty) described the dismay of the miners:

*"... It was difficult to find the right colour when the desert was hot in the summer, the hills are red with iron, and the colours are cloudy..."*

And again,

*"... Certainly, there is still mafkat in the mountains, but not of the right colour during the bad summer season..."*

Chrysocolla dehydrates under the heat of the sun and the blue surface becomes whitish. The reference to the change of colour of chrysocolla shows remarkable knowledge of the minerals of the desert. Turquoise and chrysocolla have the same colour in winter. But the mineral that was prospected seem to have been turquoise, which does not change colour in summer. These texts show that the turquoise outcrops were exhausted under the 12th dynasty, leaving only chrysocolla.

According to Egyptologists, turquoise is essentially sought as a semiprecious stone for religious offerings; no explanation is given for the enormous quantity that was extracted from the mines compared with the insignificant number of turquoise objects found by archaeologists. In a recent work published in 1991, the French Egyptologist Professor Sydney Aufrère[1] takes up the problem of the volume of mafkat extracted. Discussing a publication by one of his colleagues, he writes:

*"... But let us come back to another argument of E. Iverson's; he was astonished at the enormous quantity of mafkat extracted... The work of 30 men working for 60 days, and corresponding to a hypothetical quantity of 35.4 tonnes..."*

Each Pharaoh sent several teams per year, and for the principal dynasties of the Old Kingdom, the quantities extracted are estimated at several thousand tonnes. Further on, S. Aufrère does recognise that:

*"... In spite of exploitations that must have produced a large quantity of this mineral in its time, it is a fact that in museums there is very little genuine turquoise..."*

The industrial use of mafkat, as opposed to its use as a semiprecious stone for jewellery or offerings, must be accepted as a fact. The sheer quantities extracted mean that it served as a chemical used in mass production. In another chapter of his book, Sydney Aufrère claims chrysocolla to have been used simply as green eye shadow; this is wrong. He writes: *"I choose the translation 'chrysocolla', a vague term used in former times to designate various copper-based substances, certain of which were used as eye shadow"*. He is thus

---

[1]S. Aufrère, L'univers Minéral dans la Pensée Égyptienne, Institut Français d'Archaéologie Orientale du Caire, 1991, Volume 2, p. 494.

neglecting the modern meaning of the word chrysocolla as defined by mineralogists.

Among all mafkats, turquoise (a double phosphate of aluminium and copper) and chrysocolla (hydrated copper silicate) are the most important minerals in the alchemical reactions of Khnum. During the third and fourth dynasties, the Egyptians were heavily exploiting the Sinai mines. In those of the Wadi Maghara, there are frescoes and bas-reliefs depicting the Pharaohs Djoser, Sneferu and Cheops.

Sneferu's activities were probably not limited to the mines of Wadi Maghara and Serabit-el-Khadim; he must have been the first Egyptian king to have made large-scale use of the Sinai outcrops, since his memory was perpetuated for a long time in this country, to the point where in the 12th dynasty the mines of Wadi Maghara and Serabit-el-Khadim were still called *the mines of Sneferu*.

Then came Cheops who, also at Wadi Maghara, left at least two steles. The two bas-reliefs sculpted one next to the other (figure 21.2) do not tell us much about the man or his mining activities. One of the tableaux only contains titles and names, while the other shows him massacring a person crouched in front of him.

Figure 21.2: The two bas-reliefs of Cheops at Wadi-Maghara.

187

It seems curious that the only archaeological references to the
Pharaoh Cheops should be those found here, suggesting a link between the mining expedition and the construction of the Great Pyramid.

What exactly was the role of the *mafkat* (turquoise or chrysocolla)
in the agglomeration of the Pyramid blocks? Maybe it was added
to the geological glue, but I think that it was especially reserved for
stones of high-quality, hard stone vases, statues and casings. The
use of *mafkat* in the production of stones or blocks for the mass of
the Pyramids was probably confined to symbolism and ritual, in con-
cordance with the act of petrification according to Khnum. Without
this ritual element, a symbol of creation, agglomerated stone production would have lost all its mythical sense. Other substances needed
to make this cement are siliceous minerals, opal and volcanic glasses.
Thus the Sinai mines could provide enough material, assuming that
they remained accessible.

# Chapter 22

# The decline

## The small pyramids of the fifth and sixth dynasties

*After the pyramids of the third and fourth dynasties, their successors are all small or even tiny. Why?*

Several frescoes from that time depict famines. The enormous industry that had been undertaken exhausted the country, causing an ecological and agricultural catastrophe. This is what we shall try to understand here.

## 22.1   The pyramids of the fifth dynasty

According to the historian Manethon of the second century BC, the fifth dynasty came from Elephantine and was thus directly linked to the worship of Khnum (figure 22.1).

The fifth dynasty (2565 to 2423 BC) marked the end of the magnificent age of the pyramids. They now become smaller then the pyramid of Mikerinos and of very inferior quality. Although the pyramid of Mykerinos is a small pyramid, it is still made from regular blocks, whereas those of the kings of the fifth dynasty are built in a completely different way.

The pyramid of Userkaf, the first Pharaoh of the fifth dynasty, is a heap of stones piled up next to the Step Pyramid of Djoser at Saqqarah (see chapter 26). The succeeding sovereigns Sahu-Re, Neferirka-Re and Neuser-Re made similar constructions on their funeral sites at Abu Sir, just to the north of Saqqarah (figure 22.2).

**Figure 22.1:** The Pharaoh Sahu-Re breast-fed by one of the goddesses accompanied by Khnum (Temple of Sahu-Re).

**Figure 22.2:** Abu Sir, pyramids of Neferirka-Re, Neuser-Re, and Sahu-Re of the fifth dynasty (2003).

The large blocks of the main bulk have disappeared leaving a mass of rubble with clay filling the gaps, the whole being held in position by sustaining walls between each section. All these pyramids are highly damaged. There only remain heaps of stone and sand sandwiched between stone walls. The casings no longer exist; they have been used as building material by the local inhabitants. Under the stone heap is the hypogeum (underground burial chamber) itself, consisting of the descending galleries, the mortuary chamber and the sarcophagus.

The builders were more concerned with the complex surrounding the pyramid, using both stone and mud bricks dried in the sun. The elegant architecture, with its sumptuous decorations and coloured bas reliefs, is now only a ruin. In the funeral complexes, the fifth dynasty builders used far fewer stones than in the pyramid itself, so that the total, including the pyramid, represented a drastic reduction in the volume of stone material used. During the fourth dynasty, even the causeways needed a large number of gigantic blocks to be laid (see for example the causeway of Mykerinos in stage 13 of the *Giza Platea Circuit*). They now followed the contour and surface of the plateau in order best to economise on stone material. The Sahu-Re causeway, for example, changes direction twice and, moreover, at seven places contains blocks that were deliberately taken from the complex of Djoser (first pharaoh of the third dynasty).

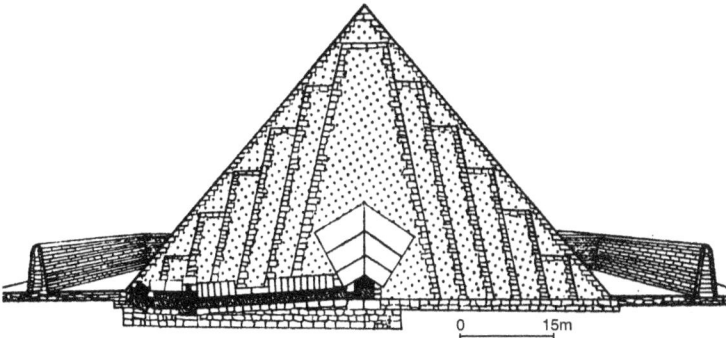

**Figure 22.3:** Cross-section of the pyramid of Sahu-Re.

On the other hand, the builders spared no effort in building the tomb itself. The roof is made of enormous limestone blocks 10 to 15 metres long weighing 40 to 80 tonnes, in three layers (figure 22.3). It is only here, around the mortuary chamber, that the concentrated use of divine incarnation in agglomerated stone is found. Obviously, the pharaohs had to economise on the use of alchemical agglomeration products, these having become very rare.

The pyramid of King Unas merits particular mention because of the discovery in the sepulchral chamber of the famous "Pyramid Texts", the oldest religious texts ever discovered. His pyramid is a heap in the centre of which are found enormous stones that were taken from the worshipping complex of his predecessor Djedkere-Isesi (see chapter 24).

## 22.2 The artistic decadence of the sixth dynasty (2423–2250)

Economic power diminished during the sixth dynasty and the king no longer reigned as an autocrat. The continuing decline in architecture was accompanied by artistic decadence. Few statues date from the fifth and sixth dynasties, the best having been made at the beginning of the fifth. This is in stark contrast to the preceding dynasty, with its formidable artistic accomplishments, no fewer than 500 sculptures having been placed in the Giza pyramid complex. The sixth dynasty pharaohs, Teti, Pepi I, Menenreh and Pepi II built their pyramids at Saqqarah by the same method as those of the fifth dynasty (figure 22.4). But they used much less material for the secondary constructions of the funerary centre.

During this period, several high officials organised mining expeditions that gained them prestige and recognition from the sovereign, who was highly dependent on the success of such enterprises. Numerous privileges were bestowed upon them and they used their new wealth in the provision of sumptuous tombs. Various explorations in foreign countries and in the Sinai mines undertaken in the name of the pharaoh enabled them to find enough minerals.

Pepi II probably continued importing cedars from Lebanon. His pyramid is built much better than those of the other kings. The ceiling of the funeral apartment is made of enormous stone beams (figure 22.4). The method used for making these beams was extremely refined, and closely similar to that used for a modern concrete beams. But the bulk of the pyramid is relatively small and simple in design. The interior of the pyramid is not made up of regular tiers, but of small stone blocks arranged in tiers.

**Figure 22.4:** The stone beams of the pyramid of Pepi II (J.P. Lauer).

They can be no doubt that if Pepi II had had the mineral resources, he would have been one of the most prolific builders in all Egypt. His reign of 94 years was one of the longest in history. He was the last of the great pharaohs of the Old Kingdom. Shortly after his death, Egypt had already ceased to be a unified nation.

## 22.3 The rise and fall of the pyramids

Egyptologists provide no explanation for this abrupt change in funerary architecture. Why, all of a sudden, did the Pharaohs concentrate their efforts and resources on buildings covered with sumptuous decorations, buildings generally made of mud bricks, and build much smaller pyramids? Neither do they explain why the builders took bricks and stone blocks from the structures of their ancestors.

The graph in figure 22.5 shows the variation in volume of the various pyramids of the third, fourth, fifth and sixth dynasties. The pharaohs Sneferu, Cheops and Chephren were the most prolific of all kings. They alone account for more than three quarters of the stone materials used in all the pyramids built during the third, fourth, fifth and sixth dynasties. Why did their successors not continue this architectural prowess?

Attempting to understand this, Egyptologists invoke the decline of Egyptian civilisation itself. In fact, they are merely basing this general decline on the decline in architectural effort, and are thus explaining nothing.

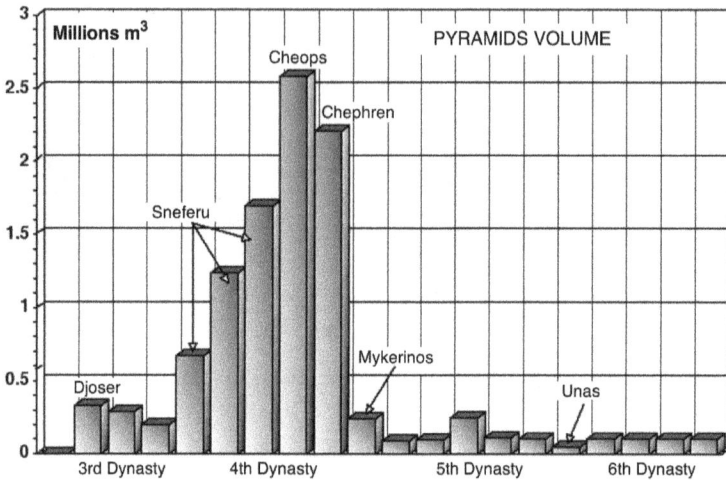

**Figure 22.5**: Variation in volume of the pyramids of the third to fifth dynasties, those of Djoser, Sneferu, Cheops, Chephren and Mikerinos.

No interpretation of the decline is given by the theory of stone hewing, this technique remaining abundantly used. Some interpreters think the decline in activity may be due to the disappearance of something that has left no trace. All agree that there is no simple explanation.

## 22.4 The reasons for the decline

With the theory of agglomeration, we can propose a logical solution. The decline in building would have been caused by a sudden reduction in mineral resources, in particular turquoise and lime-ash.

## 22.4.1 The Sinai minds become exhausted

In 1972, the expedition of Beno Rothenberg[1] found evidence that the principal mines were exhausted at the end of the fourth dynasty and that Sahu-Re was lucky enough to find a new vein of modest size not far from Wadi Maghara in the Wadi Nasb, in particular the Wadi Kharit. This vein also ran out rapidly.

The Bedouins of Sinai kept the kings of the fifth dynasty very busy. Steles of the Wadi Maghara and Serabit el-Khadim commemorate the narrow victories over the Bedouins in the neighbourhood by Sahu-Reh, Neuser-Re, Mykerinos (Menkaure) and Djekare-Isesi. But very little mineral was brought back after these missions, sometimes nothing at all.

## 22.4.2 Lime-ash production causes an ecological disaster

Technically speaking, the most important substances in the agglomeration reaction for the production of limestone blocks for the pyramids were natron (a salt containing mainly sodium carbonate, very abundant in Egypt) and lime (calcium oxide, $CaO$). As we know, natron reacts with lime and water to give caustic soda, the chemical needed to catalyse the geosynthesis reactions (this reaction is also described in chapter 6).

The geochemist D.D. Klemm[2] found that the mortars used in the pyramids of Djoser, Meidum and Chephren and in general the pyramids of the third fourth and fifth dynasties contained lime, while, according to Klemm:

*"... In the sixth dynasty, lime disappeared from practically all mortars. Should we interpret this as being due to a shortage of fuel (wood) and consequently, could this be the proof of an economic crisis?"*

Klemm's study does show that lime was used but, in his interpretation, the technology used to make mortar involved the calcination of limestone as a source of lime, $CaO$. He fails to point out that the

---

[1] B. Rothenberg, Sinai Explorations 1967-1972, Bulletin, Museum Haaretz Tel Aviv, 1972, page 35. B. Rothenberg, Bible et Terre Sainte, April 1973, No. 150. B. Rothenberg and Helfried Weyer, Sinai, Kümmerly+Frey ed., Berne Switzerland, 1979.

[2] D.D. Klemm and R. Klemm, Mortar Evolution in the Old Kingdom of Egypt, Archaeometry '90, Birkhäuser Verlag, Basel, Switzerland, pp. 445-454 (1990).

ashes from the calcination of wood or other plants, during simple daily operations such as cooking bread and other food, could have been used (see chapter 21 above). Nevertheless, he does show that this lime, which we call lime-ash (from ashes), was used in the third, fourth and fifth dynasties, but not in the six dynasty. What was the cause of this sudden shortage of lime? Was it because wood had now become a rare commodity and there was no more enough fuel to cook food? Had a radical change in climate led to an ecological disaster, wiping out agriculture? This is possible; I.E.S. Edwards suggested that at the end of the fifth dynasty (Unas) there was a very severe famine in Egypt. He writes:

*"... One of the scenes shown in the frescoes may depict the victims of famine, for their bodies are shown so emaciated that they look like skin and bone"* (figure 22.6).

A similar scene was recently discovered in the funerary complex of King Sahu-Re at Abu Sir. The famine therefore existed long before Unas. The most commonly held hypothesis is that these tablets represent the King (Sahu-Re or Unas) bringing help to the starving population. Some, such as Christiane Ziegler of the Louvre Museum think that the bas-relief depicts *"... difficulties met by the Egyptians in finding the most suitable stones..."*

Under the Pharaohs Sneferu, Cheops and Chephren, the whole country was involved in accomplishing gigantic undertakings, part of which consisted of supplying the fuel to prepare lime-ash. In chapter 21 (cf. the table) we calculated the production capacity of 100 000 Egyptian households on ash duty. This intensive exploitation of food resources, pushed to the extreme, in order to achieve these objectives was probably the cause of an ecological disaster. With the exhausting of the Sinai outcrops and the agricultural catastrophe came the decline in pyramid building.

Today, visiting the Nile valley to the north of Meidum, it is easy to imagine what happened. This is the most fertile part of Egypt and it is likely that modern agricultural techniques are very similar to those used four thousand years or more ago.

We find ourselves in an immense palm plantation (figure 22.7) under which the peasants grow a whole range of food plants, vegetables and cereals. In the warm dry climate of this latitude, the palm trees not only give dates, but also shade to protect the harvest from the fierce heat of the sun. Yields are phenomenal.

Demand for lime-ash became greater and greater under the pharaohs

**Figure 22.6:** Starving Egyptians at the time of Unas. Louvre Museum.

**Figure 22.7:** The palm plantation north of Meidum (2003).

Sneferu, Cheops and Chephren. Ever more palm trees were cut down and the planting and growing of new trees lagged further and further behind. Palm trees grow very slowly and 50 to 100 years must pass before a palm plantation tended to agricultural use. In less than 60 years, plantations had disappeared from the pyramid region. Food crops withered under the sun, causing an ecological agricultural catastrophe. And the cut palms were only replaced during the sixth dynasty. But it was a lesson for the Egyptians, who now turned away from the massive use of lime-ash.

# Chapter 23

# The mud brick pyramids of the Middle Kingdom, 1870 BC

*The saga of the pyramids continues: the Pharaohs of the Middle Kingdom placed their tombs inside monuments of this type. But how different they are from the Great Pyramids of the Old Kingdom! Are we still in the same technical and religious paradigm of divine incarnation with agglomerated stone?*

A cruel lack of raw materials seems to have led the pharaohs to regress technologically, abandoning stone and going back to mud bricks. This was a hard time for the priests of Khnum, who could no longer build pyramids worthy of their god and king.

There are not many stone objects in the pyramids of the Middle Kingdom; what are striking are the enormous intact monolithic sarcophagi — but they are empty. Then during the 12th dynasty, a curious and symbolic architectural feature was introduced into the construction of the pyramid itself. Once again, Egyptologists give no satisfactory explanation for this sudden change.

All technologies have a more or less pronounced impact on the history of civilisations and, of course, the production of stone is no exception. Sudden technological regressions greatly affect sociological progress. To understand the repercussions of the degradation in agglomeration techniques, imagine how our modern society would react to a prolonged boycott of petroleum resources. However, the disappearance of one practice can foster the emergence of another.

In ancient Egypt, bronze metallurgy to make new cutting tools and chisels gradually replaced the alchemical production of stone. As always, it is difficult to know whether the change in technique was caused by historical circumstances or whether it was the evolution of technology that had a profound effect on the course of history. Bearing this in mind, we can try to understand the main events that took place in Egypt around 2000 BC.

## 23.1 The birth of ideological rivalry between Khnum and Amun

Around 2000 BC, there was a new king, Mentuhotep, born in the south and impregnated with sudden culture and Nubian customs. At this moment in history, the royal residence of Mentuhotep was no more than a small provincial town, Waset, later named Thebai or Thebes by the Greeks. Memphis, the capital of Egypt since distant times, was replaced by this modest underdeveloped community. During the 51 years of his reign, Mentuhotep focused all his efforts on making Thebes worthy of its rank. Although there remain very few monuments at Thebes that can be ascribed to this period, we know that the town grew in importance during the 11th dynasty.

In the calm that Mentuhotep restored throughout the country, the idolatry of a minor local god, Amun, spread. The centre of worship of Amun had always been the town of Thebes where the priests claimed to come from a long line of predecessors. Their Heracleopolitan rivals from the North continued to worship Khnum. The god Khnum was deified in Egypt under several entities: Khnum-Ra, Khnum-Hapi, and Hershef at Heracleopolis which had meanwhile become the seat of the mythology of Khnum.

The two doctrines, that of Khnum and that of Amun, were based on fundamentally different religious philosophies. We know little or nothing of the cult of Amun during the Old Kingdom. Thus, we do not know if the ideology dates back to antiquity or whether it developed and became predominant when the priests of Amun assumed more and more importance in Egypt. In Theban mythology, sandstone and pink granite represent the body of Amun. Sandstone blocks were extracted with great care so as to cause no injury to the essence of the deity. The granite obelisks of Aswan were designated as the fingers of Amun. At the time of the New Kingdom, statues were carved out of the quarry with such great care that today it is still possible to locate precisely the place from which they came. The marks of the tools and chisels left in the face from which they were carved correspond exactly with those on the statues.

It was at this pivotal time, under the reign of one of the Mentuhotep sovereigns, that the sculptor Irtysen engraved his famous funerary stele (see chapter 15). This stele attests in a certain manner to the fact that the statues were moulded according to a secret religious technique used with a special authorisation of the Pharaoh Mentuhotep.

## 23.2 The pyramids of stones, earth and sand, 12th dynasty (1990–1780 BC)

As soon as he had been crowned king, Amenemhaat I immediately re-established the royal power over governors and nomes, transferred the royal residence to the town of Ithtawi, not far from the old town of Meidum, southern Memphis, alongside the modern town of el Lisht, at the entrance to Fayum.

His pyramid of the classical type and complex are decorated in the style of the Old Kingdom. In Egyptology it is named: *"the Museum of the art of the Old Kingdom"*. The complex does indeed contain numerous ornate blocks taken from monuments at Saqqarah, Dashur and Giza. Some experts even state that certain granite items come from the temple of the valley of Cheops and Chephren. The mortuary temple was decorated with reliefs copied from those of the Old Kingdom.

The pyramid of Amenemhaat I is of identical construction to that of the sixth dynasty. The site includes a system of interlocking main walls from which secondary walls proceed (figure 23.1).

Within these stone walls, the bulk of the pyramid is made up of limestone rubble, earth and even sand, held together by a limestone casing. Today it is in ruins and all that can be seen are the enormous granite blocks still in place and a funeral chamber now permanently underwater because of a substantial increase in the level of the Nile.

His successor Sesostris I reigned for 35 years, sent expeditions to the Sinai mines at Wadi Kharit and built his pyramid near to that of his father at el-Lisht, using similar architecture. The compartments inside, between the sustaining walls, contain mud bricks and stones.

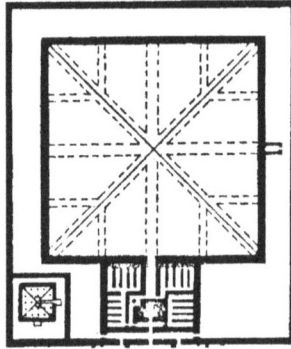

Figure 23.1: Section of the pyramids of the 12th dynasty.

The flooded passage down to the funeral chamber is covered with granite. Sesostris I practised religious compromise: he embellished Heliopolis with a magnificent temple of the sun and obelisks. Today, one obelisk is all that remains of the site.

His son, Amenemhaat II, maintained the traditions at Dashur; however, there was a new decline in stone making technology. The pyramid casing, in ruins, appears to have come from the Red Pyramid of Sneferu nearby, and there do exist causeways linking the two monuments, going back to Amenemhaat II (see chapter 24).

## 23.3    The mud brick pyramids

It was around 1870 BC that the next pharaoh, Senusert II (Sesostris II), introduced an architectural revolution into pyramid building. Situated at the entry to the Fayum basin near the village of el-Lahun, his pyramid contains neither stone, nor rubble nor sand; it was made entirely of mud bricks. Since the mud brick enclosure of Khasekhemwy built 800 years previously, it was the first of the giant mud brick pyramids built by the kings of the twelfth and thirteenth dynasties (figure 23.2). When, at the end of the nineteenth century the English Egyptologist W.M.F. Petrie first entered the granite funeral chamber, what he saw left him speechless: a red granite sarcophagus which he described as one of the most refined masterpieces made in such a hard and difficult to work material. The walls were perfectly parallel to within a millimetre.

His successor Sesostris III was one of the great pharaohs of the Middle Kingdom. He built a mud brick pyramid at Dashur. The monument, now in ruins, was covered with a casing of limestone blocks and his funeral chamber had a lining and sarcophagus in granite.

**Figure 23.2:** The mud brick pyramid of Sesostris II, after Faucher Gudin.

Like his father and grandfather before him, Sesostris III ordered numerous mining expeditions to Sinai. Despite providing unlimited funds, he brought back very little mafkat, even though by that time metal tools had replaced the old flint tools. Many documents show that numerous expeditions returned empty handed.

Sesostris III had problems too with a rebel prince of Hermopolis, the town that counted Amun among the nine deities of the original cosmic group. The monarchs of Hermopolis had their own naval fleet and army. The town's sculptors, following the traditions of their religion, carved a large statue representing their sovereign Djehutihotep, in a block of very soft alabaster from the Habnu quarries. On a fresco in the tomb of this sovereign we can see this colossus being pulled on a sledge by hundreds of men — an illustration of one of the false proofs advanced by Egyptologists to support the standard theory of pyramid building in the Old Kingdom (see chapter 24).

## 23.4 The return of Khnum

With the pharaoh Amenemhaat III, conditions were favourable for a renewal of Egyptian culture. During his 46-year reign he fostered the arts and architecture. Egypt owes to him the creation of Lake Moeris in the Fayum region. Two brick pyramids are attributed to him; the first was built at Dashur. It is highly degraded and appears to have been abandoned by its builders, probably because it proved to be too close to the Nile.

The second is at Hawara and overlooks the Fayum region. Its vast temple was frequently visited by Roman tourists in antiquity; they called it the Great Labyrinth; the temple is now completely destroyed. The pyramid is in an excellent state of conservation, the mud bricks having remained intact after 3800 years. Why? Had the technology been perfected? Was the knowledge of agglomeration according to the god Khnum once again being used? Apparently the worship of Khnum had taken on new life as is demonstrated in the text attributed to one of the king's administrators. This person had the habit of giving written 'instructions' to his children on the morals practised at the time, the correct behaviour to observe toward he who had once again become the absolute master and the incarnation of God: the pharaoh.

*"... I am addressing these important words to you and I count on you to understand them.... Venerate the King in your body, that he might live forever, and be faithful in your souls to His Majesty. He is the intelligence in the hearts (of men) and his gaze penetrates all bodies. He is Ra by the rays by which one sees. He is who illuminates the two earths (better still than) the solar disc.... He feeds those who serve him and he submits to the needs of those who follow his road. The King is Ka and his word is life. Whosoever be born is his work, for he is (the god) Khnum from whom come all the bodies, the progenitor ... "*

At this time in Egyptian history, the priesthood of Amun had not yet attained its power and Amun had not been proclaimed the progenitor. It was still Khnum who created humanity, with the help of a process of agglomeration. In building his pyramid, Amenemhaat III was perpetuating the ancient rite of agglomeration, and since the pyramid had to be eternal, he added the necessary ingredients such as natron and lime-ash. The clay came from the bottom of Lake Moeris and its special mineralogical composition ensured geopolymeric cohesion.

Inside, the pyramid has a highly complex system of galleries leading to the funerary chamber. The architects designed a whole series of endless corridors in a sort of labyrinth. When Petrie entered the pyramid and reached the tomb, he found an extraordinary structure, a monolithic chamber that was actually a solid enclosure executed in a single piece of yellow quartzite. Petrie writes:

*"The sepulchre is an elaborate and massive construction. The chamber itself is a monolith 267.5 inches [6.8 metres] long, 94.2 inches*

*[2.4 metres] wide and 73.9 inches [1.9 metres] high to the top of the enormous block with a course of bricks 18.5 inches [0.5 metres] high upon that. The thickness of the chamber is about 25 inches [0.6 metres]. It would accordingly weigh about 110 tonnes [metric tons]. The workmanship is excellent; the sides are flat and regular and the inner corners so sharply wrought that — though I looked at them — I never suspected that there was not a joint there until I failed to find any joints in the sides. "*

So if the block had been hewn, its original weight would have been around 110 tonnes, for a final weight of 72 tonnes. But without high-performance tools, carving a monolithic block of these dimensions in one of the hardest of materials is a feat that is difficult to conceive. It is this type of object that people used to support theories claiming the existence of ultramodern tools or the presence of a super-civilisation. Had the block been extracted in the form of a monolith, we should have found the original quarry. This is not the case. But this type of stone, quartzite, can quite easily be reagglomerated if a convenient geological source is available as raw material.

## 23.5 The paradox: the return to mud bricks

After the extravagant use of gigantic stones by the builders of the Old Kingdom, the return to a material like mud bricks comes as a severe shock for anybody studying the architecture of the pharaohs. For now that bronze tools and chisels were available, we should expect to find monuments built in hewn stone. This paradox is illustrated in figure 23.3. In the first pyramid, that of Djoser (third dynasty), the limestone bricks used by Imhotep were made in the same way as the mud bricks of the enclosure of Khasekhemwy (second dynasty).

Subsequently, the dimensions of the limestone bricks (and those of the moulds) increase little by little. In the pyramids of the fourth dynasty, the blocks are made on the spot and a characteristic feature of the temple is the use of gigantic blocks weighing several hundred tonnes. The mortuary chambers of the fifth and six dynasties are protected by enormous beams, the bulk being filled with stone rubble. In the pyramids of the 12th dynasty, the tomb is made of a hard stone monolith, but the body of the pyramid is of mud bricks.

These mud brick pyramids seem an aberration unless we introduced the technology of agglomeration; mud brick production and

**Figure 23.3:** The paradox in pyramid building. 800 years after the invention of limestone bricks by Imhotep, the pyramid building material of the 12th and 13th dynasties is once again the mud brick.

alchemical stone production would have been parallel techniques.

This evolution in the art of pyramid building remains inexplicable if we cling to the standard theory of stones that have been hewn and hauled into place. For as we pass from the Stone Age (second dynasty and beginning of the third dynasty) to the Copper Age (fourth, fifth and sixth dynasties) and then to the bronze age (eleventh and twelfth dynasties), it seems to be more and more difficult to carve stone, whereas logically the opposite should have been true. Why did Amenemhaat III only use mud bricks (made from silt) when it would apparently have been easier, 1000 years after Djoser, to use small hewn stone blocks? Why is it that the first archaeological proof of the extraction of limestone from the Tura quarries is a stele of this self-same Amenemhaat III? Before him, no vestige of this nature left by pyramid-building pharaohs has been found. Why did the dimensions of the blocks increase from Djoser onwards (a few kilograms) up to the monolithic chambers in hard stone of Amenemhaat III, while the quantity of stones used in the pyramid decreases? Only the theory of reagglomerated stone can give answers.

# Chapter 24

# The seven false proofs of Egyptology

*Now that we are beginning to get a better understanding of this brilliant period in Egypt's history, can we account for the so-called proofs given by Egyptology to defend the traditional theories?*

In most of these false proofs, knowledge about the history of the civilisation of the New Kingdom, up to Roman times, i.e. 1000 to 2500 years after the pyramids, is used to interpret what happened in the Old Kingdom and before. They do not take account of the fact that the history of Egypt is a history, not of a single civilisation, but of a whole succession: Predynastic, Old Kingdom, Middle Kingdom, New Kingdom, the Lower Period, the Ptolemaic Period.

## 24.1   The pyramids: an exception to the rule of Jean-Pierre Adam

Everybody agrees that the pyramids were built by workers using simple stone tools. But consider what the French architect and egyptologist Jean-Pierre Adam[1] had to say:

*"... We can readily understand that to obtain one cubic metre of building stone, it was easier to make it in one single piece than out of a lot of smaller blocks, where the amount of surface to be dressed would have been considerably multiplied... "*

---

[1] J.-P. Adam, l'Archéologie devant l'imposture, Ed. Robert Laffont, Paris, 1975, page 135.

If we follow this reasoning, the first pyramids should have been made with enormous blocks. As tools became more and more efficient, the sizes of the blocks should have diminished (figure 24.1). In fact it was the opposite that happened. The pyramid of Djoser (2710 BC), the very first, is built entirely of small stones measuring 20 cm high at the start, and in general weighing several dozen kilograms. The blocks of the Great Pyramid, the seventh of eight in the Chronology, are much larger: from two to twenty tonnes. In vaults inside the pyramids of the fifth and sixth dynasties we find beams weighing an estimated 30 to 40 tonnes. As we can see from figure 24.2, the dimensions of the stones increase in regular fashion.

Thus, conventional theory is totally at odds with the evolution of pyramid building.

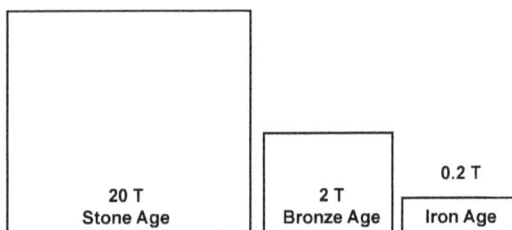

**Figure 24.1:** Variation in the dimensions of stone blocks with the efficiency of the tools according to J.P. Adam.

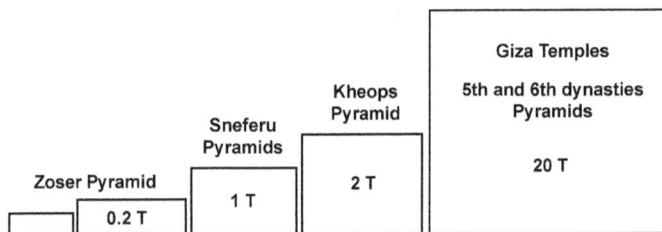

**Figure 24.2:** Actual variation in the dimensions of the blocks of the pyramids of Egypt.

## 24.2   Hewing blocks

To the north of the second pyramid of Giza (at Q in figure 24.3a) there exist the remains of the extraction of blocks from a trench. There are also inscriptions on the vertical face of this quarry (at

H) and a cartouche bearing the name of the New Kingdom pharaoh Ramses II (1298–1235 BC), figure 24.3b, who, as we know, demolished many monuments to use the stones for his own constructions.

(a) The trench of Chephren, stone extraction (Q).

(b) Hieroglyphs (H) (1988).

**Figure 24.3**

This inscription was engraved to honour the chief architect of Ramses II, who is suspected of having plundered numerous blocks from the casing of the second pyramid. He is also said to have dismantled some parts of the nearby temple. This happened 1400 years after the building of this pyramid. No other inscription that might date this quarry to an earlier time has been found (for more details, see the appendix on the Giza circuit).

In this "quarry", the stone hewing left the marks of tools. These have been dated as belonging to the reign of Ramses II. How is the dating of the various techniques for the extraction of stones in Egypt carried out? A comprehensive survey was carried out by a team led by the German geologist, Dietrich D. Klemm[2] of the University of Munich, concentrating essentially on the large sandstone quarries at Gebel-el-Silsilis. D.D. Klemm presented the results of this research during the second International Congress of Egyptologists in 1979 at Grenoble. He was able to give precise dates to the various methods of extraction used historically in Egypt, and therefore to the tool marks left in the quarries.

Figure 24.4 summarises the work of Klemm. In the earliest part of the quarry (around 1600 BC), tool marks have random orientations. During the New Kingdom, around the 18th dynasty (1400 BC), we find a herring bone pattern. During the 19th dynasty (1250 BC), Ramses II introduced a different technique producing parallel chisel marks, and this continued up to the latest periods and the Ptolemaic Period. But at the southern extremity of Gebel-el-Silsilis, we find quarries that were exploited by the Romans.

Now, however, there are no carving marks left by chisels; instead, we find notches left by metal or wooden wedges or dowels. The Egyptians quarried their stone with extreme care, and continually improved their technique. During the Middle and New Kingdoms, as we have seen, the quarry itself was considered to represent the eternal body of the god Amun. Rough quarrying of the stone would have been seen as an act of sacrilege on the body of Amun. The stones were carefully extracted one by one according to a sacred rite. But this typically Egyptian method would not have been productive enough for the pyramids.

In the southern part of the quarry of Silsilis, only the imprints left by iron or wooden wedges are found. Wooden wedges were driven into the rock, then soaked with water so that they swelled and the rock split. This process is often described in books about pyramid building. But the dating carried out by D.D. Klemm clearly shows that the process was never used by the Egyptians. Here in this

[2]D. D. Klemm et R. Klemm, The archaeological map of Gebel el Silsila, 2nd International Congress of Egyptologists, Grenoble 1979, Session 05.

| Third - First Century BC | 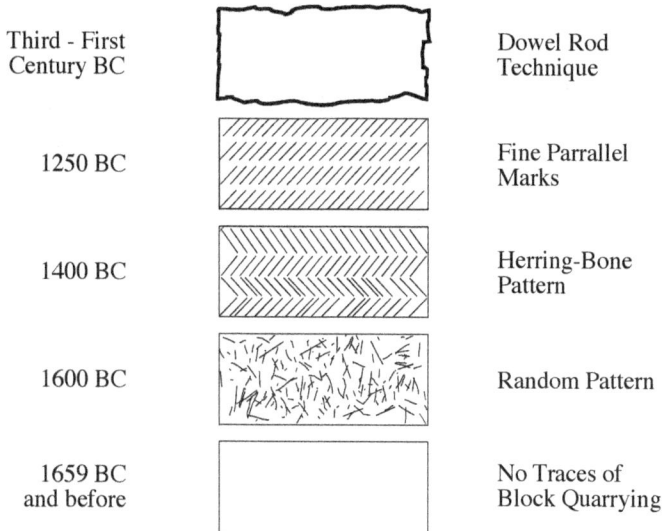 | Dowel Rod Technique |
| 1250 BC | | Fine Parrallel Marks |
| 1400 BC | | Herring-Bone Pattern |
| 1600 BC | | Random Pattern |
| 1659 BC and before | | No Traces of Block Quarrying |

**Figure 24.4:** Tool marks left in the quarries at Gebel-el-Silsilis, after D.D. Klemm.

quarry, it was the Romans who used his technique at the end of the Egyptian civilisation, someone 1500 years later.

So how did Egyptians work at the time of the pyramids? Clearly, if this method of the Romans had been used for pyramid construction, the amount of debris left in the form of millions of unusable blocks and carving waste would have been enormous. And any traces of this primitive dowelling method should be found in the oldest part of the quarry. But D.D. Klemm shows that the opposite is true: the dowling technique was used by a civilisation later by 2500 years than the Old Kingdom, long after the time of the Great Pyramids.

## 24.3   The transport of the statue of Djehutihotep: the sledge

A twelfth dynasty (1800 BC) bas-relief from the tomb of Djehutihotep depicts the transport of a colossal statue of this ruler of Hermopolis (figure 24.5). This was 800 years after the Great Pyramid was finished, yet it is used as evidence to support the traditional theory of pyramid construction.

The colossus no longer exists but according to the inscriptions it stood 6.5 metres high and weighed about 60 tonnes. It is shown

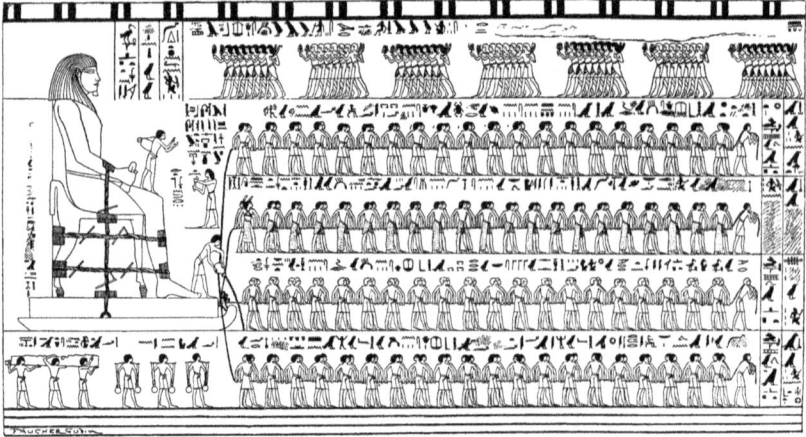

**Figure 24.5:** Transport of the statue of Djehutihotep, after Faucher Gudin.

on the bas-relief being hauled on a sledge, to which it was solidly secured by thick ropes tightened by means of tourniquets; at the corners of the statue under the ropes, protective pads have been inserted. There is a water carrier perched at the foot of the Colossus pouring water in front of the sledge to ease its movement over the surface of the silty causeway. At the bottom on the left, three more carriers can be seen, and three overseers carrying sticks. Between these two groups, three workers are carrying a wooden beam, one face of which is notched; In front of the statue are 172 haulers in four lines and behind there follow twelve men ready to replace any who fall by the wayside. Architect and egyptologist Jean-Pierre Adam[3] finds this document extremely important:

*"The existence of a document of this order (and there are others both in Egypt and Mesopotamia) enables us to consign to the dustbin all the far-fetched theories on the moving of megaliths in ancient Egypt".*

Is this proof as blinding as he claims? Archaeologists have demonstrated the fact that this massive 60 tonnes could easily have been hauled over flat terrain. Experiments such as those carried out by Henri Chevrier, an architect, have shown that the effort each man had to supply was only one sixth of the load to be pulled. In other words, using a wooden sledge on a silty causeway, a load of 150 kg can be pulled by a person making an effort of 25 kg. 60 tonnes can

---

[3] J.-P. Adam, *ibid*, page 158.

therefore easily be hauled by a team of 400 men. So a block of the Great Pyramid weighing around six tonnes could be hauled by 40 men on the flat. But what would happen on a ramp?

The French Egyptologist Jean-Philippe Lauer[4] has suggested that an inclined ramp with a slope of between 26 % and 35 % could have been used. In that case, the number of men necessary to reach the summit of the Great Pyramid would not have been 40, but 150 to 200. Is this compatible with the enormous quantity of blocks that would have to be manipulated into place every day?

A commonly agreed calculation is that 2.6 million blocks weighing on average about two tonnes would have been transported from the quarries over a period of about 20 years (the approximate reign of the pharaoh Cheops), i.e. 130 000 blocks per year. If, as the Greek historian Herodotus tells us, the construction of the Great Pyramid took place during the three month period of the Nile flooding, approximately 1400 stones would have to have been handled each day. Each stone of average weight two tonnes would need a team of 60 people. If a team made only one trip per day, there would be at least 80 000 people on the construction site (Herodotus mentions 100 000 workers). But this weight of two tonnes is only an estimate. As we have seen in the previous chapter, the stones weigh between 1.5 tonnes and 15 to 20 tonnes, distributed over the whole height of the pyramid. A block of 20 tonnes needs 600 people to haul it up a ramp, which seems hard to conceive.

As we know, the quarries are situated below the pyramids and at some distance. The length of ramp, too, would have added to the problems. A team could have made at most one or two trips a day. Under these conditions there would have been around 40 000 to 50 000 people per day solely employed in shifting blocks from quarry to pyramid site. Such a large number of people could not have been working in the same place together without being shoulder to shoulder in an area the size of a sports arena.

In 1984, I went to Cairo and visited Dr. Rainer Stadelmann who, with his wife Hourig Souroukian, had just published the first reports on the digs at Dashur on the site of the Pyramids of the pharaoh Sneferu, the father of Cheops[5]. They had discovered pyramid blocks

---

[4] J.P. Lauer, Le Mystère des Pyramides, Presses de la Cité, Paris 1974.

[5] R. Stadelman and H. Sourouzian, Die Pyramiden des Snofru in Dahschur, Mit. des Deutschen Archäologischen Intituts, Abteilung Kairo, Vol. 38, pp. 379-393, 1982.

bearing several marks and graffiti, some oddly engraved upside down (see the seventh false proof below). They also told me about tracks laid down in the Middle Kingdom linking Sneferu's Pyramid of the north with the site of the pyramid of Amenemhaat II in the twelfth dynasty. Thus, 700 years later, the workers of Amenemhaat II had used these tracks for the transport on sledges of stones taken from the pyramid of Sneferu, using the pyramid as a mere quarry. As evidence of the use of sledges in the building of the pyramids of the Old Kingdom, Egyptologists cite the existence of these sledges, used much later and for a quite different task. Such chronological confusion is a regrettable habit of some Egyptologists.

## 24.4 The Tura stele dating back to Amosis, New Kingdom

A stele discovered in the Tura quarries is attributed to the pharaoh Amosis (1580–1558 BC). This stele was destroyed in the nineteenth century, and today there remains only a sketch made by the English Egyptologists Vyse-Perring[6] (figure 24.6). The sketch shows a stone block on a sledge being pulled by oxen. Although the wheel was known in Egypt at that time , this stele implies that it was not used in stone hauling.

Figure 24.6: Tura detail, adapted from Vyse-Perring.

The pharaoh Amosis opened the Tura quarries to obtain soft stone for the temple of the god Ptah of Memphis. But the Tura stele is not acceptable as evidence to support the traditional theory of Pyramid construction because it was produced almost 1000 years after the Great Pyramid was built.

So while the Tura stele, together with other documents, appears to support the traditional explanation, they are merely the product of a society which, as we have seen, was developing different tech-

---

[6]Vyze-Perring, The Pyramids of Gizeh, Vol. III, page 99.

niques from those used by their ancestors. In any civilisation, new technologies come to replace the old. Archaeologists are not given to presenting far-fetched hypotheses; however, they do recognise that there must have existed a special method, known to the builders of the Great pyramids. Thus, according to the English archaeologist I.E.S. Edwards[7]:

*"Cheops, who may have been a megalomaniac, could never, during a reign of about twenty-three years, have erected a building of the size and durability of the Great Pyramid if technical advances had not enabled his masons to handle stones of very considerable weight and dimensions."*

Edwards implies that some clever method was being used. But with few exceptions, historians regard ancient civilisations as technologically inferior to our own.

## 24.5   The fresco of Rekhmire

The frescoes discovered in the tomb of Rekhmire, an important individual in the New Kingdom (1400 BC) are famous for their illustrations of the technological knowledge of the time. One of the frescoes shows blocks being carved with bronze tools (figure 24.7). This painting was produced 1300 years after the construction of the Great Pyramid. Unlike some frescoes of the Old Kingdom showing the carving of wooden statues, it does not show stone or copper tools being used. What it does show is a celebration of the arrival of bronze tools. It is therefore irrelevant.

## 24.6   The bas-relief of Unas

Another of the false proofs of Egyptology is the bas-relief decorating the wall of the ascending causeway of the pyramid of the pharaoh Unas (2356–2323 BC) at the end of the fifth dynasty (figure 24.8).

This bas-relief shows a boat being used to transport monolithic temple columns 6 metres high weighing 11 tonnes, together with temple architraves or cornices placed on their sledges. Since the columns found on the causeway are of granite, they must logically come from the quarries of Syene (Aswan). The bas-relief is used to explain that the columns were brought by boat up to Saqqarah.

---

[7]I.E.S. Edwards, The Pyramids of Egypt, Penguin Books, 1961.

**Figure 24.7:** Painting from the tomb of Rekhmire in which stonemasons are dressing blocks with bronze tools, after Faucher Gudin.

**Figure 24.8:** The bas-relief of the causeway of Unas, Saqqarah, after J.P. Lauer.

But historians of the Old Kingdom tell us that the pharaoh Unas destroyed a monument of his predecessor, Djedkare-Isesi, in order to reuse the stones. So what the bas-relief actually shows is a boat transporting columns along the Nile from the old temple of Unas' predecessor. The funerary site of Djedkare-Isesi is only 2 km from that of Unas. While visiting the site I noticed that some of the columns are not monoliths, as seen in the bas-relief, but consisted of sections joined together by mortise and tenon. The bas-relief cannot therefore be used to generalise as to the monolithic nature of the columns. It does show how the columns were brought to the temple of Unas, but does not show that they were hewn from blocks of granite that could previously have been extracted from the Syene quarries, 700 km further south.

## 24.7   Marks of the quarriers

The discovery of painted or engraved marks on the pyramid blocks and in certain quarries is the basis of another major proof. We find the names of teams and dates showing the existence of a hierarchy as in all well-organised work sites. For Egyptologists, these marks explain how the work was shared between the quarriers, the transporters and the block layers. The implication is that working with agglomerated stone, there would not be any hierarchy: no foreman, no inspector; this reasoning is simplistic and false.

Let us examine these marks. The first thing which we observe is that no marks are found on the pyramid of Djoser, the Step Pyramid, the first pyramid of all. Neither are there any on Cheops, whereas beside the pyramid of Chephren there are some splendid hieroglyphs. But these date back to the time of Ramses II (see figure 24.3b above). Those found on the Red pyramid of Sneferu require more serious study and we shall be coming back to them. On the pyramids of Mykerinos and those of the fifth and six dynasties, nothing is found.

Most of the marks are from the Middle Kingdom at a time (see chapter 23) when:
- Amenemhaat II reused stones from the pyramid of Sneferu;
- Sesostris I built his pyramid using a filling of stones and mud bricks;
- Sesostris II and Amenemhaat III built their pyramids in mud bricks.

The stones in question (generally casing stones) are small; all had been transported or handled. Again, we have a false proof.

Regarding the marks discovered on the pyramid of Sneferu at Dashur, Hourig Stadelmann-Sourouzian[8] wrote in 1982 in his article "Marks and graffiti at northern Dashur": "... *we observed that approximately one in ten of the (casing) blocks bore a mark... the marks were painted in red ochre in a single stroke of the brush and the engravings cut and painted at the same time...* " See figure 24.9a,b.

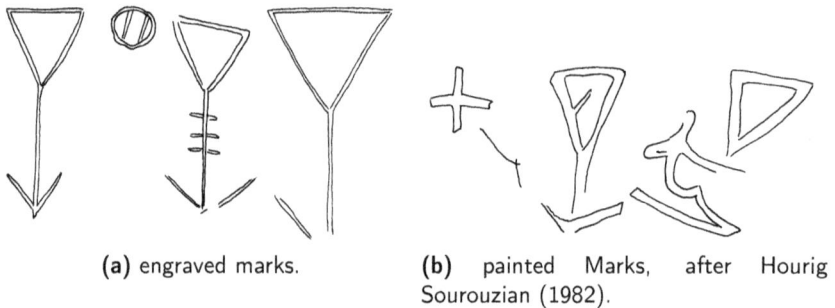

(a) engraved marks.

(b) painted Marks, after Hourig Sourouzian (1982).

**Figure 24.9**: Marks at Sneferu pyramid.

Mrs Hourig Sourouzian explains that:
— the painted marks are always found on the face opposite to the inclined face and back to front. The worker was perched on the block with his head looking over the edge!
— the engraved marks are always found on the lower face of the block (underneath) with the point directed towards the pyramid. The block thus marked is found upside down. To engrave it, the worker must have slid under the block, but when?

These marks all show that the way the casing blocks were laid according to Egyptology is false. We are told that the casing blocks were an integral part of the pyramid tiers and that they were cut at an angle when the pyramid was finished. But in that case, why are all these marks upside down and inaccessible? The evidence is that they were made at a time when the block was in an inverted position (see figure 24.10), the arrangement that would have been necessary for the block to be made by reagglomeration.

---

[8]R. Stadelman and H. Sourouzian, Die Pyramiden des Snofru in Dahschur, Mit. des Deutschen Archäologischen Intituts, Abteilung Kairo, Vol. 38, pp. 379-393, 1982.

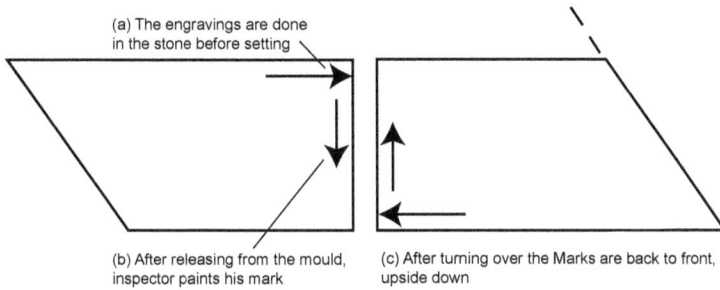

Figure 24.10: The explanation for the position of the marks in the casing block in reagglomerated stone conforms to archaeological discoveries. The arrows show the sense of the writing.

The engravings were made in the material before it hardened completely, on the upper face, just after filling and packing. They are the marks of the team leader. After releasing from the mould, the inspector used a brush to paint a mark on the rear face, this being the face that would be hidden, and in the normal sense from top to bottom. This is the sign that the stone is a good one. Then, once the block had hardened, it was turned over and slid into its final position. This is a more detailed explanation of what we referred to in chapter 19, concerning the casing of the Red Pyramid of Sneferu.

# Chapter 25

# Egypt after the pyramids

## The return of agglomerated stone under Amenhotep III and Akhenaton (18th Dynasty)

*Divine incarnation in carved stone became the rule under the New Kingdom and the hegemony of the god Amun. The soft sandstone from the Silsilis quarries is so easy to carve that everything appears simple. So why should there be any controversy about the monuments and objects dating from this period?*

It is true that 1200 years after the great pyramids, agglomerated stone was again being used, albeit sporadically, under the domination of Amun. After all these years, the worship of the god Khnum and initiation into his mysterious technology had not been forgotten. The pharaoh Amenhotep III used his alchemical secret to build amazing statues. And the heretical king Akhenaton did the same thing in order to rival the supremacy of Amun and carved stone.

## 25.1 The Colossus of Memnon

Geologists fail to agree between themselves in determining the origin of the stone used to the famous statues built for the eighteenth dynasty pharaoh Amenhotep III (1350 BC), in the Valley of the King, figure 25.1.

To summarise, French and German archaeologists[1] claim that the

---

[1]M. G. Daressy, in Ann. Serv. Antiq. Egypt., 13 (No. 2), page 43 , 1913. See aslo in Baedecker's Egypt, 1929, page 345. L. Habachi, Mitt. Deut. Archaeol. Inst. Cairo, Vol. 20, page 85, 1965.

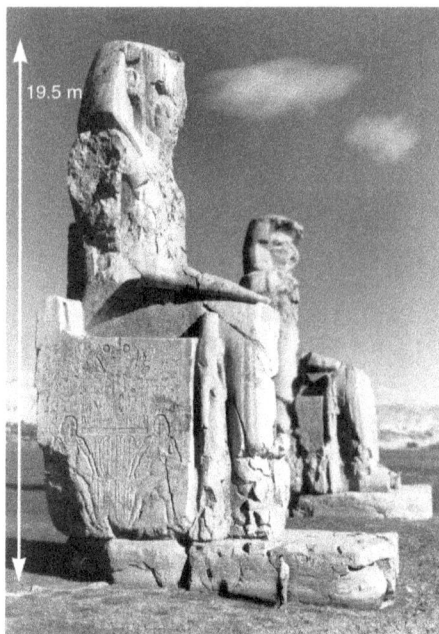

**Figure 25.1:** The Colossus of Memnon, with the author in the foreground (1979).

Colosses of Memnon were sculpted in a quarry 70 km further south down the Nile and that they were brought up by boat. Other British and American[2] researchers propose an even more extraordinary exploit. According to them, the statues were carved then transported upstream on the Nile from a place 700 km downstream near to Cairo. Each team of scientists uses more and more sophisticated methods in pursuing their research, including atomic absorption, x-ray fluorescence and neutron activation. When applied to the most enigmatic of Egyptian monuments, these new techniques shed more confusion than light.

In antiquity, the statues commanded respect; the colosses of Memnon are monoliths — they are made from a single block of stone weighing nearly 1000 tonnes and standing on a pedestal of 550 tonnes. They are 20 metres high, equal to a seven storey building. The stone

[2]R.F. Heizer, F. Stross, T.R. Hester, A. Albee, I. Perlman, F. Asaro, H. Bowman, The Colossi of Memnon Revisited, Science, Vol. 182, pp. 1219-1225, 1973. See also : H. Bowman, F.H. Stross, F. Asaro, R.L. Hay, R.F. Heizer and H.V. Michel, The Northern Colossus of Memnon: New Slants, Archaeometry 26, 2, pp. 218-229 , (1984).

from which they are made is quartzite, which is practically impossible to carve. The members of the Egyptian expedition organised by Bonaparte at the beginning of the nineteenth century recorded several notes on the stages and on the Egyptian quartzite quarries. Thus we can read in La Description de l'Égypte[3]:

*"... none of the great quartzite blocks bear any trace of tools that is so common in the sandstone and granite quarries: a material that is so hard, so refractory in the face of sharp tools cannot, it is true, be worked by the same methods as ordinary sandstone nor even of granite... We know nothing of how the blocks of such a rock were squared, how their surfaces were dressed or how they were given the beautiful polish that can still be seen in some places; but though we cannot guess the means, we are no less obliged to admire the results. There is nothing that can give a better idea of the highest state of advancement of the mechanical arts in antiquity as the beautiful execution of these figures and the pure lines of the hieroglyphs engraved in this material, harder and more difficult to work than granite. The Egyptians recoiled in front of none of these difficulties; nothing seemed to hinder them; the working is free throughout. Did the sculptor, in the middle of engraving a hieroglyphic character, strike one of the flints or pieces of agate that are encrusted in the material, the line of the character continued in all its purity, and neither the agate nor its enveloping stone bear the slightest crack."*

The consequences of this last observation are very important. What is the technology that could enable hieroglyphs to be engraved in this way? The Pharaoh Amenhotep III puts these statues down to a "miracle". Later on, in hieroglyphic documents, the stone is designated as *"biat inr"*, which means "stone obtained after a miracle". To what miraculous technology is Amenhotep alluding?

Once we accept the technique of agglomeration we can understand how Amenophis, scribe, sage and son of Hapu, was able to make this quartzite rock and cast to the colosses of Memnon, these enormous statues more than seven storeys high. With the technique of agglomeration, we can also explain the controversy surrounding the different interpretations of the analysis results obtained by various scientific teams.

On his biographical statue at Karnak, the Royal scribe Amenophis

---

[3] Jollois et Devilliers, Description de l'Egypte, Volume II, Chap.IX, Section II, page 153.

(1350 BC) describes the building of these colossal statues by the technique of agglomeration "as bread is made" using a box (a mould) specially made by his workers. Here are lines 16 and 17 of his biographical inscription, in a translation that differs from that of A. Varille[4] in the interpretation of the key technical words:

*"... My master (the Pharaoh Amenhotep III) appointed me head of all works... I have not imitated what was done before me... Nobody before me has done such a thing, since the founding of the Two Earths. I have carried out work to make statues of great girth and taller than the colonnade, finer than the pylon 40 cubits tall; this magnificent mountain of miraculous quartzite is near Re-Tum. I had a vessel of 8 built I had it ascend the Nile to set its image (its statue) in its great temple, according to our calculations (with the technology), as for the making of bread. Here is what I testify to those who come after us. An entire team built a single box (mould) of ingenious design. They fashioned (the statues) with the lightness of their heart, without hesitation, then worshipped the perfect image of the god (pharaoh) thus created. Then came those of Thebes, rejoicing in the colossal statues and satisfied that they would stand for all eternity."*

## 25.2 The agglomerated stone statues of Akhenaton and Nefertiti: the Mansoor collection

The period of el-Amarna, under Akhenaton (the son of Amenhotep III) around 1350 BC, was characterised by an unprecedented explosion of culture and the arts. The bust of Queen Nefertiti, found in the ruins of el-Amarna, is one of the most gracious and beautiful sculptures to have survived from antiquity. It was found in the workshop of the chief sculptor Tutmosis. His workshop was filled with original portraits waiting to be copied by other less skilled artists, in plaster moulds with agglomerated stone containing geopolymeric binders, a method that was also used to produce a whole variety of stone objects.

---

[4]A. Varille, Inscriptions concernant l'architecte Amehotep Fils de Hapou, IFAO, Bibliothèque d'Étude, T. XLIV, Le Caire (1968), texte No. 13, pp.41–42. J. Davidovits, La Bible avait raison, T. 1, ed. J.-C. Godefroy, Paris (2004), chap. 6, sec. 4., p. 99.

The evidence for this is based on an examination of around 150 limestone sculptures dating from the period of el-Amarna, and representing Akhenaton, Nefertiti and members of their family. They all belonged to the Mansoor collection, figure 25.2.

**Figure 25.2:** Two pieces in the Mansoor collection (on the right, the head of Queen Nefertiti).

They appeared in the United States at various times between 1947 and 1950. The Metropolitan Museum of arts of New York decided to acquire several examplars of these Amarna statues, but the museum curator had some doubt as to their authenticity and had them sent to William J. Young[5], the director of the laboratory of the Museum of fine arts in Boston. Young's report came as a terrible shock for the Mansoor family. He writes:

"... The larger of the two heads was examined from a minute fragment and appears not to be a natural material. It shows all the indications of being a made stone which could have been fabricated in a great many ways."

In the course of the 20 years following this analysis, several geologists tried to convince the Museum of Boston that the statues were authentic, i.e. that the limestone is natural, but in vain! In 1975, the Mansoors sent the sculptures to another expert, Richard L. Hay[6], Professor of geology at the University of California, Berkeley, who heavily criticised the results of the previous scientific analysis.

---

[5]W. J. Young, Technical Examination of Nine Tell El-Armana Objects, Property of Mr. William Monsoor, Report, Boston Museum of Fine Arts, April 14, 1949.

[6]R. L. Hay, Report on two sculptures from El-Armana, Feb. 10, 1975.

In a summary of his investigation (dated 10th of February 1975) he stated:

*"... I have gone farther than necessary in documenting what is really a simple matter. The intact nature of the delicate foram tests (shells) together with the euhedral shape (rhomb-shaped) dolomite crystals shows that this limestone could not have been made by cementing crushed limestone; ... It can perhaps be conjectured that a technology might exist (say beings from another planet technologically much more highly advanced than Homo sapiens) for artificially duplicating the several geological processes required... "*

Between 1950 and 1975, if an object had been detected to be made of artificial stone, this would have been taken to imply the presence of contemporary material and therefore of fraud. However, the geological investigation undertaken on the request of the Mansoors showed that the patina covering the statues had all the features of an antique patina which could not have been imitated by a modern forger. It was in 1984, while I was presenting the results of my research on the analysis of the pyramid stones, during the congress Science in Egyptology organised by the Museum of Manchester, England, that the director of this Museum, Dr Rosalie David, told me of the existence of the Mansoor collection.

I can confirm that these are genuine antique objects made in the workshops of el-Amarna, 3350 years ago and that they are copies that were probably obtained by casting a liquid mixture of geopolymeric limestone in plaster moulds. The statues are both antique and in artificial stone. Tutmosis, the chief sculptor and his colleagues had simply continued using the technique described 700 years earlier by the sculptor Irtysen in stele C14 in the Louvre (see chapter 15). Recently, while preparing a documentary for American television, I was able to examine two reliefs from the collection. The "hollow relief" is in red limestone produced from a mixture of two limestone pastes, one dark red, the other white. They were blended in the way the pastries are made, using a pastry roller for example. The hollow imprint was not carved, but simply modelled by pressing a pattern in relief on the very plastic paste. The other object in relief, of lighter colour, was not modelled but sculpted in an even softer material using a metal or wooden tool.

# Chapter 26

# The new history of the Pyramids

*Has anybody other than yourself ever suggested that the men of antiquity used this astonishing yet so simple knowledge in their architecture?*

In France, in the 18th century, there was much excitement at the reports of Paul Lucas, entitled *Voyage of Sir Paul Lucas to the Levant, Paris 1704; third voyage made from 1714 to 1717 by order of Louis XIV to Turkey,... Upper and Lower Egypt*, etc. (Rouen, 1719). His peregrinations around the Near East had taken him as far as Egypt, where he applied his observational skills. But although his ideas on the pyramid casings — which he judged to have been made of cement — are interesting, they are not entirely satisfactory. As we have seen, the few casing blocks still in place are exceptional, so smooth and with such perfect joints that Paul Lucas thought they must have been made with a mortar or binder. But he was clearly not referring to the blocks themselves; his ideas are the fruit of his own personal assumptions and are not scientifically based.

*The theory of agglomerated stone as applied to the pyramids is relatively recent; how much excitement has it provoked in the scientific community?*

Closer to home, several researchers have followed my lead, publishing papers on the agglomeration hypothesis, showing that this is a thriving field. For example, the Egyptian Mustapha Gaddala, the American Margaret Morris, the Russians Igor Davidenco and Jaroslav Kesler, the Frenchman Joël Bertho, the South-Africans Guth

227

and Maria Walton and the Belgian Guy Demortier.  An Internet search on the subject yields a surprising number of sites where the theory is discussed, with contributions both for and against.  The criticisms are levelled, not so much at the concept itself as at the book I published in New York in 1988, *The Pyramids: An Enigma Solved*. At that time, though the foundations of my hypothesis were solidly laid, I had not completed my research. I nevertheless decided to publish the general principles in the absence of certain evidence, evidence which has subsequently been brought to light.

In their arguments, my detractors have often used investigations carried out by insufficiently scrupulous geologists, and their criticisms are as ill-founded as they are ferocious. Some are simply in bad faith, from people whose sole aim was publicity and its associated rewards. Others at best show a lack of understanding of geopolymeric systems, at worst a total ignorance, in formulating totally erroneous conclusions with no scientific foundation. And a handful of them seize on the investigations carried out on a few of the natural stones that are found on various sites. These people arrive at the site, not to examine any of the blocks that really do raise questions, but merely to unearth that one block of natural stone that has the misfortune to be sitting among millions of other, more anonymous, stones. Holding aloft their find, they announce, *"There you are, the stones are all natural!"* This hasty procedure speaks volumes about the quality of the opposition. The reader may judge the relevance of the various criticisms in Appendix B. *The Giza Plateau Circuit*, gives the locations where natural stone and reagglomerated stone co-exist (stages 5, 6, 12 and 19). See also chapter 2, figure 2.5.

Other critics have focused on the unjointed stones in the pyramids of Meidum and the Bent Pyramid of Dashur, with a view to discrediting the whole theory of artificial stone. Until 1995, access to the pyramids of Dashur was forbidden for military reasons, and I could not therefore include these in my evidence. This omission has now been corrected following my visit in 2003, and I have been able to provide satisfactory replies to these criticisms. They have been given in chapter 19.

Opposition of this sort has the merit of forcing me to go further with my research.

Of all criticisms, the most virulent has involved the small pyramids of the fifth dynasty, which have the appearance of heaps of natural stones (see chapter 22).

## 26.1   The pyramid: a heap of natural stones?

The Saqqarah site is particularly interesting; there, we can compare the variations in the architecture of pyramids from different dynasties.

Figure 26.1: The pyramid of Djoser (2003).

Figure 26.2: Left: Background, the pyramid of Djoser; foreground, the pyramid of Userkaf and the author. Right: Close-up view showing the type of block (2003).

From an observatory north-east of Saqqarah there can be seen the Step Pyramid of Djoser, almost intact and built of small, carefully laid uniform blocks (figures 26.1, 26.2). The structure is homogeneous, only the casing having disappeared. It is even legitimate to wonder whether the pyramid ever had a casing, for seen from afar it does not appear to have suffered the ravages of time. The pyramid of Userkaf in the foreground of figure 26.2, however, looks totally different: it is merely a heap of stones.

When Userkaf, the first king of the fifth dynasty, returned to Saqqarah, he had his pyramid built very close to the Step Pyramid of Djoser, in the north-east (see figure 17.8). This location must have had a particular significance for the king. His reign was very short — less than ten years — and his pyramid is much smaller than that of his predecessor Mykerinos, with a height nevertheless of 49 metres and a base of 73 metres. It was originally covered with a limestone casing that hid from view the mass of natural limestone blocks piled irregularly one on top of another. With the subsequent exploitation of this casing by the Arabs, this pyramid was considerably damaged.

It appears obvious that the stone blocks came directly from the geological stratum of hard siliceous limestone at Saqqarah, with its alternating hard and soft layers as shown in figure 26.3. The soul of the tomb of Userkaf, the divine incarnation in agglomerated stone, was no longer the pyramid itself, a mere heap of stones. As we have seen in chapter 22, this pyramid is one of the vestiges of the period of decline, when the pharaohs of the fifth dynasty, threatened with ecological disaster, had decided to make sparing use of alchemical substances. Divine incarnation and esoteric functions were now focused on the funerary chamber, protected by enormous reagglomerated limestone lintels.

So in the case of the pyramids of Djoser and Userkaf, we have two totally different building methods. One used material from the soft geological stratum, reagglomerated into blocks using wooden moulds to build a monolithic, homogeneous, stable, weather-resistant monument: the Step Pyramid of Djoser, the invention of Imhotep. The other used make-shift methods with material from the immediate environment. Stones from the hard layer were merely gathered and broken up. The blocks, of random dimensions, were heaped up to form a pyramid of precarious appearance.

Thus, to my detractors I would say: *"Yes, there does exist a pyramid in hewn stone. This is what it is like. But it is the best the Egyptians could achieve using tools of stone and copper."* What is more, the pyramid of Userkaf is more recent, which ought to mean that it should be as well built, if not even better than its predecessors. This hewn stone pyramid, built after the fabulous pyramids on the

**Figure 26.3:** Alternating layers of hard and soft limestone at Saqqarah (2003).

Giza plateau, are proof to the incredulous that the technology used was radically different from before, and that Egyptian society had had to adapt to a new context.

I must now address a number of other issues that have cropped up from time to time in pyramid investigations, issues that do not seem to have unduly worried tenants of the traditional theory. How can the building of pyramids in mud bricks in the Middle Kingdom be accounted for (see chapter 23), when the Egyptians had at their disposal hard bronze tools, quite suitable for hewing stone? Nearly everybody prefers to remain silent on this question, or to ignore it altogether. The religious context, too, and the hieroglyphs discovered on steles are put aside or considered irrelevant.

## 26.2 The granite blocks in Cheops King Chamber: carved or agglomerated?

One of the preferred arguments against the re-agglomerated concrete limestone technology is based on the presence of natural granite ashlars in the King Chamber and above it. The reasoning is simple: because these granite blocks are made of natural stone, this is proof that the entire pyramid is built with natural limestone, not re-agglomerated limestone concrete.

Heating stone and applying water is applicable for reducing large pieces of granite into smaller ones. For example, granite blocks in the base of Chephren's pyramid have only one flat side. The other surfaces of the stone are irregular, showing the remaining shape of the boulder (figure 26.4)

**Figure 26.4:** Irregular granite blocks on the west side of the pyramid of Chephren (2003).

To understand why we have both technologies in Cheops, let us come back to the political and religious aspects of Egyptian civilization. We have learned in chapter 13 that Egypt was never unified. It was a federation of two adjacent states: North and South. Pharaoh was the King of the Two Earths. He wore the white crown of the South and the red crown of the North (figure 13.1). The pyramid represented the Egyptian people, i.e. both countries. It is therefore obvious to find in the pyramids the two different esoteric representations of the divine incarnation: agglomerated stone (according to Khnum) and carved stone (according to Amun). Cheops pyramid builders used two different technologies and hired two different gangs of workers: those from the North for re-agglomerated core stones, the others from the South, from the Aswan region, for split granite boulders. The granite ashlars were not carved in a quarry, but simply taken from individual boulders found in great quantities in the Aswan region. The boulders were split (with fire) to fine dressed faces, leaving a typical rough undressed back.

We had two separate building sites: one in the center, in charge of the King Chamber made of split granite ashlars, the second around it, in charge of the massive core with its millions of re-agglomerated limestone concrete blocks. The two work sites were independent. To reach the King Chamber level and drag up these huge granite ashlars, they needed a sort of ramp located on the south side, on the opposite of the Great Gallery (see in figure 26.5).

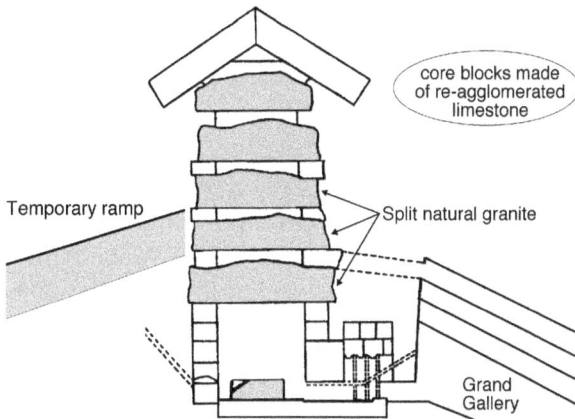

**Figure 26.5:** Cheops pyramid, the King Chamber, position of the temporary ramp needed to drag the split granite boulders up to the King Chamber.

I shall discuss other occurrences of natural granite blocks in Appendix A, *The Circuit of the Pyramid Plateau at Giza*, especially at the Stages 10 and 17.

## 26.3 In memory of the great Egyptian geniuses

To be sure, Egypt is a fascinating field of study, and the inconceivable prowess shown in that eternal image of the pyramid of Cheops, built in stones carved with such difficulty and hauled up on sledges and ramps, contributes to the fascination. Should our sense of wonder diminish because it appears that the Egyptians very pragmatically made use of the natural geological resources around them, sparing themselves much superhuman effort in the process? Is this, the first of the Seven Wonders of the World no longer to be marvelled at?

But if we consider the process of building by agglomeration, elegant and simple, rich in religious significance, do we not find, here too, a formidable lesson in technical skill and the mastery of materials? A lesson that has been handed by one ancient civilisation to another — western civilisation — that is wrongly boasting of having more wisdom than the others before.

The Egyptians were fully aware of the importance of this major discovery, as evidenced by their perpetration of the memory of two individuals. Thus, the inventor of the technique of building in agglomerated stone was glorified throughout Egypt's history. He was the first great scientist, great scribe and great universal genius. He was deified and went down in history as "Imhotep, son of Ptah". Later he was joined in this pantheon by another no less ingenious individual, the royal scribe Amenophis son of Hapu, who was also deified and named "Houy the sage, son of Hapu". Whereas Imhotep invented the agglomeration of limestone to build the pyramid of his master the pharaoh Djoser, around 2700 BC, Amenophis son of Hapu discovered the agglomeration of quartzite, using it around 1350 BC to make the colosses of Memnon for his sovereign, the pharaoh Amenhotep III (figure 25.1, chapter 25). And because his tale must also be told, the fascinating story of Houy, son of Hapu will be the subject of the next book.

# Appendix A

# Circuit of the Pyramid Plateau at Giza, Egypt

## An introduction to the study of pyramid construction methods

The present circuit is the compilation of several excursions performed by the author between 1979 and 2003, namely:

1. A standard touristic visit in 1979.

2. A seven-day long survey in October 1984 performed with an Egyptian geology student and subsequent discussions with members of the Geology Faculty at Ain Shams University, Cairo.

3. A seven-day stay in November 1988, in connection with the 5th International Congress of Egyptologists (the author presented a paper on the subject).

4. A four-day visit in October 1991, in connection with the shooting of the TV show NOVA entitled "This Old Pyramid" and produced by the American team for the PBS network (Broadcast in September 1992).

5. A seven-day stay in November 2003 for the outside filming of the TV series "Ari-Kat" for Relevant Television.

Dates given after figure captions correspond to one of these trips.

## Preliminary recommendations

The excursion requires at least five hours. It is not a substitute for the standard tour, which every pyramid visitor should undertake before focus-

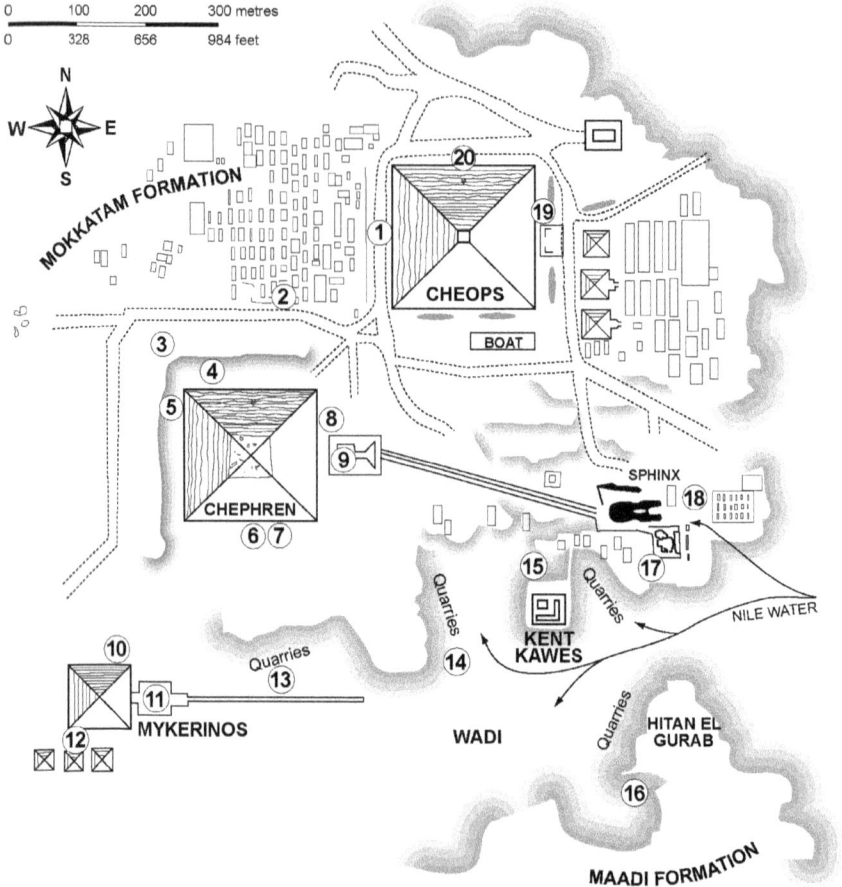

**Figure A.1:** The Giza Plateau circuit, Stages 1 to 20.

ing on the several issues which are raised in this circuit. A minimum stay of two days in a hotel located in the vicinity of the site is recommended, the first day being spent simply enjoying the environment. I would recommend starting the tour early in the morning (when the site opens) with Stage 1 and then following the order of the stages, from 1 to 20. You should be properly dressed for protection from the harsh sun glowing over the sand. You should also take sufficient drinking water with you for the tour. Starting at 8 am will bring you back to Cheops pyramid at around 1 pm. The best time for taking pictures is either early in the morning for locations looking east and south, and late in the afternoon (after 4 pm) for areas looking west and north; otherwise, there is a risk of getting overexposed pictures with no contrasted features. Amateurs may anticipate a second trip to the site in the afternoon after a suitable rest.

**Figure A.2:** J. Davidovits and M. Lehner in the TV film "This Old Pyramid", WGBH, Boston, 1992.

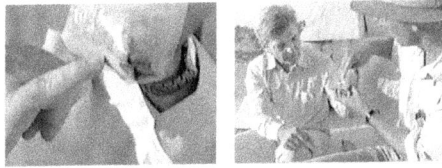

**Figure A.3:** After 24 hour soaking in a plastic bag with water, the limestone chunk separated into clay and nummulites. In the presence of an excess of water, the heavier clay settles, leaving the nummulites separated from each other. "This Old Pyramid" WGBH, Boston, 1992.

Before continuing, you should review chapter 7 describing the special geology of the Giza Plateau. As we have seen, the builders made advantageous use of softest limestone in the marly layers of the southern part of the Mokattam formation in the Wadi, but they built their pyramids on the base formed from hard nummulitic limestone bed in the north. The soft marly limestone of the wadi is a very suitable raw material for the agglomeration of limestone blocks as it readily disaggregates in water after a certain time.

In October 1991, during the shooting of the TV production "This Old Pyramid" by NOVA, aired on the American PBS network on September 1992, I had the opportunity to demonstrate this unique property of the Giza limestone (figures A.2, A.3).

The circuit starts at Stage 1 and ends at Stage 20. It is an introduction to the issues related to the study of the pyramid construction methods. It should be undertaken by those who favour the casting and packing system as well as by those who defend the traditional carving and hoisting method. Visitors often wish to take stone samples for further analysis. However, do not take fragments from the Pyramids because the Egyptian authorities do not allow unauthorized sampling; moreover, fragments picked up here and there on the ground are not representative samples.

# Introduction to a study of the Mysteries of the Pyramids

From an engineering point of view, with the agglomeration process we can easily understand how the giant blocks were laid at often impressive heights up the Great Pyramids; the technology was quite compatible with the knowledge at the disposal of any architect at the time. We can understand how the perfectly level tiers of the Great Pyramids were produced, enabling perfect summits to be achieved. We can understand how 200 tonne blocks were placed in the temples.

We can rid our minds of the old scenario with tens of thousands of labourers working shoulder to shoulder on the Giza site, most of them doing forced labour hauling enormous blocks to great heights, like those shown in Stage 2.

Stage 3 poses the question of the structural stability of the monument resulting from a plan prepared in advance by an architect. The remains of the quarry, with from five to seven blocks of different sizes, also raise a few questions. No one postulating the technique of transporting carved stones to build the pyramids could explain the advance preparation of two million blocks conforming to a set of different dimensions. Blocks with dimensions calculated in advance could not have been extracted, carved, stored and then selected according to size. But in the agglomerated stone scenario, stones of the dimensions required by the architect could be cast on the spot; it would have been a very simple matter to determine the length and height and to adjust the dimensions of the mould.

In Stages 7 and 8 we discover the problems arising from the restoration and repair work carried out on the eastern parts of the pyramids, and especially the part which connected the mortuary temple with the pyramid. This restoration work has left marks that are still visible today, and it could explain the presence of carved blocks at that location.

In Stages 11 and 17 we shall find traces of tools on various temple blocks. Egyptian masons used their tools — stone pickaxes and copper chisels — to roughen the surfaces of the blocks so as to make the decorative coating stick better and to give an imitation of granite. In Stage 12 we shall discuss the small narrow carved stones that were vertically aligned in the nummulitic beds and we shall consider their purpose as a point of anchorage for the moulds and as reference levels.

In Stages 14 to 16 in the quarries, we do not find vestiges of inclined planes that would have linked the bottom of the quarry and the top of the plateau for the transporting of carved blocks on sledges. Traditionally, throughout Antiquity, quarriers extracted their blocks from quarries located above the monument to take advantage of gravity, but this is not so at Giza; why?

In the agglomerated stone scenario, it is absolutely vital for the limestone extracted from the quarries (Stages 14 to 16 and Stage 18) to disaggregate easily in water. The numerous studies on the severe degradation of the Sphinx have all revealed erosion by water and the presence in the limestone of large quantities of water-sensitive substances. All these studies show how easily the limestone located at these places disaggregates in contact with water. The large amount of clay and silt of kaolinitic composition is exactly what my research has shown to be necessary. The disaggregated limestone slurry (containing kaolinitic clay) served as a glue or cement to bind together those lumps of limestone that had not disaggregated. Water is thus indispensable. This implies that water had to be abundant and easily accessible down in the quarries, at least during the annual Nile flooding (see the details on the general map of the circuit).

## Stage 1: Cheops west

The variation in quality of the blocks composing the Giza pyramids is striking. Some blocks are unweathered whereas the majority has become extremely eroded by wind, rain, and the sunlight; the degradation is most severe from the south and west (figure A.5).

On the west side of Cheops and Chephren's pyramids, the first several tiers have for centuries been protected from weathering because until about 50 to 100 years ago, they were buried under desert sand. This can clearly be seen on the drawings made by the French Description de l'Egypte in 1802 and by the German Expedition of Lepsius around 1845, which distinctly show the bottom of each pyramid covered with sand, up to a very high level, which I have represented by the line on figures A.4, A.5. Little erosion occurred after the sand was cleared. Because the blocks were exposed quite recently, the blocks located underneath the line are relatively unweathered (figure A.6)

**Figure A.4**: Stage 1, looking towards the western face of the pyramid of Cheops from the opposite side of the road, while leaning on a hillock (the remains of a mastaba) (1984).

However, the majority of these unweathered blocks exhibit a light, weaker top layer, which cannot be attributed to weathering, despite the statement by geologists that it is the result of "... the differential weathering of a relatively soft limestone layer caused by the burrowing of animals during the Eocene period ... "

In the agglomerated stone scenario, this top layer is a feature of the technology employed. One type of mould is illustrated in figure A.7. The side planks of the mould are blocked by an existing stone (A) or fixed by means of a hole in the stone below (B). During casting or packing, the bottom and centre part of the blocks become denser, while the top does not experience the same compression, resulting in a lighter density. It is striking that the height of this layer is rather uniform, from one block to another.

Figure A.5: The highly eroded blocks are above the sand line (1984).

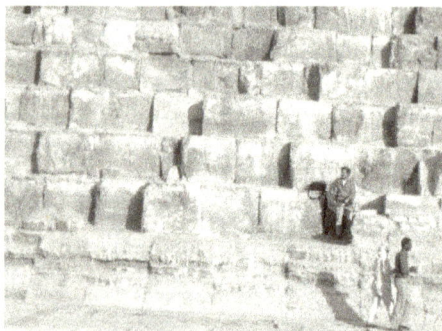

Figure A.6: Blocks with no erosion that were protected by sand (1984).

In the pyramids of Cheops, Chephren, and Mykerinos, one sees from time to time a thick, pink mortar. This mortar was applied to a thickness of 20 mm beneath the base of the trapezoidal blocks. These blocks are positioned with their widest area upward. Mortar was used to fill cracks and level imperfect blocks and also to cement a minority of rough trapezoidal-shaped blocks to neighbouring blocks. Sometimes, the mortar was applied thickest at the bottom, with that thickness gradually decreasing as it neared the top of the blocks. Practically no mortar is visible at the top edges, because there is no room. The presence of this thick mortar indicates that these particular blocks were moved into place, as opposed to having been cast in situ. These blocks represent only a small minority and their trapezoidal shape is intriguing. They may have been cast nearby and placed during the final construction phase to plug passageways that had remained open to provide ventilation and allow ingress and egress of materials.

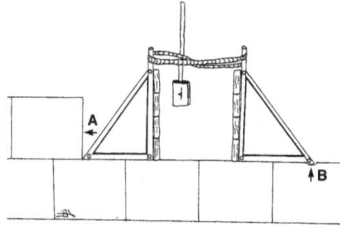

**Figure A.7:** Mould for packing (or casting) wet limestone material.

# Stage 2: Cheops west, a view on the height of the steps

The list of anomalies about the Great Pyramid grows longer when we consider the dimensions of the blocks. There is a misconception about the blocks of the Pyramids which archaeologists perpetuate. They claim that the heights of the blocks at the base are always greater than those near the summit. If accurate, this would make logistical problems far less complex.

It is true that the height of the blocks at the base of Cheops is 1.41 metres (4.62 feet) and that the heights of blocks progressively diminish to 0.59 metres (1.93 feet) in the first seventeen tiers. With the exception of the huge cornerstones, the weight of blocks in the first seventeen tiers diminishes from approximately six to two tonnes. Beyond the seventeenth step, however, blocks once again weigh more than two tonnes, even reaching fifteen to twenty tons apiece in some places, showing that their dimensions certainly do not diminish regularly as we go up the pyramid.

The only way to determine the exact heights of the tiers is by measuring them. Because it is difficult and potentially dangerous to climb to the top of the pyramid, it is likely that most specialists have mounted only the first few steps.

**Figure A.8:** Stage 2, looking to Cheops Pyramid, standing 300 metres west, on the rocky plateau (1984).

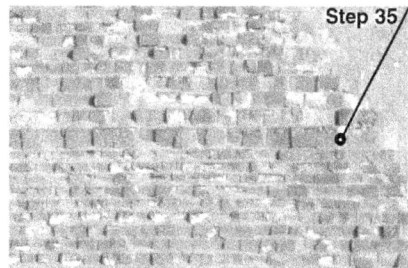

**Figure A.9:** Close-up on tier 35 with its large blocks (1984).

This is not obvious when one is standing at the bottom of the pyramid

241

looking up, because the heights of blocks forming the tiers appear to diminish. However, this does become obvious when standing at Stage 2 (figure A.8, A.9). The Egyptologists' remark that, "naturally, the heights continuously decrease" was meant as a general statement, and was not intended to account for all blocks in the pyramid. It certainly does not apply to the hundreds of blocks weighing from fifteen to twenty tonnes situated near the King's Chamber, and at level 35. Blocks of this size are so large that they occupy the space of two tiers. Nevertheless, this general statement is always cited, whereas the precise detailed reports on the variation of the heights are rarely, if ever, taken into consideration.

Because of the difficulty of raising such large stones to great heights, the data given here pose a serious threat to the accepted carving and hoisting theory.

# Stage 3: Chephren north-west, a view of the trench

**Figure A.10:** Stage 3, standing above the trench on the west side of Chephren Pyramid. On the far left, Cheops Pyramid. (1988).

There exist the remains of quarrying activity (label Q) in a trench on the north-west side of the Chephren Pyramid (figure A.10). Egyptologists use this as evidence to support the traditional carving and hoisting theory. For example, French Egyptologist G. Goyon states that the blocks were easy to cut because advantage was taken of natural divisions in the bedrock. Occasionally, a stratum (lift line) can be observed in very large pyramid blocks. When one does appear, however, it is not as high as the divisions of strata found on the Giza plateau. The divisions of strata in the bedrock near the pyramid of Chephren are about 4.5 metres (15 feet) apart (labelled H), three to four times greater than the heights of the pyramid blocks.

Goyon provides also an interesting sketch of the quarry Q (figure A.11)[1] . The most striking feature is that blocks Q are of different sizes. Apart from one fracture crossing obliquely at the end of the quarry, the outcrop is homogeneous and it does not make sense to have cut blocks of different dimensions.

**Figure A.11:** sketch of the quarry remains (Q), adapted from Goyon.

The northern vertical face of this quarry bears hieroglyphic inscriptions (labelled H) with a large cartouche containing the name of the New Kingdom pharaoh, Ramses II (1298–1235 BC) (figure A.12), who demolished numerous monuments to obtain ready-made blocks for his own constructions or to hew blocks for his buildings or restored temples, the remains of which are seen here under (Q). But, why are they not all of the same size? Any logical explanation on this issue would focus on the fact that Ramses' architect deliberately followed an architectural plan by hewing blocks of different sizes. From Goyon's sketch it can easily be deduced that the architect wanted blocks having five to seven different dimensions.

I have studied the dimensions of the Chephren pyramid blocks and have noticed that almost all the 2000 blocks I photographed in Chephren's pyramid conform to ten uniform lengths. To obtain these ten lengths distributed among the 22 tiers I examined, only five mould sizes would have been needed, because the blocks were set in place alternately lengthwise and widthwise.

The longest blocks all have the same length, and this is evidence for reconstituted stone. These very long blocks are always found directly above or below much smaller blocks, an ingenious method of building designed to avoid a succession of aligned vertical joints. The height of the tiers is much more variable than the range of lengths of the blocks. The desired height could easily have been obtained simply by marking the level to which the mould was to be filled. This would enable the striking variation in tier

---

[1]G. Goyon, Le Secret des bâtisseurs des grandes Pyramides Cheops, Pygmalion ed., Paris, 1990, Fig. 29 bis on page 107.

height that the architect appears to have stipulated, giving an extremely stable structure. It explains how the Great Pyramids remained unscathed by the earthquake of 1301 that devastated Cairo.

# Stage 4: Chephren north-west, hieroglyphs, cartouche of Ramses II

**Figure A.12:** Stage 4, at the quarry remains (Q), inscription in honour of Mey, with the cartouche of pharaoh Ramses II. (1988).

The hieroglyphic inscription (H) is in honour of Ramses II's architect Mey, chief architect in the temple called "Ramses shines in the Great House of the Prince" and son of Bek-en Amun, chief architect of Thebes. It is assumed that during the reign of Ramses II, Mey either systematically demolished the temple of Chephren or restored it. The discussion is still open. He also took parts of the facing of the pyramid to obtain materials for building a temple at Heliopolis. Ramses II and other pharaohs took a number of ready-made blocks from various pyramids to use in their own projects.

# Stage 5: Chephren north-west, in the trench, natural bedrock

To form a level base on the incline of the Giza plateau, five tiers on the west side of the pyramid of Chephren were shaped in situ from natural bedrock (figure A.13). There are no individual blocks in these bedrock steps. Here we must look at the transition between the natural tiers and those of reconstituted limestone blocks. The blocks in the sixth tier (figure A.14) were covered by sand and so, like the five natural tiers (figure A.15), have not been eroded. The variation in density of the individual blocks is thus not the result of erosion but of the method of fabrication. If the blocks of the pyramid were of natural limestone, the difference in density would have to be accounted for by a difference in the stratum — which is the explanation of standard Egyptology.

Above these natural steps, and where they have been covered by sand and protected against differential weathering, the pyramid stones bear the traditional density pattern encountered in Stage 1 (figure A.14). The natural tiers show no sign of weathering (figure A.15) and therefore it can be concluded that this pattern does not come from weathering but from the block manufacturing process itself.

**Figure A.13:** Stage 5, Chephren west, floor of the levelled plateau. View on the natural tiers (arrows) (1988).

**Figure A.14:** Pyramid, blocks on sixth tier with density pattern (1988).

**Figure A.15:** Unweathered natural tiers (1988).

If the pyramid blocks were natural limestone, the unnatural density pattern could be explained only if two adjacent strata of different qualities had been included in the cut. But in fact nearly all the blocks show this difference in density, the upper part being less dense than the lower part. Now, the geological strata at Giza, with a thickness of 4.5 metres near the pyramid of Chephren or in the quarries of the wadi, are three or four times thicker than the height of the pyramid blocks. (See Stages 13, 14, 15, 16).

# Stage 6: Chephren south, inclined bed rock and pyramid stones

A good place to study the transition between the homogeneous natural bedrock tiers and the individual pyramid limestone blocks is near the middle of the south side of the base of the pyramid of Chephren (figures A.16 and A.17). At the base, on the inclined bedrock (marked with a thick line, inclination 3°), the individual blocks automatically correct the inclined level to produce a perfectly horizontal base. The bedrock is quite homogeneous in density. The nummulites in the bedrock tiers are oriented horizontally, characteristic of natural sedimentary layering.

**Figure A.16:** Stage 6, middle of the south side of Chephren Pyramid. Inclined bedrock, thick line (1984).

**Figure A.17:** Pyramid blocks above inclined bedrock (dotted line) (1984).

On the other hand, the shells in the pyramid blocks lying just above the bedrock are jumbled, not horizontally oriented. This feature distinguishes agglomerated limestone from carved limestone.

# Stage 7: Chephren south-east

**Figure A.18**: Stage 7, Chephren Pyramid, south-east. Blocks showing curved jointing. (1984).

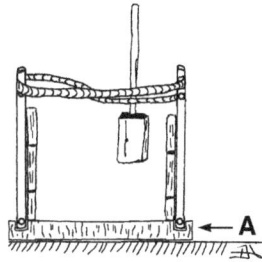

**Figure A.19**: Mould with wooden stays (A) for packing and casting wet limestone material.

The curved joint to the left of figure A.18 strongly suggests that the stones were made with the face of one serving as the side of a mould for the next, ensuring perfect jointing. This type of joint is found in all the large blocks making up the eastern parts of the temples of the Giza plateau, which we shall be visiting in the next stages. In figure A.18 at the bottom of the large block there can be seen holes that have been filled with mortar. This suggests the use of a mould (figure A.19) in which the boards were held in place by several wooden stays passing from one side to the other

(A). These would have been pulled out before final hardening of the stone, leaving holes that were filled with mortar.

# Stage 8: East side of the pyramids

It is worthy of note that the first tiers on the east side of Chephren's pyramid are made of enormous individual blocks (figure A.20). When looking at the first and second tiers of the three great pyramids (Cheops, Chephren and Mykerinos) one notices that the blocks have been subject to intensive repair or restoration work. They bear marks and lines, which have sometimes been taken for natural bedding (horizontal and vertical). The Egyptians used to flank the pyramids with subsidiary buildings. The Mortuary Temples seemed to have been separated from the east face of the Pyramid (at Cheops and Chephren). But in the other pyramids, for example Mykerinos and those from the fifth and sixth Dynasties, the mortuary temple is contiguous and the first tiers of the pyramid are part of the temple walls. In other words, the architecture of the east sides of the pyramids may have been considerably adapted and changed during the various periods, and what we see today may not represent the original construction.

**Figure A.20:** Stage 8, Chephren Pyramid, east. Enormous blocks and angle stones (1988).

This is how the marks shown in figure A.18 should be interpreted, i.e. as the result either of repair work or of demolition. The marks are horizontal and located in the middle of a series of adjacent blocks.

# Stage 9: Chephren east. Mortuary Temple, enormous blocks

I have closely examined blocks in the Mortuary Temple, Valley Temple, and the Temple of the Sphinx in the Chephren complex, and the Mortuary Temple in the Mykerinos complex. These walls were originally covered with granite facing or with a coating, an imitation of granite, which has now disappeared.

Walls protected from weathering are smooth and light grey. Large areas of blocks composing the walls that have been attacked by weather display the same density variations as in the pyramid blocks. The blocks in the temples of the Chephren complex are gigantic. They stand approximately 2 to 3 metres (6 to 10 feet) high and weigh up to 500 tonnes. The weathered faces of the largest of these blocks sometimes exhibit two or three irregular wavy strata (figure A.21).

**Figure A.21**: Stage 9, Mortuary Temple, Chephren Pyramid east. Block with strata, on right hand when looking east and toward the valley. Notice the close vertical fit between the blocks and the thin mortar separating each block (1984).

These strata are narrower than the natural divisions of strata in the Giza plateau. The geologists I met from Ain Shams University in 1984 claimed that the strata prove the stones to be natural. They were unaware that most types of concrete can also exhibit strata, known as lift lines.

Like those visible in the largest pyramid blocks, these lift lines can be explained by the method used to produce the blocks. To cast blocks of such enormous size might require three days. After the workers quit for the day, the unfinished block hardened. As it set, a surface (lift line) formed. The process was repeated daily until the block was complete. The lift lines are visible now that the outer surface has been destroyed by weathering and they are wavy, unlike those of geological strata which are straight. They are similar to the lines left by the form panels used to cast a concrete wall in stages. They have all the characteristics of a material packed into a mould, just as in concrete constructions.

# Stage 10: Mykerinos north, carved granite casing

**Figure A.22**: Stage 10, north side of Mykerinos Pyramid, entrance and casing with carved granite (1988).

The pyramid of Mykerinos has an exceptional history. Most of its casing blocks, now disappeared, were limestone. Those appearing on the lower quarter of the pyramid are made of carved granite (figure A.22). Some of the blocks are irregularly shaped, typical of carved blocks. The Mykerinos pyramid probably fell victim to the New Kingdom pharaoh, Ramses II, who routinely used pyramid casing blocks to build or restore temples dedicated to his god Amun. Maybe, the pyramid of Mykerinos was stripped starting at the bottom, but only one-third was denuded. A subsequent ruler restored the pyramid with carved syenite granite from Aswan, a material which was commonly carved during the New Kingdom. Far from supporting the traditional theory of construction, the carved blocks contribute to my theorem. Their appearance clearly demonstrates the difference between carved and agglomerated blocks: tool marks are visible on the former, but not on the latter.

# Stage 11: Mykerinos east, tool marks on Mortuary Temple

The stone blocks or mud bricks were covered with a layer of stucco imitating granite or with a white coating of plaster, both on the internal and external faces. In the mortuary temple, close to the pyramid, the surface exposed to the north is covered with very obvious tool marks (figures A.23, A.24). These tool marks are also observed on the blocks of other temples and have been taken as proof against the agglomerated stone theory. They are not proof. As mentioned above, the blocks were not bare, but covered with a decorative coating and the stone surface must be roughened in order to achieve good mechanical adhesion between the plaster and the stone surface. This is traditional practice in all civilizations when applying a decorative coating, plaster or stucco upon a smooth stone or brick surface.

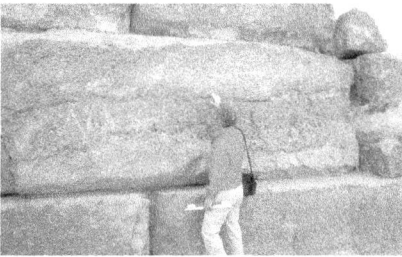

Figure A.23: Stage 11, Mortuary Temple, Mykerinos Pyramid, east, on the right hand when facing the valley. Blocks with tool marks.

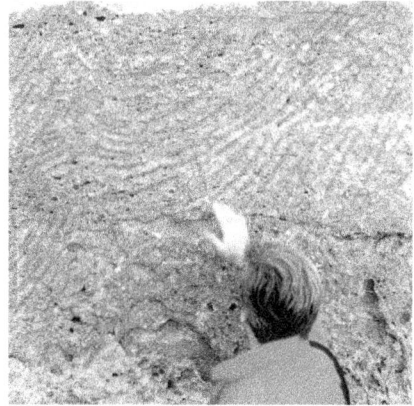

Figure A.24: visible tool marks (1988).

It is likely that these tool marks were specially worked on the agglomerated stone because Mykerinos' architect did not have the time or the budget to face the pyramid wall with massive granite stones. Remains of coloured plaster (coating) are often visible on pyramid blocks, essentially those located on the east sides, sheltered from erosion.

The shape of the bottom edge of the block in figure A.23 suggests the use of another type of mould (figure A.25) where the side planks are maintained in position by a special fillet of wood running lengthwise (A), the assembly being shored up with a pole to the ground.

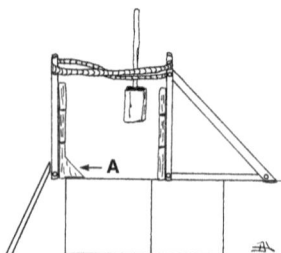

**Figure A.25**: Another mould type for packing and casting wet limestone material.

# Stage 12: Mykerinos stepped satellite pyramids, razor-thin joints, stone with vertical strata as part of mould

The route now leads to the southwest of the Mykerinos pyramid. Here stand three small pyramids belonging to near relatives of King Mykerinos. Those of interest are the stepped pyramids, made of gigantic blocks. A place of curiosity is the north side of the second of these small pyramids.

**Figure A.26**: Stage 12, west end of Mykerinos satellite pyramids (1991).

In 1991, I noticed there a cavity of particular interest. You can see how the huge horizontal blocks are lying perfectly flat over one another, separated by a 1 mm wide white line (figure A.27). In the carving and hoisting scenario, this thin white coating would have been entirely destroyed during the dragging, adjusting and pushing of the upper block against the one situated below. On the other hand, in the agglomerated stone system, this thin layer would have been spread over the finished packed material. Today's concrete blocks are often covered with a thin layer of impervious coating to prevent or restrain the evaporation of water. Geopolymeric hardening also requires water for the reaction to happen and evaporation must not occur during the preliminary phase of hardening. The upper block would have been cast later (after hardening of the lower one) and packed against this white coating, providing a close fit with its underlying neighbour.

252

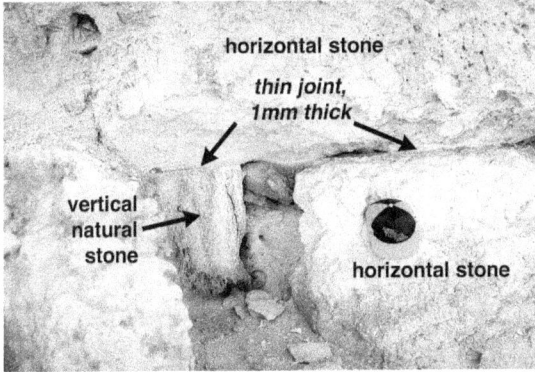

**Figure A.27:** Huge blocks with 1mm thin white joint and stone with vertical strata on the left (1991).

The same spot provides a more intriguing element. In figure A.27, the small narrow block on the left is made up of nummulitic strata with a vertical orientation. If this stone was cast, the nummulitic bed orientation would be jumbled, perhaps horizontal, but of course not vertical. This is therefore probably natural limestone hewn in the nearby quarry. It is not heavy, weighing at most 0.5 tonnes. In comparison, the majority of the Step pyramid blocks are gigantic, in the 5 to 20 tons range.

This light block could easily have been moved in and stood with its narrow side on the horizontal level. It constituted the first solid reference element, on which the other parts of the mould (wood planks, crude bricks) would be anchored. Neighbouring stones would be packed against it, providing close fit and stability. Similar narrow blocks with vertical bedding are present in all pyramids and may easily be detected by their lying between two much larger stones. Yet their number is very small with regard to the main population of the pyramid blocks. They were probably used as stable mould parts as well as a reference point.

# The quarries: Stages 13 to 16, in the wadi

The basic geology of the Giza plateau reported at the beginning of this circuit accounts for why the stone material was extracted from quarries located at the edges of the wadi from the layer containing soft, yellow marly limestone. In 1993, the German geochemist Klemm published analytical data on the origin of the core stones for the three pyramids, Cheops, Chephren and Mykerinos. The chart summarizes the results of Klemm's study performed on 72 core block samples for Cheops, 77 for Chephren and 22 for Mykerinos. They are statistically representative of the material representing each pyramid. Look again at the results of analyses in the investigation into the origin of the stones of the three pyramids, Cheops, Chephren and Mykerinos (cf. chapter 7).

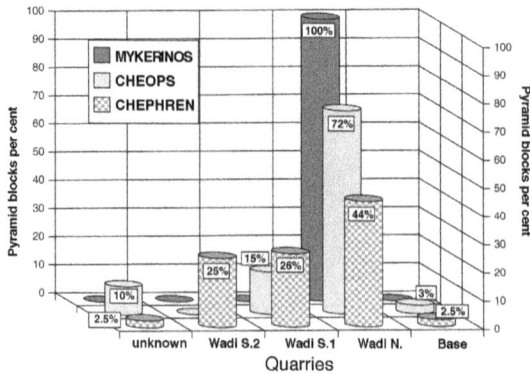

**Figure A.28**

1. Up to 100 % (100 % Mykerinos, 72 % Cheops, 44 % Chephren) are attributed to the quarries located at the north edge of the wadi, in the soft marly layer, some in the vicinity of Khent Kawes (Stages 14 and 15).

2. Up to 26 % (0 % Mykerinos, 15 % Cheops, 26 % Chephren) are attributed to a quarry located at the south edge of the wadi at the place called Hitan el Gurab (Stage 16).

3. For Chephren, 25 % of the stones are attributed to an unidentified quarry; analytical data appear to confirm that these stones could have come from the southern edge of the wadi.

4. Up to 10 % (0 % Mykerinos, 10 % Cheops, 2.5 % Chephren) are attributed to an unknown quarry that is not located in the vicinity of the pyramid platform.

5. Only 3 % (0 % for Mykerinos, 3 % Cheops, 2.5 % Chephren) come from the Mokattam formation right next to the pyramids.

Analysis results confirm unequivocally the basic geological data above: the pyramid builders did not extract the limestone rocks from the hard grey geological stratum of the Mokattam formation that makes up the pyramid platform (Stages 3, 5 and 18), but got 97 % to 100 % of their limestone raw material from the soft marly limestone stratum near the wadi, down from the plateau (Stage 14 to 16).

# Stage 13: Mykerinos east. Causeway and quarries

The Mykerinos Causeway leading from the Valley Temple to the Mortuary Temple consists of an embankment of nummulitic limestone blocks upon which was built a crude brick corridor overlaid, both inside and outside, with white plaster and roofed with wooden logs. As in other places, this site was covered with sand for centuries. The blocks we see today have therefore been relatively well protected, though they do show a weak differential weathering pattern.

Figure A.29: Stage 13, the Mykerinos Causeway (1984).

The nummulite shells are jumbled and the blocks exhibit the typical density pattern with the top less dense, typifying agglomerated pyramid blocks. To the north of the causeway are quarry sites, probably for Chephren's pyramid, filled with debris and sand.

# Stages 14 and 15: wadi north, quarries, Khent Kawes

Figure A.30: Stage 14, west side of the quarry (1984).

Figure A.31: East side of the quarry, Khent-Kawes (1984).

Figure A.32: East side of the quarry basin, Khent-Kawes, W-E canal (line and dot (1988).

A large basin quarry is located between Stages 14 and 15 (figure A.30, A.31). The basin is presently filled with stone rubble and debris. After Mykerinos, a queen of the sixth Dynasty (after Mykerinos), married to the Pharaoh Shepseskaf (whose tomb is the huge Mastaba Fara'un in Saqqarah), had her sepulchre built on an open space lying between the quarries. The tomb was essentially similar to the Mastaba Fara'un. Its superstructure was in the form of a sarcophagus mounted on a high, rectangular podium (figure A.31, A.32).

Today the basin is filled with all manner of debris. According to Lehner, the quarry had a width (E-W) of 230 m, a length (N-S) of 400 m and was 30 m deep. His volume calculation gives 2,760,000 m$^3$ of stone to be compared with the estimated 2,590,000 m$^3$ of stone for the Cheops pyramid. At its lowest point the basin is 30 m deep, and if cleaned of debris would be 1 to 5 m below the level of the Nile flooding. In figure A.32, the visible trench (line and dot), running W-E towards the bottom of the wadi and the Nile

Valley, could be the remains of the water canals that brought the Nile water into the basin for the disaggregation of the limestone chipped down from the quarry edges.

At Stage 15, you can do a water soaking disintegration experimentation (allow 5–10 hours); sampling can be made ideally in the vicinity of the geological separation (line and dot in figure A.33). The selected sample should contain nummulites (disk like shells) 1–3 cm in diameter (0.5 to 1 inch). Limestone with smaller nummulites needs more soaking time, preferably alternate soaking and drying cycles. An easy access to the sampling site is provided when descending the Chephren Causeway, between the Mortuary Temple and the Sphinx. Remember that permission must be obtained from the authorities before taking samples.

Note: In 2003, access was practically impossible owing to work in progress. A replica of a mastaba was built there.

**Figure A.33:** Stage 15, middle of the east quarry side, sampling site (line and dot) (1991).

# Stage 16. Maadi Formation, quarries, gypsum bed

This stage is not mandatory. Those visitors interested in the mineralogy of this outcrop should take a look at the beautiful layers of gypsum crystals and clay that alternate with the limestone beds (figure A.34).When heated and calcined, gypsum (dot in figure A.35), clay and limestone materials provide some of the reactive geopolymeric reactants which are necessary to catalyse the hardening of the agglomerated limestone blocks.

Figure A.34: Stage 16. Summit of the Maadi formation with gypsum and clay beds (1984).

Figure A.35: Gypsum bed (1984).

# Stage 17: Chephren Valley Temple and Sphinx Temple granite blocks used as mould

The Chephren Valley Temple remained buried under the desert sand until the 19th Century and was only completely excavated in 1910. It was not described by the French Napoleonic Expedition in 1799–1802. The walls of the Chephren Valley Temple and of the adjacent Sphinx temple are formed of huge parallelepipeds of limestone with irregular surfaces (line and dot in figure A.36).

However, as for the other temples on the Giza Plateau (see Stages 9 and 11), the walls were originally faced with granite cladding, still intact on the inside of the Chephren Valley Temple (figure A.37).

What strikes the casual observer is the modest size and irregular shape of the granite blocks. Their outside surface is smooth and level whereas they have a rather irregular face in contact with the limestone core. On the outside, with the exception of the east temple entrance, these granite casings were stripped away during antiquity. The bare limestone with its impressive irregular surface remained unweathered because it was buried under the desert sand. The limestone surface appears to be the negative imprint of the face of the granite claddings (figure A.38). To match such granite casing slabs to the limestone blocks may have required some masonry work on their surfaces and edges. Some experts claim that the limestone core was worked and sculpted in order to provide a close match with the irregular granite surface. Other experts state that, on the contrary, the carving and sculpting had to be performed on the granite casing to make it match the irregular limestone blocks. On both temples (Chephren and Sphinx) this cladding, or demolition/recuperation work, have left marks, which may be seen running horizontally through adjacent blocks. Some geologists have used these horizontal marks as evidence of the geological nature of these immense blocks, claiming them to be sedimentary stratification layers.

**Figure A.36:** Stage 17, Chephren Valley Temple south, enormous concrete-like blocks (line and circle) (1984).

There is a more practical explanation directly connected with the limestone agglomeration technology. The granite casing formed the exterior moulding for the huge limestone concrete blocks. What we see now is the imprint of the moulds. We know several examples of concrete walls and structures built with a similar technique in modern and ancient times. The ancient Romans had a special word for this, namely *opus caementicium*. This involves the casting of concrete like mixes in shuttering made of natural stone or baked brick. Generally the outside face of the natural stone (limestone, marble, and sandstone) is worked smooth and flat. The natural irregular stone is actually cut or split into two parts, providing two stone blocks, each one with a smooth plane face (the split). The rear side of the stone remains rough. A spectacular example of this technique is provided by the Roman Coliseum in Rome (Italy) with its travertine limestone cladding serving as mould for its brick-concrete core.

# Stage 18: The Sphinx, water sensitive limestone

Visitors to this part of the circuit will gain an insight into why the head of the Sphinx (sculpted in a local protuberance of the dark hard Mokattam Formation) has so wonderfully withstood 4,500 years of harsh weathering conditions.

The body of the Sphinx, in contrast, is what remains from the extraction of stone from the softer marly layers (figure A.39). It is assumed that the quarried stone material was used in the making of the Chephren Valley Temple as well as for the Sphinx temple. The body of the Sphinx is severely eroded, and for some experts this is "erosion due to rain and flooding", i.e. disaggregation through water soaking. The body of the

**Figure A.37:** Chephren Valley Temple (inside); casing of small granite blocks (arrowed) with fine flat exterior surface and irregular interior face in contact with the limestone core (R. Temple, 2000).

**Figure A.38:** Stage 17, Chephren Valley Temple (south side), limestone surface represents the negative face of the granite claddings (1984).

**Figure A.39:** The Sphinx seen from the Chephren Causeway, head sculpted in hard grey Mokattam Formation, body resulting from quarrying the soft yellow marly limestone (1988).

Sphinx was continually restored during antiquity and is today the subject of a very substantial conservation programme. But this degradation is no normal climatic erosion; for the body of the Sphinx was covered in sand for thousands of years and therefore protected against weathering. All experts today agree that the erosion was caused by water, but the origin of this water is the subject of much controversy.

Now, as we have seen, to make reagglomerated stone we need to disaggregate soft limestone in water (the same limestone in which the body of the Sphinx was carved). What the ancient Egyptians would have done was to build ponds for the soaking, water absorption and disaggregation of limestone right at the side of the quarries or directly within them. These ponds would have been flooded, and later during the dry period the water would have evaporated; again they would have been flooded, until the desired degree of disaggregation was obtained. Those large lumps of limestone that did not disaggregate easily would then have been enveloped in limestone slurry and would end up within the blocks.

# Stage 19. Return to Cheops Pyramid, east; geologists find natural stone blocks

In the previous stages, we focused our attention on the two different sorts of limestone occurring in the Mokattam formation: an upper bed containing hard grey limestone, on which the pyramids were built, and a soft yellowish layer (marl with clay layers) from which the building materials were essentially extracted. Notwithstanding this basic and visible geological knowledge on the two different outcrops within very close range of the monuments, two American geologist teams, Folk and Campbell on the one hand, Harrell and Penrod on the other, strongly challenged the casting and packing theory. But they never mentioned the existence of the two varieties of limestone.

Immediately upon arriving at the Giza plateau in January 1990, Folk and Campbell observed stone blocks that appeared to them to be natural limestone. In an article published in the Journal of Geological education, they wrote:

*"Within the first minute at Cheops pyramid, we knew that the pyramids were built of real limestone blocks, not of concrete (reagglomerated stone) ..."*

Folk and Campbell went directly to the north-east corner of the pyramid of Cheops. In their article, they do not explain the reason for this choice. There, they did in fact find natural limestone, from an elevation in the Mokattam formation.

In 1983, Lehner had mentioned the existence of this natural geological layer, rising to 4 metres above the base in the north-east corner. Folk and

262

**Figure A.40:** Block discussed by Folk and Campbell.

Campbell took all their evidence against the agglomerated limestone theory precisely from this area. They identified natural stones where previous studies had already shown that they exist. The reader will find details of their arguments in appendix B.

## Stage 20. Access to the interior of the pyramid of Cheops; the irregular blocks

Today all tourists enter the pyramid through a tunnel between the sixth and eighth tiers. This tunnel is said to have been opened by the caliph Al Mamun at the beginning of the ninth century. In fact it is agreed that the Arabs merely opened a corridor previously hollowed out by other treasure seekers in antiquity. The tunnel was unknown to visitors from the sixteenth to the nineteenth centuries, who never mention it in their descriptions — instead, they used the official entry located higher up at the fifteenth tier. The Description de l'Egypte of Bonaparte does not mention it either. In plate 9, access to the official entry is by climbing up a sand dune that covers the first fifteen tiers; in the section of the pyramid, plate 14, Al Mamun's tunnel is not visible. The plates from the expedition led by Lepsius, which are representative of the state of the site halfway through the nineteenth century when the sand dune had been partially cleared, show the entry. The visitors in Napoleon's expedition do not mention it and it is likely that it was filled with debris, making it inaccessible. The debris is not desert sand; it comes from inside the pyramid itself, from the partial collapse of the tunnel. Today, this mass of debris gives a false impression of stones that have not been dressed, with gaps between them.

From the entry, the tunnel makes its way through a succession of seven enormous blocks, all of parallelipipedal shape. The block patterns then change; some have no right angles, and have oblique planes. The upper and lower faces nevertheless remain perfectly horizontal, and the jointing is exemplary. Between some faces there is a 10 to 15 cm thick filling, suggesting the use of the lost mould technique, with a tafla (clay) mortar and cobbles. In the section 20.4 in chapter 20, I discussed the use of these lost moulds made of highly friable material that disaggregates easily. The ceiling is well jointed; some blocks have a trapezoidal rather than a rectangular base. However, part of the material of the corners of the blocks has disappeared, leaving a 15 to 20 cm deep void giving the blocks an ovoid appearance. When reagglomeration is carried out using pisé clay, a stiff material, the corner parts of the mould cannot be thoroughly packed. If the work is done hurriedly, this part will have little cohesion and will tend to crumble down from the ceiling as the tunnel is bored. The voids may then result both from the disintegration of the crumbly walls of the lost mould, and from the destruction of the weaker lumps of stone.

# Appendix B

# Objections to my theory

When I started to propagate my theory in 1979, I wished to be confronted with serious opponents; those that could take my arguments one by one, counter them with solid and valid scientific evidences, in geology, mineralogy, chemistry, hieroglyphic studies, religion and Egyptian history... I only got sloppy studies, miserable reviews from people that have one thing in common: none of them have seriously studied my theory or worse, some of them used hearsays and preconcieved ideas instead of quoting my work. The problem is that these published sloppy articles are taken for serious references by the opponents of the re-agglomerated theory. In addition, almost all of these opponents wrote their papers for only one purpose: to make easy publicity for themselves.

## Absence of knowledge of the Giza Plateau geology

In chapter 7, we focussed on the two different limestone outcrops of the Mokattam Formation: a hard grey superior bed on which the pyramids are founded, and a soft yellowish (with clay beds) where the pyramids core materials were extracted. Notwithstanding the basic and visible geological knowledge on the two different outcrops within very close range of the monuments, the American geologists Harrell and Penrod challenged the casting and packing theory. In a paper published in Journal of Geological Education in 1993, they state: "... *Our objection to the geopolymeric process (agglomerated stone process) has to do with disaggregating limestone by soaking it in water — it does not work! We soaked the Mokattam limestones whose composition is given in Table 1 for seven weeks and after this time the samples were just as hard and solid as the day we first immersed them....*[1]

They never mentioned noticing any difference between the pyramid blocks and the hard Mokattam Formation that constitutes the surrounding plateau. Harrell and Penrod, who published on ancient Egyptian limestone quarries, ignored the presence of the two different outcrops. They relied only on the generic denomination of the Giza Pyramids bedrock, namely the name Mokattam Formation. Mokattam is the name of a Cairo suburb in the vicinity of the Citadel, made of hard limestone. The quarry at Gebel Mokattam supplies squared stones for the Cairo monuments. In the cited Table 1 of their publication, Harrell and Penrod provide the location of their tested samples, namely: Gebel Mokattam, Tura and Masera. There is no mention of any Giza sample.

For their demonstration, Harrell and Penrod deliberately took hard Mokattam limestone instead of the soft material from the wadi quarries or the Sphinx trench. In addition, the soaked sample did not come from the Giza Pyramids site at all. These ancient Egyptian quarries specialists ironically collected this piece of hard limestone from the modern quarry behind the Citadel on Gebel Mokattam, Cairo, 20 km east of the Giza Pyramids, on the other side of the Nile.

Two other American geologists, R. Folk and D. Campbell[2], vigourously challenged the theory essentially in publications that do not have the "Peer review" system and therefore were not edited, such as Journal of Geological Education or The Epigraphic Society Occasional Papers. There are several statements made by Folk/Campbell in these papers that demonstrate their lack of knowledge on the geological uniqueness of the Giza Plateau. Yet, they wrote with arrogance:

*"... we feel it is the duty of professional geologist to expose this egregiously absurd archeological theory before it becomes part of entrenched*

---

[1] J.A. Harrell and B.E. Penrod., The Great Pyramid Debate – Evidence from the Lauer Sample, Journal of Geological Education, Vol. 41, pp. 358–363 (1993). In the cited Table 1, Harrell provides location of the samples, namely: Gebel Mokattam (the suburb of Cairo behind the Citadel), Tura, Masara and Lauer. There is no mention of any Giza sample. See also the rebuttals: M. Morris, How Not to Analyze Pyramid Stone, Journal of Geological Education, Vol. 41, pp. 364–369 (1993). R.G McKinney, Comments on the Work of Harrell and Penrod, Journal of Geological Education, Vol. 41, pp. 369 (1993). McKinney, a geologist concludes with the following statement: *"... Finally, I am not a "geologist sympathetic to the geopolymer theory" as Harrell suggests. I was asked to participate in this project by Marshall Payn, President of the Epigraphic Society of America, and financier of R.L. Folk's trip to Egypt. He wanted an impartial observer with no knowledge of the theory to render an opinion on the results of the visit. I have since read Davidovits' book and do think his approach to the problem of pyramid construction is the most analytical I have read, but this has nothing to do with thin-section analysis... "*

[2] R.L. Folk and D.H. Campbell, Are the Pyramids built of poured concrete blocks, Journal of Geological Education, Vol. 40, pp. 25-34 (1992).

*pseudoscience... We believe that had Davidovits had any understanding of basic geologic principles and understood the implications of simple geological evidence at Giza, he would have realized that this geopolymer theory had no basis in fact... We have also shown how geologic commonsense can destroy archaeological quackery, but not, unfortunately, before it has enjoyed widespread publicity among the gullible and sensation-minded... The geopolymer theory is defunct; we still remain in awe of the enigma of Egyptian skill and engineering."*

They did not study the soft marly limestone bed and its peculiar property, at all:

*"... A fundamental and obvious objection to the geopolymer theory is that, had the Egyptians wanted to make "permastone", why would they have gone to the excessive labour of crushing limestone and gluing back together when it would have been much easier to use the abundant, nearby, loose desert quartz sand that would have surely made a more homogeneous concrete... "*

The theory never states that the limestone has to be crushed. It is obvious that Folk and Campbell did not understand the feasibility of the system based on water disaggregation.

Immediately upon arriving at the site in January 1990, Folk and Campbell observed features that they interpreted to indicate that the blocks are natural, they state:

*"Within the first minute at Cheops pyramid, we knew that the pyramids were built of real limestone blocks, not of concrete (reagglomerated stone)... ".*

For a reason which is not explained in their papers, Folk and Campbell went directly to the North East corner of the Cheops pyramid, and found there, natural limestone, an outcrop of the Mokattam Formation.

A major part of their preliminary geological study was carried out precisely on this location (see in figure A.40). They deliberately ignored the elementary fact that the pyramid was built on a levelled plateau, which left some natural bedrock as part of the monument.

In 1983, Lehner[3] had mentioned that this natural bedrock shows to a height of 4 metres above the base, at the North-East corner. Nevertheless, Folk and Campbell based all their demonstration against the agglomerated limestone theory, on superficial investigation. They identified real stones where previous studies showed them to be located, thus proving on one hand their expertise in geology and on the other hand their scientific misconduct. They used this North-East. corner natural stone to demonstrate that

*"... they are tectonic fractures in many pyramid blocks, filled with calcite (the vertical tectonic fracture T in the photo)... These fractures*

---

[3]M. Lehner, Some Observations on the Layout of the Khufu and Khafre Pyramids, J. American Research Center in Egypt, Vol. 20, p. 7 (1983)

*generally are only about 1 mm wide, and run in a more or less straight path all across a single block... These are obvious tectonic fractures formed when the block was flexed millions of years ago, and demonstrate that the pyramid core stones were quarried blocks, not poured geopolymer... ".*

They also used these natural blocks to demonstrate that specific weaker parts of pyramid blocks were caused by the presence of burrows (label B in the picture), stating that there are:

*"... numerous burrows and tubes formed by animals when the sediment had a muddy consistency on the Eocene sea floor. Similar burrows are readily seen in nearby outcropping limestones. Burrowing and churning of the soft sediment by sea-floor organisms produces inhomogeneities in sediment composition, texture, and porosity, which control to a great extent the processes of hardening into rock as the pore spaces are filled with a secondary geologic cement, in this case calcite. When the rock is weathered, the inhomogeneities are strikingly brought out as generally irregular, elongated, discolored features on the rock surface. Consequently, the inhomogeneities in the rock result in its differential weathering... "*

Other natural limestone blocks located on the lower two courses of the same East side were also given as proof for the explanation of density changes and lift lines presence in pyramid blocks. Taking the marly layer labelled M as example, they stated that all layers were merely geological stratification produced in the ancient Eocene seas.

In response to another of their papers also published in 1991 but in a different technical journal, Concrete International[4], I published[5] in 1992 in the same journal, the sketch focusing on the N-E corner of Cheops pyramid and the obvious occurrence of natural stones.

Folk and Campbell never publicly admitted their error. Some of their 1990-1991 published papers are still used today by those who wants to discredit my theory. They do not know that Folk confessed his mistake in private. In March 1992, I received a letter from him dated of February 18th, 1992, that reads:

*"... I was impressed by your reasonable and interesting letter in Concrete International, Feb. 1992... Your argument that the lower two courses of Khufu (Cheops), on the east face, are in place bedrock is intriguing and I must admit was a new thought to me. This morning, thanks to your citation, I went over and read Lehner (1983) on Khufu (Cheops) and he does indeed show the NE corner of Khufu to be bedrock in his sketch. Our photo was of that corner. So I concede that, on the North-East corner, you*

---

[4]D. H. Campbell and R. L. Folk, The Great Pyramid Debate, The Ancient Egyptian Pyramids - Concrete or Rocks, Concrete International, Vol. 13, No. 8, pp. 28-39. (1991) See also, the rebuttal by M. Morris, The Great Pyramid Debate: The Cast-in-Place Theory of Pyramid Construction, Concrete International, Vol. 13, No. 8, pp. 29-44. (1991)

[5]J. Davidovits, J., Great Pyramid debate, Concrete International, Vol. 14, No. 2, pp. 17-18, (1992)

*are correct as the bedrock idea had not entered my head at the time we were there. . . "*

The geologist and limestone specialist Robert L. Folk admitted that he did not have any basic geological knowledge of the Giza plateau when he made his survey and triumphally claimed: *". . . Within the first minute at Cheops pyramid, we knew that the pyramids were built of real limestone blocks, not of concrete (reagglomerated stone). . . ".*

# Approximate science

A scientific paper was published by a team from the University of North Texas, USA in the December 1993 issue of the Journal of Archaeological Science. The paper titled *"The Pyramids – cement or stone?"* by K. Ingram, K. Daugherty and J. Marshall, outlines the results of a series of tests performed in 1989 on samples of limestone from the pyramids of Chephren and Mykerinos at Giza. Their conclusion reads: *". . . We found no evidence that support his (Davidovits) ideas . . . ".* This conclusion is wrong because the paper contains at least three data which proves the contrary. What would have upset any fair geologist seems normal to these scientists. Trained experts will decide whether the three following uncommon scientific data must be qualified as 'normal' or 'abnormal' results:

1 - To determine the chemical content of the limestone, one proceeds generally with a calcination at 900°C of a powdered sample. The calcite (calcium carbonate) decomposes and gives off carbon dioxide. In general, the calcination material loss for Egyptian limestone (and other limestones) ranges between 40-41 % of its mass. In Ingram/Daugherty's paper, the material lost 60 % of its mass during decarboxylation. This is an unusual result for ordinary limestone. This excessive loss should have been tentatively assigned to bounded water and therefore suggesting geopolymeric re-agglomeration.

2 - The chemical analysis determined with a sophisticated tool called Inductively Coupled Plasmagraphy (ICP) provides a high amount for aluminum, 3.9 % expressed in aluminum oxide $Al_2O_3$. The authors wrote: *". . . the sample appears to be normal limestone, not a geopolymeric cement blend. . . "* This is again very unusual. We know that the limestone of the hard grey Mokattam bed does not contain more than 0.5 % aluminum oxide $Al_2O_3$. On the other hand this high aluminum amount is found in the soft yellow marly limestone of the Sphinx trench and the wadi quarries and that it is not appropriate for standard constructional purpose, yet a dedicated raw material for the re-agglomeration process as depicted in the previous chapter.

3 - The third mistake relates to the Infra-Red Spectroscopy investigation. The infra-Red spectrum differentiates between calcium carbonate calcite and silico-aluminate (clay constituent of geopolymeric cement). A

shoulder in the spectra around 1000 cm$^{-1}$ characterises silico-aluminate. Both Chephren and Mykerinos stones spectra display this shoulder. Yet for Ingram/Daugherty "... *this is a minor variation...* ". Why did they refrain from enlarging their spectra, as would have done any scientist in order to focus on this very peculiar band which pertains to routine geopolymeric characterisation?

To sum up: this paper provides additional data supporting the agglomeration theory. It shows how untrained scientist, who are ignorant of the geopolymer chemistry potential, can improperly assign the analysed samples to natural stones despite their uncommon features. K. Ingram, K. Daugherty and J. Marshall assumed that since the agglomeration stone theory is against orthodoxy, it must be incorrect; therefore, it is not worthy of serious study and hence their sloppy science and incorrect conclusion.

# A cheap and easy way to make advertisement

In 2005, to inaugurate the acquisition of its new tool, a rotating crystal spectrometer (RCS), Dr. Menno Blaauw[6], of the Technische Universiteit Delft in the Netherlands, was looking for a cheap and easy way to get publicity on a non-serious topic. He decided to analyse a small piece of stone stolen from the Queen's chamber in Cheops' pyramid, high up in the rear of a niche for a statue. His purpose, and obvious conclusion, was to demonstrate that the chunk of stolen limestone was natural stone, and not a piece of concrete. His main argument was that the inside of the stone has not seen daylight for at least 400 000 years.

Firstly, Dr. Menno Blaauw is making the same mistake as all other opponents to the theory. He deliberately ignores the fact that the pyramid stones are made out of 95 % by weight of natural limestone. By doing this type of analysis, they have 95 % chance of analysing natural stone elements. It is like analysing the aggregates in a modern concrete; they will claim that the aggregates are natural stones, which is obvious. Any scientific investigations must be based on multiple sampling in different parts of the block, not just on a single one.

Secondly, the natural limestone from the Giza plateau belongs to the Eocene period. It is therefore at least 30–40 million years old. The 400 000 years do not refer at all to a geological material of this period. On a time scale, 400 000 years is much closer to 4000 years (date of the pyramid building) than 40 million years. This means that Dr. Menno Blaauw is rewriting geology. This young age (it is 100 times younger in comparison with the genuine Eocene age), could on the contrary suggest that this piece

---

[6]M. Blaauw, The Kheops sample and the Reactor Institute Delft, TU Delft, Faculty of Applied Science, advertisement brochure (2005).

of natural stone did receive some photons during the re-agglomeration of the block.

He also analysed the composition of the stone. He found: *"Sodium (Na, 0.86 %) and chlorine (Cl, 1.45 %) levels are quite high for limestone. The concentrations nicely match the composition of ordinary salt — the sample was taken high up, but nevertheless the use of the niche as a public bathroom may explain it."* So, the presence of a high amount of salt (quite abnormal for a natural limestone) is explained by the fact that the Queen's chamber in Cheops pyramid was used as a public bathroom, and men urinated up to 2 metres high (quite impressive!), thus explaining why the stone sample is spoiled with salt! In chapter 6, I develop a more reasonable explanation of the presence of salt.

So, on setting aside Dr. Menno Blaauw's wrong conclusions, his analysis can be interpreted as a good clue for re-agglomeration.

# How not to write a scientific paper

Now, this is one of my favourites. It combines everything: scientific disinformation, ill will and self-publicity. This person has not read any of my works. My books were written in English, French, Portugese, Italian, Czech languages. Even, my oldest English book published in New York in 1988 is still available as a used book at internet bookstores. They were superbly ignored by this fellow who used hearsays or preconceived ideas to criticize the theory. A parody of science. Even the general public will acknowledge how ignorance is often synonymous with arrogance.

Mr. Ioannis Liritzis[7], from the Laboratory of Archaeometry at the University of the Aegean, Rhodes, Greece, wrote in 2008 in the Journal of Cultural Heritage a paper titled: *"Mineralogical, petrological and radioactivity aspects of some building material from Egyptian Old Kingdom monuments"*. One of its aims is to prove that the re-agglomeration theory is wrong, based on the critique of a paper I published in... 1984, 24 years ago. I have produced many publications since that date, many new analyses and discoveries. I have written three books on the subject and we have manufactured 15 metric tonnes of reagglomerated limestone. Since 1996, the Geopolymer Institute website has been well documented, open to any member of the public. Yet Liritzis has chosen to ignore them. Why? Moreover, in his study he cites a total of 84 scientific references, but only one, my 1984 paper is referred to and discussed. Around 60 % of his paper and analysis are dedicated to countering my theory, and I will prove that he has not even taken the time to study it. Let's take a closer look at his arguments.

---

[7]I. Liritzis, C. Sideris, A. Vafiadou, J. Mitsis, Mineralogical, petrological and radioactivity aspects of some building material from Egyptian Old Kingdom monuments, Journal of Cultural Heritage 9 (2008) 1–13.

First, in order to better understand the background of this act of scientific disinformation, let us have a look at my 1984 paper, with its following abstract, the only source of my theory according to Liritzis:

*X-Ray Analysis and X-Ray Diffraction of Casing Stones from the Pyramids of Egypt, and the Limestone of the Associated Quarries*[8]: The hypothesis that the limestone that constitutes the major pyramids of the Old Kingdom of Egypt is man-made stone, is discussed. Samples from six different sites at the traditionally associated quarries of Turah and Mokattam have been studied using thin-section, chemical X-Ray analysis and X-Ray diffraction. The results were compared with pyramid casing stones of Cheops, Teti and Seneferu. The quarry samples are pure limestone consisting of 96–99 % Calcite, 0.5–2.5 % Quartz, and very small amount of dolomite, gypsum and iron-alumino-silicate. On the other hand the Cheops and Teti casing stones are limestone consisting of: calcite 85–90 % and a high amount of special minerals such as Opal CT, hydroxyapatite, a silico-aluminate, which are not found in the quarries. The pyramid casing stones are light in density and contain numerous trapped air bubbles, unlike the quarry samples which are uniformly dense. If the casing stones were natural limestone, quarries different from those traditionally associated with the pyramid sites must be found, but where? X-Ray diffraction of a red casing stone coating is the first proof to demonstrate the fact that a complicated man-made geopolymeric system was produced in Egypt 4700 years ago.

My 1984 paper was not dealing with the bulk of pyramid construction and their millions of core stones. It was only dedicated to one casing stone pertaining to Cheops which happens to present a special coating, highlighting very complex chemical knowledge. It was my first scientific report, at a time when knowledge was scarce. During the 24 years that followed, we acquired a vast amount of technical, historical knowledge, which I shared with my colleagues at the International Congresses of Egyptology as well as in my books. Well, Liritzis strongly ignores them and focuses on the beginning of our research project, as if nothing happened in between.

Now, let's read some excerpts of his work:

**"3.3. Egyptian monuments: Casting or carving?**

---

[8] J. Davidovits, X-Ray Analysis and X-Ray Diffraction of Casing Stones from the Pyramids of Egypt, and the Limestone of the Associated Quarries, Science in Egyptology Symposia, R. David ed., Manchester University Press, U.K., pp. 511–520, 1984. Paper available at the Geopolymer Institute website www.geopolymer.org

*The building blocks of the Egyptian monuments are made of limestone, sandstone or granite. The huge blocks are well carved, perfectly aligned and considerable engineering and labour was involved (52)."*

Note 52 refers to a paper written in 1930; could he not find a more recent one? Has no Egyptologist worked on the pyramids since then?: C.F. Engelbach, Ancient Egyptian Masonry, Oxford University Press, Humphry Milford, 1930.

*"This amazing building has provoked thoughts to readdress manufacturing techniques, however against the theory of Davidovits (53)* [The only reference to my work in 1984] *, who maintained that these blocks were not cut and carved but cast from parent rock ground down and binders such as gypsum and fossils."*

Wrong, I never wrote this, never mentioned the use of gypsum. Here is the exact quote: "A problem of analysis, assuming that this stone is made by agglomerating crushed limestone using lime as a binder, is that lime hardens over a period of time and becomes recarbonated into calcium carbonate, calcite. It is impossible to distinguish a natural calcite microcrystal from a microcrystal of calcite which is the result of the recarbonation of lime. This is an obstacle involved in the detection of geopolymeric setting and new techniques must be developed to resolve it".

*"Several points reject the casting hypothesis. (1) No reference is made on trace remains, paintings, sculptures or texts etc. of the referred moulds or bucketful."*

You have read this book and you know that we have numerous genuine texts and frescos; the irony is that it is precisely the carving theory that does not have any texts, paintings and sculptures supporting it.

*"(2) Muddy limestone is not reliably interpreted."*

How funny — I did not address the subject in the 1984 paper and it was not my purpose; I discussed the casing stone, not the core blocks that are made of this muddy, easy to disintegrate, limestone. See chapter 7 in this book.

*"(3) No attempt to interpret the quarrying of natron and the construction of lime (CaO) is made, which requires time, labour and energy from the poor wooden vegetation of the Nile area."*

Of course, this is not discussed in the 1984 paper because it was not its topic, but it is clearly referred to in my books, here in chapter 9, chapter 21. Again, where are the references?

*" (...) (4) The limestone rocks, even this soft local rock, cannot be diluted with water within 24 h, as maintained by Davidovits, but with prolonged dilution only in powder form with hydrochloric acid HCl 2 N, and after all, if the calcitic material so easily dissolves in water, how have these monuments stood for so many thousands of years, in limestone either porous or soft."*

How strange. Acording to Liritzis, I am claiming that limestone rock is dissolved by water as if it were like sugar. He does not make the difference between dissolution (of sugar), and disaggregation or destructuring by the action of water or weathering agent. He does not know that a great quantity of soft core stones are presently eroding, since the protecting casing has been removed and stripped away by the Cairo populace. The west sides of Cheops, Chephren and worse, of the Seneferu Red pyramid at Dashur, are totally eroded. The body of the Sphinx is in a miserable state and needs to be constantly repaired, because of water. Again, like his colleagues, he does not know anything about the Giza plateau geology. He did not take a chunk of limestone from the official quarries in the Wadi, but apparently a sample from an extra hard grey limestone on which the pyramids stand. He is repeating the same mistake as Harrel and Pernod (see above). I already mentioned at the beginning of the *Circuit of the Pyramids* (Appendix A) that in October 1991, during the shooting of the TV production *"This Old Pyramid"* by NOVA, aired on the American PBS network on September 1992, I had the opportunity to demonstrate this unique property of the Giza limestone, before the American Egyptologist Mark Lehner. A chunk of limestone taken in the quarry was very easily disaggregated within 24 hours, leaving the nummulites and the clay gently separated from each other, whereas a chunk of the hard Mokkatam limestone did not disintegrate at all. In 1996, we put this information on the internet, at the Geopolymer Institute Archaeology page. Lirizis does not mention it.

*" (...) (6) Concerning the 'problem' with Opal CT's presence in the pyramid casing stone, it is known that this crystal phase is not a rare mineral for limestones but often exists in varieties."*

This is exactly what I wrote in my 1984 paper; I quote: "There are two possible interpretations for Opal CT's presence in the pyramid casing stone: man-made stone, since it would be the fingerprint of amorphous silica and silicates, a necessary ingredient, or a rare occurrence in natural stone.(...) The presence of Opal CT in the casing stone of Cheops does not indicate that it is naturally occurring, since Opal CT is not found in the natural limestone of the quarries."

*" (...) (1) The presence of undamaged fossils."*

He is convinced that we crushed stones, which is wrong. I keep the best for the end:

*" (...) Limestones from Valley and Sphinx Temple in Giza (ST1, VT6, VT7, VT9A, VT9B) together with Cheops and Chephren pyramids are grouped together and thin section examinations indicate provenance from Mokattam formation from Tura and Ma'sara quarries. (...)"*

In other words, all pyramid and temple limestone samples analysed by Liritzis belong to the Tura and Ma'sara quarries, located on the other side of the Nile, bringing fuel to the extravagant theories set forth in our chapter 3. However, Egyptologists and geologists agree on the fact that the limestone used to build the pyramids at Giza does not come from the other side of the Nile, but from the wadi quarries, at the bottom of the Giza plateau. Archaeological evidence found on the spot is discussed in dozens of scientific, geological and archaeological papers. They disagree on the fact that the pyramids' builders crossed the river Nile to ship millions of limestone blocks from the Tura and Ma'sara quarries, and its tremendously complicated logistics. Has Lirizis read any of these?

To sum-up Lirizis' work: nothing has been done since 1984 and everybody is wrong. In fact, the problem is not Liritzis' article per se but the fact that it was accepted for publication by *"Journal of Cultural Heritage"* without any regular peer-review system. This is not an accident but a deliberate decision from the archeological establishment, which does not like bold new ideas that would dramatically change history.

# The dogma: a scientific truth

Speaking more generally and setting aside my theory, the media always relay and emphasize works which destroy bold new ideas that go against the main stream (in science, medicine, environment, biology, etc.).

Here from the field of medicine is another example of this institutional conservatism. The Nobel Prize of medicine and physiology for 2005 was awarded jointly to two Australian researchers Barry Marshall and Robin Warren, who discovered the role of the bacterium *"Helicobacter pylori"* in the formation of stomach or duodenum ulcers. Before Marshall and Warren identified this bacterium, at the beginning of the Eighties, way of life and stress were considered as the principal causes of ulcers. It is now common knowledge that *"Helicobacter pylori"* is implied in 90 % of the ulcers.

It was in Perth, Western Australia, at the Royal Perth Hospital and the University of Western Australia, very far away from the large American and European scientific communities that the researchers made their discovery, more than 25 years ago. I have often been to Perth these last few years, because we maintain a very effective collaboration with the geopolymer group at the University of Technology Curtin. I can thus imagine what the "scientific desert" of this area looked like, more than a quarter century ago. After their discovery, Barry Marshall and Robin Warren planned to submit it to the scientific community. They, the small ones, the unknown ones, suffered absolute rejection, because what they were claiming was contrary to what was taught at the Faculties of Medicine all over the world, namely: everybody knows that it is stress that causes the ulcers. They were prohibited from publication and heavily criticized for several years, were rejected by the so-called serious scientific journals, like *"Nature, Science"* and the others, and for almost 15 years.

This example can be put alongside another, in the same discipline: the scandal of the false clones of the Korean Hwang Woo-suk. It was a popular subject, which brought huge publicity to these serious scientific journals. It is in May 2005 that Hwang published his article, as famous as smoky, in *"Science"*, in which he disclosed the first results of human cloning. The story is now well known. These are the same people who, 25 years ago, refused to publish the work of Barry Marshall and Robin Warren, because it was in counter to what the mainstream scientists believed and taught, at that time. These are also the same people (*"Nature, Science"*) who, more recently, refused the well documented publication made by an international group of renown scientists, who were presenting their analyses carried out on stones of the Egyptian pyramids. Their analyses showed that the stones in their possession were artificial, see our chapter 6. Here too, my theory on the building of the Egyptian pyramids with re-agglomerated stone (artificial stone), instead of carved stone, conflicts with what is commonly taught at the Faculties. Here too, like for the researchers from Perth, I was prohibited from publication in these so-called serious scientific journals.

The German physicist Max Plank wrote: *"In science, one does not convince anybody. The opponents die and the young people, more flexible adopt the new theory"*. Thus, after more than a quarter century of struggle, my theory was officially presented to the public in an exhibition at the French science museum, Palais de la Découverte, in Paris, in 2006–2007. More and more media are now less afraid to pass on the theory.

This book was typeset using the LaTeX typesetting system and the memoir class. The body text is set in 11pt with Computer Modern Roman designed by Donald Knuth. Other fonts include Sans, SMALLCAPS, *Italic*, and *Slanted* are all from Knuth's Computer Modern family.

Photo credits:
All photos dated 1979, 1984, 1988, 2000: Joseph Davidovits
All photos dated 2002, 2003: Ralph Davidovits
Experimentation, chapter 10: Ralph Davidovits
Cover: Ralph Davidovits, Igor Zehl

Dépôt légal janvier 2009

www.ingramcontent.com/pod-product-compliance
Lightning Source LLC
Chambersburg PA
CBHW051820040426
42447CB00006B/301